# THE AUTOBIOGRAPHY

## and Selections from His Other Writings

## The American Heritage Series
OSKAR PIEST, FOUNDER

The American Heritage Series

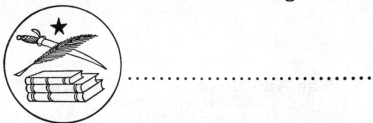

# THE
# AUTOBIOGRAPHY

and

### Selections from His Other Writings

## BENJAMIN FRANKLIN

Edited, with an introduction, by

### HERBERT W. SCHNEIDER

*Professor Emeritus of Philosophy and Religion*
*Columbia University*

· · · · · · · · · · · · · · · · · · · · · · · · · · · · · · · · ·

The American Heritage Series

*published by*

THE **BOBBS-MERRILL** COMPANY, INC.
A SUBSIDIARY OF HOWARD W. SAMS & CO., INC.
*Publishers* · INDIANAPOLIS · NEW YORK

Benjamin Franklin: 1706-1790

THE AUTOBIOGRAPHY

COPYRIGHT ©, 1949

UNIVERSITY OF CALIFORNIA PRESS

INTRODUCTION AND NOTES

COPYRIGHT ©, 1952

THE LIBERAL ARTS PRESS, INC.

# CONTENTS

· · · · · · · · · · · · · · · ·

# BENJAMIN FRANKLIN'S WRITINGS

# CHRONOLOGY

1706    Born, January 17, in Boston, Massachusetts, to Josiah and Abiah (Folger) Franklin.

1718    Apprenticed to his brother, James, in his printing shop.

1722    The "Silence Dogood" letters published anonymously in the *New England Courant*.

1723    Goes to Philadelphia and finds employment there as a printer.

1724    Leaves for London. There, as a printer, sets type for Wollaston's *Religion of Nature Delineated*.

1725    Publishes *A Dissertation on Liberty and Necessity, Pleasure and Pain*.

1726    Returns to Philadelphia.

1729    The "Busybody Papers" published in the *Weekly Mercury*.

1730    Appointed Public Printer by the Assembly of Pennsylvania.
Marries Deborah Read.

1731    Founds the first subscription library in America, the Pennsylvania Library Company.

1733    Publishes first issue of *Poor Richard's Almanack* (published regularly thereafter until 1758).

1736    Chosen clerk of the Pennsylvania General Assembly.

1744    Founds American Philosophical Society.

1746    Begins experiments with Leyden jar and other electrical apparatus.

1748    Retires from the printing business.

1749    Founds the academy later to become the University of
        Pennsylvania.
        Publishes first paper on electricity.

1750    Serves as one of the commissioners to conclude a treaty
        with the Indians at Carlisle.

1751    Elected member of the Pennsylvania General Assembly.
        Publishes first book on electricity.

1752    Collinson's edition of Franklin's works published in
        French.
        Instrumental in establishing first American fire insurance
        company.

1753    Appointed as Deputy Postmaster General of the Colo-
        nies.
        Awarded the Godfrey Copley Medal by the Royal So-
        ciety of London and made a Fellow.
        Awarded the honorary degree of Master of Arts by
        Harvard and Yale.

1754    Goes as delegate from Pennsylvania to discuss plan for
        union of the Colonies at the Albany Congress.

1756    Made a Fellow of the Royal Society of London.

1757    Goes to London as commissioner for the Colony of
        Pennsylvania.

1759    Chosen honorary member of Philosophical Society of
        Edinburgh.

1762    Awarded honorary degree of Doctor of Law at Oxford.
        Returns to America.

1764    Appointed agent for Pennsylvania to petition Crown for
        a change in their status from Proprietary to Crown
        Colony and leaves for London.

1766    Wins temporary repeal of the Stamp Act.
        Chosen foreign member of the Royal Society of Sciences,
        Göttingen.

1768–70 While in London, requested to serve as colonial agent
        for Georgia, New Jersey, and Massachusetts.

1771    Chosen member of the Learned Society of Sciences, Rotterdam.

1772    Becomes foreign member of the Royal Academy of Science of Paris.

1775    Returns to America.

Elected member of the Second Continental Congress.

Appointed Postmaster General under the Confederation.

1776    Serves on committee to draft and sign Declaration of Independence.

Appointed one of three American agents in France.

1777    Chosen member of the Royal Medical Society of Paris.

1778    Signs Treaty of Alliance with France.

1781    Serves as one of the commissioners negotiating peace with England.

1783    Signs Treaty of Paris with John Jay and John Adams.

1785    Resigns as minister to the French Court and returns to America.

1787    Chosen delegate to the Constitutional Convention, Philadelphia.

1787–90 President of the Pennsylvania Society for the Abolition of Slavery.

Founds Society for Political Enquiry, and elected its first president.

1790    Dies, April 17, in Philadelphia.

# INTRODUCTION

Benjamin Franklin is one of the few men in history who, by personal achievement and public service, have become examples not only in their own times but for future generations as well. John Adams reports that "his name was familiar to government and people" in Europe, and, "If a collection could be made of all the Gazettes of Europe for the latter half of the eighteenth century, a greater number of panegyrical paragraphs upon *'le grand Franklin'* would appear, it is believed, than upon any other man that ever lived." [a] In *Dichtung und Wahrheit* Goethe tells us that as a youth, when he hoped to amount to something (*"etwas Tüchtiges werden wollte"*), he was enormously impressed with Benjamin Franklin and recognized in him an extraordinary union of "deep insight and emancipated outlook" (*"tiefe Einsicht, freie Übersicht"*). In 1757, on his second trip to England, he was acclaimed as one of the outstanding men of his time, a Fellowship in the Royal Society of London having been bestowed on him in the previous year in recognition of his contributions to the "fluid" theory of electricity, a theory which is still preserved in our common electrical terms ("current," "flow"), though it has lost its experimental value. In France he was not only accepted but idolized as "the good Dr. Franklin," the embodiment of all those virtues which were inspiring both the decadent polite society, into which Franklin was first received, and the revolutionary circles, into which he later was drawn. He was at once a "noble barbarian" and a complete republican. This image still lives among Europeans, especially among those who make a firsthand acquaintance with him through his writings and who do not accept the stereotype of "Americanism" for which Franklin has been made to stand in academic texts and journalistic ideology.

The grounds on which his fame rests vary from reader to reader

---

[a] Quoted in Max Farrand: *Benjamin Franklin's Memoirs*. University of California Press, Berkeley, 1949, p. xix.

and from age to age; some have called him "the Newton of electricity," others "the first civilized American," others "the schoolmaster of the American Revolution," and still others "the saint of bourgeois capitalism" and "the apostle of modern times." Strictly speaking, he was none of these, but vaguely he combined all these traits. In the United States the memory of Franklin as it is still cherished centers less about his science and his "goodness," more about his usefulness to America as a public servant in time of need. He was the American incarnation of "public spirit." Whether he was editing a newspaper or forming a scientific academy or devoting himself to the American Revolution, he did it wholeheartedly and without regard to personal gain. This spirit is reflected in his *Autobiography,* and this is probably the secret of its unique success since its publication. More than one hundred editions have been published in the United States, and it has been translated into almost all languages. It is still an inspiration for those who wish to unite virtue with happiness and personal achievement with public service. His own public services are too numerous to list completely here. Among others, he managed, on his first public mission to England (1757-1762) in behalf of the citizens of Pennsylvania, whose interests were conflicting with those of the Proprietors of the Colony,[1] to lay the ground for the transformation of Pennsylvania from a Proprietary to a Crown Colony. Thus he gained the respect of the very politicians whom he opposed and was, therefore, able to command attention on his second mission to Great Britain (1766-1775), when, as agent for Massachusetts and for the rebellious Colonies generally, he had a peculiarly delicate and difficult objective. To win, as he did, even a temporary repeal of the Stamp Act [2] was no small diplomatic triumph. His most important political service to the United States, however, was his patient labor in France (1777-85), then the enemy of Great Britain, to secure military intervention in behalf of the American rebellion. Had he merely labored among military circles and amid military intrigues, his mission would have had a more limited value. But he portrayed the independence of the American colonies as something much more significant than a rebellion; to him it was the outbreak of a universal moral and intellectual revolution, a revolution in which French "citizens" had a much deeper interest than in the so-called "French and Indian Wars" (1754-1763). It is largely through Franklin in Paris and his able successor there, Thomas Jefferson, that the framers of the French Revolution could derive strength and hope from the American Revolution.

Benjamin and his older brother grew up in eighteenth century Boston, Massachusetts, surrounded by Puritan preachers and Yankee skippers. He would have gone to sea had not his father apprenticed him to his brother's business and thus forced him into the printer's trade. It was almost inevitable in Boston that a printer must also become a journalist and take part in the debates which were then raging in pulpit and press and which made an explosive mixture of preaching holiness on sabbaths and practicing indepɛndence during the week. He imbibed in childhood the twin gospels of "doing good" and "being thrifty," but he transformed both these gospels. He took the hypocrisy out of Puritan benevolence and the greed out of Yankee business.

The learned but bigoted Reverend Mr. Cotton Mather, the last of the Puritan theocrats,[3] organized a vigorous inquisition under the hypocritical caption of *Essays to Do Good*. The young Benjamin Franklin and his older brother, James, used their *Courant* to satirize such puritanical doing good, and Benjamin's newspaper column, signed "Mrs. Silence Dogood," was so effective that he was practically forced to flee Boston. Settled in Philadelphia among the Quakers, he immediately organized his own club, which he called a "Junto," to "do good." His amusing description in the *Autobiography* makes it clear that this Junto was both a benevolent club and a continual satire of the Puritan inquisition: "Have you lately heard of any citizen thriving well, and by what means? Do you think of anything at present, in which the Junto may be serviceable to mankind, to their country, or to themselves?" After each of these queries there was a pious pause "while one might fill and drink a glass of wine."

When he went to London in 1724, he carried his freethinking and his "enlightenment" still further, satirizing not only Calvinism but also natural religion. He composed a *Dissertation on Liberty and Necessity, Pleasure and Pain* and *Dialogues Concerning Virtue and Pleasure*, and he argued that "vice and virtue are empty distinctions." But these youthful attempts to play *le philosophe* were soon abandoned, and when he set to work as a printer in Philadelphia, he soon realized that vice and virtue needed no theological justification but were "of the utmost importance" in practical affairs. This discovery he mentions in the *Autobiography* with his characteristic simplicity. "I grew convinced that truth, sincerity, and integrity, in dealings between man and man, were of the utmost importance to the felicity of life." [b]

In short, Franklin placed the frontier morality of the Puritans on a secular, utilitarian footing, summing it up as follows:

"Revelation had indeed no weight with me as such; but I entertained an opinion that though certain actions might not be bad *because* they were forbidden by it, or good *because* it commanded them, yet probably those actions might be forbidden *because* they were bad for us, or commanded *because* they were beneficial to us, in their own natures, all the circumstances of things considered." [c]

He preached this gospel with simplicity, good sense, and humor. Most influential were his "Sayings of Poor Richard," published in his *Almanacks* which circulated widely among the rural population. The most popular of these sayings he compiled in *The Way to Wealth*, which is included in this edition. [d]

Philosophers are offended by the simplicity, almost simple-mindedness, of Franklin's morality. Surely there can be nothing profound in a doctrine which a Pennsylvania farmer could understand. Though more recent instrumentalists have succeeded in putting this doctrine in language which appeals more to "university men, and men of all sorts that have been bred at Edinburgh," [e] any intelligent analysis usually reveals the validity of Franklin's contentions; and though it may be more systematically developed and more elaborately conceived, the implications for conduct will be substantially the same. Certainly no method or presentation of utilitarian ethics could have been more effective than Franklin's, for he is to this day the patron saint of those who are interested in achievement.

---

[b] See p. 57.   [c] *Ibid.*   [d] *Ibid.*, p. 202.   [e] *Ibid.*, p. 15.

But more important than Franklin's utilitarianism in business was his practical sense as a humanitarian. He devoted the major part of his energies and resources to making benevolence practical by planning public improvements as scientific experiments. Throughout his life he proposed public plans—a plan for uniting the American colonies, a plan for the abolition of slavery and piracy, a plan for bringing the comforts of civilization to the natives of New Zealand, a plan for a "United Party for Virtue" organized internationally, a plan for a civil militia, a plan for transforming debts into philanthropy, a society for the promotion of science, a plan for conversion of the masses to Christianity (by converting first a few popular "grandees"; "for," said he to the evangelist George Whitefield, "men fear less the being in hell than out of fashion"). His numerous experiments in public welfare were much more important to him than his applications of science to lightning rods, bifocal spectacles, smokeless fireplaces, musical glasses, etc. As early as 1748 he wrote to his fellow scientist, Cadwallader Colden of New York:

"I am in a fair way of having no other tasks than such as I shall like to give myself, and of enjoying what I look upon as a great happiness, leisure to read, study, make experiments, and converse at large with such ingenious and worthy men as are pleased to honor me with their friendship or acquaintance, on such points as may produce something for the common benefit of mankind, uninterrupted by the little cares and fatigues of business." [f]

Since practical humanitarianism or intelligent public service is so dominant in Franklin's character and career, the publisher and editor of these selections are especially pleased to have the opportunity of calling attention to a few of his informal essays which are relatively little known. They are not literary masterpieces, but they exhibit vividly a master public "planner." He took ideals which were not new even in his day, but which needed practical embodiment, and he concentrated his mind on giving them concrete realization. Note particularly his observations on war, piracy, slave trade, penal reform, and freedom of the press; there is little

---

[f] Letter of July 6, 1749. John Bigelow: *The Complete Works of Benjamin Franklin*, Vol. II, p. 151.

theoretical elaboration of the grounds on which the abolition of basic evils should rest, but an intense conviction that something practical can and must be achieved at once in each of these fields of reform. Note also the characteristic simplicity and practicality of his suggestion for transforming debts into benefactions.[g]

Franklin's "art of virtue," outlined in his *Autobiography*,[h] is one more expression of his passion for "living usefully." He was no saint, and he specifically excluded the Christian virtue of humility from his table of virtues for practical cultivation. For a brief time in Franklin's life he concerned himself more or less seriously with religious reform. He tried to work out in detail a religious system which would give sincere expression to his moral ideas. To a certain extent Freemasonry and the Junto were his substitutes for churches. But above all he wrote little on religious subjects in order to avoid stimulating more theological contro-versy. Though it was his policy to disturb no one in his religious practices and beliefs, he himself contributed to the support of various religious groups. Thus he made his peace with all religions and devoted himself to none. His *Parable Against Persecution* and his *Letter on Religious Toleration*, which have been included in this volume of selections from his writings,[i] seem today to be elementary good sense and liberality, but in his day they were fighting words hammered out of bitter experience.

Though Franklin was no churchman, he reasserted the stern Puritan morality, divorced from its theocratic aims, and he made it serve the public needs of a struggling country. Wherever and when-ever the problem of maintaining *morale*, either personal or public, becomes a central concern, Benjamin Franklin's life and art and science continue to serve humanity. And readers of his *Autobiog-raphy* can still join him in "the reflection of a long life spent in meaning well."

HERBERT W. SCHNEIDER

---

[g] *A New Mode of Lending Money*, p. 191. [h] See pp. 80 ff. [i] See pp. 178, 180, respectively.

# SELECTED BIBLIOGRAPHY

## The Author's Writings

*A Dissertation on Liberty and Necessity, Pleasure and Pain.* London, 1725. Reprinted, with a bibliographical note by Lawrence C. Wroth, by the Facsimile Text Society. New York, 1930.

*Experiments and Observations on Electricity, made at Philadelphia, in America, by Mr. Benjamin Franklin, and Communicated in several Letters to P. Collinson, of London, F.R.S.* London, 1751.

*Poor Richard's Almanack.* Philadelphia, 1733-1758. The *Almanacks* of 1733, 1749, 1756, 1757, and 1758 have been reprinted in a facsimile edition, with a foreword by Phillips Russell. Garden City, New York, 1928.

*Political, Miscellaneous, and Philosophical Pieces.* Collected and edited, with explanatory plates and notes, by Benjamin Vaughan. London, 1779.

*The Works of Benjamin Franklin, L.L.D.* 3 vols. London, 1806.

*Memoirs of the Life and Writings of Benjamin Franklin.* Collected and edited by his grandson, William Temple Franklin. 3 vols. London, 1818.

*The Works of Benjamin Franklin.* Edited by Jared Sparks. 10 vols. Boston, 1836-1840.

*Letters to Benjamin Franklin, from his Family and Friends, 1751-1790.* Edited by William Duane. New York, 1859.

*The Complete Works of Benjamin Franklin.* Compiled and edited by John Bigelow. 10 vols. New York, 1887-1889.

*The Writings of Benjamin Franklin.* Edited, with a Life and Introduction, by Albert Henry Smyth. 10 vols. New York, 1905-1907.

*The Ingenious Dr. Franklin; Selected Scientific Letters of Benjamin Franklin.* Edited by N. G. Goodman. Philadelphia, 1931.

*Benjamin Franklin. Representative Selections.* Edited, with an Introduction, Bibliography, and Notes, by Frank Luther Mott and Chester E. Jorgenson. New York, 1936.

*Benjamin Franklin's Memoirs.* Parallel Text Edition, edited, with an Introduction and Explanatory Notes, by Max Farrand. Berkeley, California, 1949.

## Collateral Reading

An extensive bibliography up to the year 1889 is to be found in Paul L. Ford's *Franklin Bibliography, A List of Books Written by, or Relating to Benjamin Franklin.* Brooklyn, New York, 1889. Since that time, close to 100 works and essays on Franklin have been published. The following list includes the more important works of recent date.

d'Aulaire, J. M. *Benjamin Franklin.* New York, 1950.

Becker, Carl, *Benjamin Franklin.* Ithaca, New York, 1946.

———— "Benjamin Franklin." *Dictionary of American Biography,* Vol. VI. New York, 1931.

Cobb, B. B., and others, *American Eagle: The Story of Benjamin Franklin.* Newton, Massachusetts, 1944.

Cohen, J. Bernard, ed., *Experiments.* With a critical and historical Introduction. Cambridge, Massachusetts, 1941.

Crane, V. W., *Benjamin Franklin.* Baltimore, Maryland, 1936.

Crowther, J. G., *Famous American Men of Science.* New York, 1937.

Eaton, J., *That Lively Man Ben Franklin.* New York, 1948.

Eislen, M. R., *Franklin's Political Theories.* Garden City, New York, 1928.

Epstein, J., and B. Williams, *Real Book about Benjamin Franklin.* Garden City. New York, 1952.

Fay, Bernard, *Franklin, the Apostle of Modern Times.* Boston, 1929.

———— *The Two Franklins: Fathers of American Democracy* Boston, 1933.

Ford, Paul L., *The Many-Sided Franklin.* New York, 1899.

Goggio, E., "Benjamin Franklin and Italy," *Romantic Review,* XIX, 302-8, October, 1928.

Goodman. N. G., *Benjamin Franklin Reader.* New York, 1945.

Gray, A. K., *Benjamin Franklin's Library.* New York, 1937.

Greene, C. R., *Benjamin Franklin and Catherine R. Greene. Their Correspondence*. Edited by W. C. Roehler. Philadelphia, 1950.

Green, P., *Franklin and the King*. Historical play. New York, 1939.

Jay, J., *Some Conversations of Dr. Franklin and Dr. Jay*. New Haven, 1936.

Jusserand, J. J., "Franklin in France," *Essays Offered to Herbert Putnam*, edited by W. W. Bishop and A. Keogh. New Haven, 1929.

Maurois, A., *Franklin, the Life of an Optimist*. New York. 1945.

Meadowcroft, E. L., *Benjamin Franklin*. New York, 1941.

Meyer, Gladys, *Free Trade in Ideas. Aspects of American Liberalism Illustrated in Franklin's Philadelphia Career*. New York, 1941.

Nolan, J. B., *Benjamin Franklin in Scotland and Ireland*. Philadelphia, 1938.

Russell, Phillips, *Benjamin Franklin, The First Civilized American*. New York, 1926.

Scudder, E. S., *Benjamin Franklin*. New York, 1939.

Timothy, P., *Letters to Benjamin Franklin*. Chicago, 1935.

Truzak, C. (illustrator), *Benjamin Franklin. A Biography in Woodcuts*. New York, 1935.

Van Doren, Carl, *Benjamin Franklin*. New York, 1938.

### Foreign Language Publications

Baumgarten, Eduard, *Benjamin Franklin, der Lehrmeister der Amerikanischen Revolution*. Frankfurt am Main, 1936.

Fay, Bernard, *Benjamin Franklin*. Paris, 1931.

Rava, L., *La fortuna di Beniamino Franklin i Italia*. Florence, 1922.

Santelmo, J., *Vida de Benjamin Franklin*. Barcelona, 1924.

Seipp, E., *Benjamin Franklin's Religion und Ethik*. Giessen, 1932.

Ssymank, P., *Benjamin Franklin und die erste Berührung deutscher und nordamerikanischer Wissenschaft*. Göttingen, 1934.

# NOTE ON THE TEXT

## The Restoration of a Fair Copy of the Autobiography

The present edition follows, with minor changes, Max Farrand's "Fair Copy" of the *Autobiography*, published in cooperation with the Huntington Library by the University of California Press in 1949 and reprinted here with the permission of the publishers.

Farrand's edition is the first critical text of this great American classic. It was the editor's aim to recreate Franklin's *Autobiography* in its original directness and simplicity of style—in the manner in which it is believed that Franklin intended it to appear. Prior to that edition, this key piece of incunabula Americana has suffered from incredible confusion as to its authentic version.

To understand why there should be any confusion as to what Franklin actually wrote, one must know something of the history of the manuscript, which is as unique as the man himself. Farrand has made a careful study of the Odyssean fate of the manuscript, and the interested reader is referred to his account published as the Introduction to the "parallel text" edition of *Franklin's Memoirs*.[*] The following details concerning the "Fair Copy" are based on his report.

The *Autobiography* was written in four installments. When Franklin was writing the first part, he intended it to be seen only by his own family. However, when he resumed writing, now intending the work for publication, he apparently revised the previously written pages, so that the manuscript, which is now in the Huntington Library, is abundant with corrections written in

---

[*] Published in co-operation with the Huntington Library by the University of California Press, Berkeley, 1949.

the margins and between the lines, very often revising the same statement several times. The difficulty now is to determine what Franklin wished the final wording to be. When Franklin had finished the third part of the *Autobiography,* his grandson, Benjamin Franklin Bache, prepared, under his supervision, two copies which Franklin called "fair copies" and which apparently represented the final text that Franklin wanted to leave for publication. The copies were sent to his friends, Benjamin Vaughan and Louis Guillaume le Veillard, respectively, for comment and with the specific instruction not to "suffer any Copy to be taken of them, or of any Part of them, on any Account whatever." [b]

Both copies are lost, but it is safe to assume that the French translation by le Veillard and the edition published by William Temple Franklin in 1818 are based on the fair copy sent to le Veillard, the latter, however, including the changes which William Temple Franklin thought necessary to polish up his grandfather's style.

The fourth part was published only in 1868, after the original manuscript was recovered in 1866 by John Bigelow, then American Minister to France. Bigelow published an edited text of the original manuscript, which became the source text of most subsequent editions. Probably due to the difficulties of the manuscript referred to above, this edition, according to Farrand, contained a number of misinterpretations; and it remained for Farrand to edit the first critical text of the *Autobiography.* The reconstruction of this authentic version was achieved by comparing existing basic texts of the work: the original manuscript (in the Huntington Library); *Memoirs of the Life and Writings of Benjamin Franklin,* edited by William Temple Franklin (London, 1818); *Mémoires de B. Franklin,* translated by Louis Guillaume le Veillard (from the manuscript in the Library of Congress); and *Mémoires de la Vie Privée de Benjamin Franklin, Ecrits par Lui-Même, et Adressés a Son Fils,* published by Buisson, Paris, 1791 [an unauthorized edition, apparently based on the fair copy which had been sent to Benjamin Vaughan].

---

[b] Quoted in Farrand: *Benjamin Franklin's Memoirs.* University of California Press, Berkeley, 1949, p. xxv.

*Humanitarian Essays and Other Writings*

The other essays are reprinted from *The Complete Works in Philosophy, Politics, and Morals, of the Late Dr. Benjamin Franklin* (London, 1806), which is a reprint of the edition of Benjamin Vaughan, published in 1779, the only edition of Franklin's non-scientific works published during his lifetime.

For the convenience of the reader, the editorial staff of the publishers has contributed a number of notes, both footnotes and appendix notes. The editorial footnotes have been set in brackets. Those contributed by Max Farrand have been marked accordingly. Spelling and punctuation have been revised to conform to present-day American usage.

O.P.

# THE AUTOBIOGRAPHY

# The Autobiography

*Twyford, at the Bishop
of St. Asaph's, 1771*

DEAR SON,

I have ever had a pleasure in obtaining any little anecdotes of my ancestors. You may remember the inquiries I made among the remains of my relations when you were with me in England and the journey I undertook for that purpose. Imagining it may be equally agreeable to you to know the circumstances of *my* life—many of which you are yet unacquainted with—and expecting a week's uninterrupted leisure in my present country retirement, I sit down to write them for you. Besides, there are some other inducements that excite me to this undertaking. From the poverty and obscurity in which I was born and in which I passed my earliest years, I have raised myself to a state of affluence and some degree of celebrity in the world. As constant good fortune has accompanied me even to an advanced period of life, my posterity will perhaps be desirous of learning the means which I employed, and which, thanks to Providence, so well succeeded with me. They may also deem them fit to be imitated, should any of them find themselves in similar circumstances. That good fortune, when I reflected on it, which is frequently the case, has induced me sometimes to say that were it left to my choice, I should have no objection to go over the same life from its beginning to the end, only asking the advantage authors have of correcting in a second edition some faults of the first. So would I also wish to change some incidents of it for others more favorable. Notwithstanding, if this condition were denied, I should still accept the offer. But as this repetition is not to be expected, that which resembles most living one's life over again seems to be to recall all the circumstances of it; and, to render this remembrance more durable, to record them in writing. In thus employing myself I shall yield to the inclination so natural to old men of talking of themselves and their own actions, and I shall indulge it, without being tiresome to those who, from respect to my age, might conceive themselves obliged to listen to me, since they will be always free to read me or not. And lastly (I may as well confess it, as the denial of it would be believed by nobody) I shall perhaps not a little gratify my own vanity. Indeed, I never heard or saw the introductory words, "Without vanity I may say," etc., but some vain thing immediately followed. Most people dislike vanity in others whatever share they have of it themselves, but I give it fair quarter wherever I meet with it, being persuaded that it is often productive of good to the possessor and to others who are within his sphere of action. And therefore, in many cases it would not be altogether absurd if a man were to thank God for his vanity among the other comforts of life.

And now I speak of thanking God, I desire with all humility to acknowledge that I owe the mentioned happiness of my past life to his divine providence, which led me to the means I used and gave them success. My belief of this induces me to *hope,* though I must not *presume,* that the same goodness will still be exercised toward me in continuing that happiness or in enabling me to bear a fatal reverse, which I may experience as others have done—the complexion of my future fortune being known to him only, and in whose power it is to bless to us even our afflictions.

Some notes one of my uncles (who had the same curiosity in collecting family anecdotes) once put into my hands furnished me with several particulars relating to our ancestors. From these notes I learned that they had lived in the same village, Ecton in Northamptonshire, on a freehold of about thirty acres, for at least three hundred years, and how much longer he knew not—perhaps from the time when the name of Franklin, which before was the name of an order of people, was assumed by them as a surname, when others took surnames all over the kingdom.[a]

This small estate would not have sufficed for their maintenance without the business of a smith, which had continued in the family down to my uncle's time, the eldest son being always brought up to that business—a custom which he and my father followed with regard to their eldest sons. When I searched the register at Ecton, I found an account of their births, marriages, and burials from the year 1555 only, there being no register kept in that parish previous thereto. By that register I learned that I was the youngest son of the youngest son for five generations back. My grandfather Thomas, who was born in 1598, lived at Ecton till he was too old to continue his business, when he retired to Banbury in Oxfordshire to the house of his son John, a dyer, with whom my father served an apprenticeship. There my grandfather died and lies buried. We saw his gravestone in 1758. His eldest son Thomas lived in the house at Ecton and left it with the land to his only daughter, who with her husband, one Fisher of Wallingborough, sold it to Mr. Isted, now lord of the manor there. My grandfather had four sons that grew up; viz., Thomas, John, Benjamin, and Josiah. Being at a distance from my papers, I will give you what account I can of them from mem

---

As a proof that Franklin was anciently the common name of an order or rank in England, see Judge Fortescue, *De laudibus Legum Angliae*, written about the year 1412, in which is the following passage, to show that good juries might easily be formed in any part of England.

"Regio etiam illa, ita respersa refertaque est *possessoribus terrarum* et agrorum, quod in ea, villula tam parva reperiri non poterit, in qua non est *miles, armiger*, vel paterfamilias, qualis ibidem *Franklin* vulgariter noncupatur, magnis ditatus possessionibus, nec non libere tenentes et alii *valecti* plurimi, suis patrimoniis sufficientes ad faciendum juratum, in forma praenotata."

"Moreover, the same country is so filled and replenished with landed menne, that therein so small a Thorpe cannot be found wherein dweleth not a knight, an esquire, or such a householder, as is there commonly called a *Franklin*, enriched with great possessions; and also other freeholders and many yeomen able for their livelihoods to make a jury in form aforementioned." (Old translation.)

ory, and if they are not lost in my absence, you will find among them many more particulars.

Thomas was bred a smith under his father, but being ingenious and encouraged in learning (as all his brothers were) by an Esquire Palmer, then the principal inhabitant of that parish, he qualified himself for the business of scrivener, became a considerable man in the county affairs, was a chief mover of all public-spirited enterprises for the county or town of Northampton and his own village, of which many instances were told us at Ecton, and he was much taken notice of and patronized by Lord Halifax. He died in 1702, the 6th of January, four years to a day before I was born. The recital which elderly people made to us of his life and character, I remember, struck you as something extraordinary from its similarity with what you knew of me. "Had he died," said you, "four years later, on the same day, one might have supposed a transmigration." John was bred a dyer, I believe of wool. Benjamin was bred a silk dyer, serving an apprenticeship at London. He was an ingenious man. I remember him well, for when I was a boy he came to my father's in Boston and lived in the house with us some years. There was always a particular affection between my father and him, and I was his godson. He lived to a great age. He left behind him two quarto volumes of manuscript of his own poetry, consisting of fugitive pieces addressed to his friends and relations, of which the following, sent to me, is a specimen:

> To my Namesake upon a Report of his In-
> clination to Martial Affairs, July 7th, 1710

> Believe me, Ben, war is a dangerous trade.
> The sword has many marred as well as made;
> By it do many fall, not many rise—
> Makes many poor, few rich, and fewer wise;
> Fills towns with ruin, fields with blood; beside
> 'Tis Sloth's maintainer and the shield of Pride.
> Fair cities, rich today in plenty flow,
> War fills with want tomorrow, and with woe.
> Ruined estates, vice, broken limbs, and scars
> Are the effects of desolating wars.

## ACROSTIC

B-e to thy parents an obedient son,
E-ach day let duty constantly be done,
N-ever give way to sloth or lust or pride,
I-f free you'd be from thousand ills beside;
A-bove all ills, be sure avoid the shelf;
M-an's danger lies in Satan, sin, and self.
I-n virtue, learning, wisdom progress make,
N-e'er shrink at suffering for thy Saviour's sake.
F-raud and all falsehood in thy dealings flee,
R-eligious always in thy station be,
A-dore the maker of thy inward part.
N-ow's the accepted time; give God thy heart.
K-eep a good conscience, 'tis a constant friend;
L-ike judge and witness this thy act attend.
I-n heart, with bended knee, alone, adore
N-one but the Three-in-One forevermore.

He had invented a shorthand of his own, which he taught me, but not having practiced it, I have now forgot it. He was very pious, an assiduous attendant at the sermons of the best preachers, which he reduced to writing according to his method, and had thus collected several volumes of them. He was also a good deal of a politician—too much so, perhaps, for his station. There fell lately into my hands in London a collection he had made of all the principal pamphlets relating to public affairs from 1641 to 1717. Many of the volumes are wanting, as appears by the numbering, eight volumes in folio, and twenty-four in quarto and in octavo. A dealer in old books met with them, and knowing me by my sometimes buying books of him, he brought them to me. It would appear that my uncle must have left them here when he went to America, which was about fifty years ago. I have found many of his notes in the margins. His grandson, Samuel Franklin, is still living in Boston.

Our humble family early embraced the Reformation. Our forefathers continued Protestants through the reign of Mary, when they were sometimes in danger of persecution on account of their zeal against popery. They had an English Bible, and to conceal it and place it in safety, it was fastened open with tapes under and within the cover of a joint stool. When my great-great-grand-father wished to read it to his family, he turned up the joint stool upon his knees and then turned over the leaves under the tapes. One of the children stood at the door to give notice if he saw the apparitor coming, who was an officer of the spiritual court. In that case the stool was turned down again upon its feet, when the Bible remained concealed under it as before. This anecdote I had from my uncle Benjamin. The family continued all of the Church of England, till about the end of Charles the Second's reign, when some of the ministers that had been outed for nonconformity, holding conventicles in Northamptonshire, Benjamin and Josiah adhered to them and so continued all their lives. The rest of the family remained with the Episcopal church.

Josiah, my father, married young and carried his wife with three children to New England about 1682. The conventicles being at that time forbidden by law and frequently disturbed, some considerable men of his acquaintance determined to go to that country; and he was prevailed with to accompany them thither, where they expected to enjoy the exercise of their religion with freedom. By the same wife, my father had four children more born there, and by a second wife ten others—in all seventeen, of which I remember often to have seen thirteen sitting together at his table, who all grew up to years of maturity and married. I was the youngest son and the youngest of all the children except two daughters. I was born in Boston, in New England.

My mother, the second wife, was Abiah Folger, daughter of Peter Folger, one of the first settlers of New England, of whom honorable mention is made by Cotton Mather in his ecclesiastical history of that country, entitled *Magnalia Christi Americana*, as a "godly and learned Englishman," if I remember the words rightly.[1] I have heard that he wrote several small occasional pieces, but only one of them was printed, which I saw many years since. It was written in 1675, in familiar verse according to the taste of the time and people, and addressed to those then concerned in the government there. It asserts the liberty of conscience, and in behalf of the Anabaptists, Quakers, and other sectaries that had been persecuted. He attributes to this persecution the Indian Wars and other calamities that had befallen the country, regarding them as so many judgments of God to punish so heinous an offense, and exhorting a repeal of those laws so contrary to charity. This piece appeared to me as written with manly freedom and a pleasing simplicity. The six last lines I remember, though I have forgotten the two first; the purport of them was that his censures proceeded from good will, and therefore he would be known to be the author.

> Because to be a libeller (says he),
>   I hate it with my heart.
> From Sherbourne Town * where now I dwell,
>   My name I do put here,
> Without offence, your real friend,
>   It is Peter Folgier.

My elder brothers were all put apprentices to different trades. I was put to the grammar school at eight years of age, my father intending to devote me as the tithe of his sons to the service of the church. My early readiness in learning to read (which must have been very early, as I do not remember when I could not read) and the opinion of all his friends that I should certainly make a good scholar, encouraged him in this purpose of his. My uncle Benjamin, too, approved of it and proposed to give me all his shorthand volumes of sermons to set up with, if I would learn his shorthand. I continued, however, at the grammar school rather less than a year, though in that time I had risen gradually from the middle of the class of that year to be at the head of the same class, and was removed into the next class, whence I was to be placed in the third at the end of the year. But my father, burdened with a numerous family, was unable without inconvenience to support the expense of a college education, considering, moreover, as he said to one of his friends in my presence, the little encouragement that line of life afforded to those educated for it. He gave up his first intentions, took me from the grammar school, and sent me to a school for writing and arithmetic kept by a then

---

* In the island of Nantucket.

famous man, Mr. Geo. Brownell. He was a skillful master, and successful in his profession, employing the mildest and most encouraging methods. Under him I learned to write a good hand pretty soon, but I failed in the arithmetic and made no progress in it. At ten years old, I was taken home to help my father in his business, which was that of a tallow chandler and soap boiler—a business he was not bred to but had assumed on his arrival in New England, because he found his dyeing trade, being in little request, would not maintain his family. Accordingly, I was employed in cutting wick for the candles, filling the molds for cast candles, attending the shop, going of errands, etc.

I disliked the trade and had a strong inclination to go to sea, but my father declared against it; however, living near the water, I was much in it and on it. I learned early to swim well and to manage boats; and when embarked with other boys, I was commonly allowed to govern, especially in any case of difficulty; and upon other occasions I was generally the leader among the boys and sometimes led them into scrapes, of which I will mention one instance, as it shows an early projecting public spirit, though not then justly conducted.

There was a salt marsh that bounded part of the millpond, on the edge of which, at high water, we used to stand to fish for minnows. By much trampling we had made it a mere quagmire. My proposal was to build a wharf there for us to stand upon, and I showed my comrades a large heap of stones which were intended for a new house near the marsh and which would very well suit our purpose. Accordingly, in the evening when the workmen were gone home, I assembled a number of my playfellows, and we worked diligently like so many emmets, sometimes two or three to a stone, till we brought them all to make our little wharf. The next morning the workmen were surprised at missing the stones, which had formed our wharf; inquiry was made after the authors of this transfer; we were discovered, complained of; several of us were corrected by our fathers, and though I demonstrated the utility of our work, mine convinced me that that which was not honest could not be truly useful.

I suppose you may like to know what kind of a man my father

was. He had an excellent constitution, was of middle stature, but well set and very strong. He was ingenious, could draw prettily, was skilled a little in music; his voice was sonorous and agreeable, so that when he played Psalm tunes on his violin and sung withal, as he sometimes did in an evening after the business of the day was over, it was extremely agreeable to hear. He had some knowledge of mechanics, too, and on occasion was very handy with other tradesmen's tools. But his great excellence was a sound understanding and a solid judgment in prudential matters, both in private and public affairs. It is true he was never employed in the latter, the numerous family he had to educate and the straitness of his circumstances keeping him close to his trade; but I remember well his being frequently visited by leading men who consulted him for his opinion in affairs of the town or of the church he belonged to, and who showed a good deal of respect for his judgment and advice. He was also much consulted by private persons about their affairs when any difficulty occurred, and frequently chosen an arbitrator between contending parties. At his table he liked to have, as often as he could, some sensible friend or neighbor to converse with, and always took care to start some ingenious or useful topic for discourse which might tend to improve the minds of his children. By this means he turned our attention to what was good, just, and prudent in the conduct of life; and little or no notice was ever taken of what related to the victuals on the table—whether it was well or ill dressed, in or out of season, of good or bad flavor, preferable or inferior to this or that other thing of the kind; so that I was brought up in such a perfect inattention to those matters as to be quite indifferent what kind of food was set before me, and so unobservant of it that to this day I can scarce tell a few hours after dinner of what dishes it consisted. This has been a great convenience to me in traveling, where my companions have been sometimes very unhappy for want of a suitable gratification of their more delicate, because better instructed, tastes and appetites.

My mother had likewise an excellent constitution. She suckled all her ten children. I never knew either my father or mother to have any sickness but that of which they died, he at eighty-nine and she at eighty-five years of age. They lie buried together at Boston, where I some years since placed a marble stone over their grave with this inscription:

Josiah Franklin
And Abiah his wife
Lie here interred.
They lived lovingly together in wedlock
Fifty-five years.
Without an estate or any gainful employment,
By constant labor and industry,
With God's blessing,
They maintained a large family
Comfortably;
And brought up thirteen children,
And seven grandchildren
Reputably.
From this instance, Reader,
Be encouraged to diligence in thy calling,
And distrust not Providence.
He was a pious and prudent man,
She a discreet and virtuous woman.
Their youngest son,
In filial regard to their memory,
Places this stone.
J. F. born 1655—Died 1744—AEtat. 89.
A. F. born 1667—Died 1752——85.

By my rambling digressions I perceive myself to be grown old. I used to write more methodically. But one does not dress for private company as for a public ball. Perhaps 'tis only negligence.

To return: I continued thus employed in my father's business for two years, that is, till I was twelve years old; and my brother John, who was bred to that business, having left my father, married and set up for himself at Rhode Island, there was every appearance that I was destined to supply his place and be a tallow chandler. But my dislike to the trade continuing, my father had apprehensions that if he did not put me to one more agreeable, I should break loose and go to sea, as my brother Josiah had done, to his great vexation. In consequence he sometimes took me to walk with him and see joiners, bricklayers, turners, braziers, etc., at their work, that he might observe my inclination and endeavor to fix it on some trade that would keep me on land. It has ever since been a pleasure to me to see good workmen handle their tools; and it has been useful to me to have learned so much by it as to be able to do little jobs myself in my house, when a workman could not readily be got, and to construct little machines for my experiments when the intention of making these was warm in my mind. My father determined at last for the cutler's trade, and placed me for some days on trial with Samuel, son of my uncle Benjamin, who was bred to that trade in London and had just established himself in Boston. But the sum he exacted as a fee for my apprenticeship displeased my father, and I was taken home again.

From my infancy I was passionately fond of reading, and all the little money that came into my hands was laid out in the purchasing of books. I was very fond of voyages. My first acquisition was Bunyan's works in separate little volumes. I afterwards sold them to enable me to buy R. Burton's historical collections; they were small chapmen's books and cheap, forty or fifty in all. My father's little library consisted chiefly of books in polemic divinity, most of which I read. I have since often regretted that at a time when I had such a thirst for knowledge, more proper books had not fallen in my way, since it was now resolved I should not be bred to divinity. There was among them Plutarch's *Lives*, in which I read abundantly, and I still think that time spent to great advantage. There was also a book of Defoe's [2] called an *Essay on Projects* and another of Dr. Mather's called *Essays to do Good*, which perhaps gave me a turn of thinking that had an influence on some of the principal future events of my life.

This bookish inclination at length determined my father to make me a printer, though he had already one son (James) of that profession. In 1717 my brother, James, returned from England with a press and letters to set up his business in Boston. I liked it much better than that of my father, but still had a hankering for the sea. To prevent the apprehended effect of such an inclination, my father was impatient to have me bound to my brother. I stood out some time, but at last was persuaded and signed the indenture, when I was yet but twelve years old. I was to serve as apprentice till I was twenty-one years of age, only I was to be allowed journeyman's wages during the last year. In a little time I made a great progress in the business and became a useful hand to my brother. I now had access to better books. An acquaintance with the apprentices of booksellers enabled me sometimes to borrow a small one, which I was careful to return soon and clean. Often I sat up in my room reading the greatest part of the night, when the book was borrowed in the evening and to be returned early in the morning, lest it should be found missing or wanted.

After some time a merchant, an ingenious, sensible man, Mr. Matthew Adams, who had a pretty collection of books and who frequented our printing house, took notice of me, invited me to see his library, and very kindly proposed to lend me such books as I chose to read. I now took a fancy to poetry and made some little pieces. My brother, supposing it might turn to account, encouraged me and induced me to compose two occasional ballads. One was called the "Lighthouse Tragedy," and contained an account of the shipwreck of Capt. Worthilake with his two daughters; the other was a "Sailor's Song on the Taking of the Famous *Teach,* or Blackbeard, the Pirate." They were wretched stuff, in street ballad style;[3] and when they were printed, he sent me about the town to sell them. The first sold prodigiously, the event being recent and having made a great noise. This success flattered my vanity, but my father discouraged me by ridiculing my performances and telling me verse-makers were generally beggars. Thus I escaped being a poet and probably a very bad one. But as prose writing has been of great use to me in the course of my life and was a principal means of my advancement, I shall tell you how in such a situation I acquired what little ability I may be supposed to have in that way.

There was another bookish lad in the town, John Collins by name, with whom I was intimately acquainted. We sometimes disputed, and very fond we were of argument, and very desirous of confuting one another—which disputatious turn, by the way, is apt to become a very bad habit, making people often extremely disagreeable in company, by the contradiction that is necessary to bring it into practice; and thence besides souring and spoiling the conversation, it is productive of disgusts and perhaps enmities where you may have occasion for friendship. I had caught it by reading my father's books of dispute on religion. Persons of good sense, I have since observed, seldom fall into it, except lawyers, university men, and men of all sorts who have been bred at Edinburgh. A question was once somehow or other started between Collins and me on the propriety of educating the female sex in learning and their abilities for study. He was of opinion that it was improper and that they were naturally unequal to it. I took the contrary side, perhaps a little for dispute's sake. He was naturally more eloquent, having a greater plenty of words, and sometimes, as I thought, I was vanquished more by his fluency than by the strength of his reasons. As we parted without settling the point and were not to see one another again for some time, I sat down to put my arguments in writing, which I copied fair and sent to him. He answered and I replied. Three or four letters on a side had passed, when my father happened to find my papers and read them. Without entering into the subject in dispute, he took occasion to talk with me about my manner of writing, observed that though I had the advantage of my antagonist in correct spelling and pointing (which I owed to the printing house), I fell far short in elegance of expression, in method, and in perspicuity—of which he convinced me by several instances. I saw the justice of his remarks and thence grew more attentive to my manner of writing, and determined to endeavor to improve my style.

About this time I met with an odd volume of the *Spectator*.[4] It was the third. I had never before seen any of them. I bought it, read it over and over, and was much delighted with it. I thought the writing excellent and wished if possible to imitate it. With that view, I took some of the papers, and making short hints of the sentiment in each sentence, laid them by a few days, and then without looking at the book, tried to complete the papers again by expressing each hinted sentiment at length and as fully as it had been expressed before, in any suitable words that should occur to me. Then I compared my *Spectator* with the original, discovered some of my faults, and corrected them. But I found I wanted a stock of words or a readiness in recollecting and using them, which I thought I should have acquired before that time if I had gone on making verses; since the continual search for words of the same import but of different length to suit the measure, or of different sound for the rhyme would have laid me under a constant necessity of searching for variety, and also have tended to fix that variety in my mind, and make me master of it. Therefore I took some of the tales in the *Spectator* and turned them into verse, and after a time, when I had pretty well forgotten the prose, turned them back again. I also sometimes jumbled my collections of hints into confusion, and after some weeks endeavored to reduce them into the best order before I began to form the full sentences and complete the paper. This was to teach me method in the arrangement of the thoughts. By comparing my work afterwards with the original, I discovered many faults and corrected them; but I sometimes had the pleasure of fancying that in certain particulars of small import I had been lucky enough to improve the method or the language, and this encouraged me to think that I might possibly in time come to be a tolerable English writer, of which I was extremely ambitious.

The times I allotted for these exercises and for reading was at night after work, or before it began in the morning, or on Sundays, when I contrived to be in the printing house alone, avoiding as much as I could the common attendance of public worship which my father used to exact of me when I was under his care— and which, indeed, I still thought a duty, though I could not, as it seemed to me, afford the time to practice it.

When about sixteen years of age I happened to meet with a book written by one Tryon, recommending a vegetable diet.[5] I determined to go into it. My brother, being yet unmarried, did not keep house but boarded himself and his apprentices in another family. My refusing to eat flesh occasioned an inconvenience, and I was frequently chid for my singularity. I made

myself acquainted with Tryon's manner of preparing some of
his dishes, such as boiling potatoes or rice, making hasty pudding, and a few others; and then proposed to my brother that
if he would give me weekly half the money he paid for my board,
I would board myself. He instantly agreed to it, and I presently
found that I could save half what he paid me. This was an additional fund for buying of books. But I had another advantage
in it. My brother and the rest going from the printing house to
their meals, I remained there alone, and dispatching presently
my light repast (which often was no more than a biscuit or a
slice of bread, a handful of raisins or a tart from the pastry cook's,
and a glass of water) had the rest of the time till their return
for study, in which I made the greater progress from that greater
clearness of head and quicker apprehension which generally attend temperance in eating and drinking. Now it was that being
on some occasion made ashamed of my ignorance in figures,
which I had twice failed in learning when at school, I took
Cocker's book of arithmetic and went through the whole by myself with the greatest ease. I also read Seller's and Sturmy's book
on navigation and became acquainted with the little geometry
it contains, but I never proceeded far in that science. I read about
this time Locke, *On Human Understanding*,[6] and *The Art of
Thinking* by Messrs. du Port Royal.[7]

While I was intent on improving my language, I met with an
English grammar (I think it was Greenwood's) at the end of
which there were two little sketches on the arts of rhetoric and
logic, the latter finishing with a dispute in the Socratic method.
And soon after I procured Xenophon's *Memorable Things of
Socrates*, wherein there are many examples of the same method.
I was charmed with it, adopted it, dropped my abrupt contradiction and positive argumentation, and put on the humble in-
quirer. And being then, from reading Shaftesbury and Collins,
made a doubter, as I already was in many points of our religious
doctrines, I found this method the safest for myself and very
embarrassing to those against whom I used it; therefore, I took
a delight in it, practiced it continually, and grew very artful
and expert in drawing people, even of superior knowledge, into

concessions the consequences of which they did not foresee, entangling them in difficulties out of which they could not extricate themselves, and so obtaining victories that neither myself nor my cause always deserved. I continued this method some few years but gradually left it, retaining only the habit of expressing myself in terms of modest diffidence, never using when I advance anything that may possibly be disputed the words "certainly," "undoubtedly," or any others that give the air of positiveness to an opinion; but rather say, "I conceive or apprehend a thing to be so or so," "It appears to me," or "I should think it so or so, for such and such reasons," or "I imagine it to be so," or "It is so if I am not mistaken." This habit, I believe, has been of great advantage to me when I have had occasion to inculcate my opinions and persuade men into measures that I have been from time to time engaged in promoting. And as the chief ends of conversation are to *inform,* or to *be informed,* to *please* or to *persuade,* I wish well-meaning and sensible men would not lessen their power of doing good by a positive, assuming manner that seldom fails to disgust, tends to create opposition, and to defeat every one of those purposes for which speech was given to us. In fact, if you wish to instruct others, a positive, dogmatical manner in advancing your sentiments may provoke contradiction and prevent a candid attention. If you desire instruction and improvement from the knowledge of others, you should not at the same time express yourself as firmly fixed in your present opinions; modest and sensible men, who do not love disputation, will probably leave you undisturbed in the possession of your error. In adopting such a manner you can seldom expect to please your hearers, or to persuade those whose concurrence you desire. Pope [8] judiciously observes,

> Men must be taught as if you taught them not,
> And things unknown propos'd as things forgot.

He also recommends it to us,

> To speak, though sure, with seeming diffidence.

And he might have joined with this line that which he has coupled with another, I think less properly,

> For want of modesty is want of sense.

If you ask why *less properly,* I must repeat the lines,[9]

> Immodest words admit of *no defense,*
> *For* want of modesty is want of sense.

Now is not the "want of sense" (where a man is so unfortunate as to want it) some apology for his "want of modesty"? and would not the lines stand more justly thus?

> Immodest words admit *but* this defense
> That want of modesty is want of sense.

This, however, I should submit to better judgments.

My brother had in 1720 or '21 begun to print a newspaper. It was the second that appeared in America and was called *The New England Courant.* The only one before it was *The Boston Newsletter.* I remember his being dissuaded by some of his friends from the undertaking as not likely to succeed, one newspaper being in their judgment enough for America. At this time, 1771, there are not less than twenty-five. He went on, however, with the undertaking; I was employed to carry the papers to the customers, after having worked in composing the types and printing off the sheets. He had some ingenious men among his friends who amused themselves by writing little pieces for this paper, which gained it credit and made it more in demand; and these gentlemen often visited us. Hearing their conversations and their accounts of the approbation their papers were received with, I was excited to try my hand among them. But being still a boy and suspecting that my brother would object to printing anything of mine in his paper if he knew it to be mine, I contrived to disguise my hand; and writing an anonymous paper, I put it at night under the door of the printing house. It was found in the morning and communicated to his writing friends when they called in as usual. They read it, commented on it in my hearing, and I had the exquisite pleasure of finding it met with their approbation, and that in their different guesses at the author, none were named but men of some character among us for learning and ingenuity. I suppose now that I was rather lucky in my judges and that perhaps they were not really so very good as I then believed them to be. Encouraged, however, by this attempt, I wrote and sent in the same way to the press several other pieces, which were equally approved, and I kept my secret till my small fund of sense for such performances was pretty well exhausted, and then I discovered it, when I began to be considered a little more by my brother's acquaintance. However, that did not quite please him as he thought that it tended to make me too vain.

This might be one occasion of the differences we began to have about this time. Though a brother, he considered himself as my master and me as his apprentice, and accordingly expected the same services from me as he would from another; while I thought he degraded me too much in some he required of me, who from a brother expected more indulgence. Our disputes were often brought before our father, and I fancy I was either generally in the right or else a better pleader, because the judgment was generally in my favor. But my brother was passionate and had often beaten me, which I took extremely amiss. I fancy his harsh and tyrannical treatment of me might be a means of impressing me with that aversion to arbitrary power that has stuck to me through my whole life. Thinking my apprenticeship very tedious, I was continually wishing for some opportunity of shortening it, which at length offered in a manner unexpected.

One of the pieces in our newspaper on some political point which I have now forgotten gave offense to the Assembly. He was taken up, censured, and imprisoned for a month by the Speaker's warrant, I suppose because he would not discover the author. I, too, was taken up and examined before the Council; but though I did not give them any satisfaction, they contented themselves with admonishing me and dismissed me, considering me, perhaps, as an apprentice who was bound to keep his master's secrets. During my brother's confinement, which I resented a good deal notwithstanding our private differences, I had the management of the paper, and I made bold to give our rulers some rubs in it, which my brother took very kindly, while others began to consider me in an unfavorable light as a young genius that had a turn for libeling and satire. My brother's discharge was accompanied with an order from the House (a very odd one) that "James Franklin should no longer print the paper called the *New England Courant*." There was a consultation held in our printing house amongst his friends in this conjuncture. Some proposed to elude the order by changing the name of the paper; but my brother seeing inconveniences in that, it was finally concluded on as a better way to let it be printed for the future under the name of "Benjamin Franklin"; and to avoid the censure of the Assembly that might fall on him as still printing it by his apprentice, the contrivance was that my old indenture should be returned to me with a full discharge on the back of it, to show in case of necessity; but to secure to him the benefit of my service, I should sign new indentures for the remainder of the term, which were to be kept private. A very flimsy scheme it was, but, however, it was immediately executed, and the paper went on accordingly under my name for several months. At length a fresh difference arising between my brother and me, I took upon me to assert my freedom, presuming that he would not venture to produce the new indentures. It was not fair in me to take this advantage, and this I therefore reckon one of the first errata of my life. But the unfairness of it weighed little with me, when under the impressions of resentment for the blows his passion too often urged him to bestow upon me, though he was otherwise not an ill-natured man. Perhaps I was too saucy and provoking.

When he found I would leave him, he took care to prevent my getting employment in any other printing house of the town by going round and speaking to every master, who accordingly refused to give me work. I then thought of going to New York as the nearest place where there was a printer; and I was then rather inclined to leave Boston when I reflected that I had already made myself a little obnoxious to the governing party; and from the arbitrary proceedings of the Assembly in my brother's case, it was likely I might, if I stayed, soon bring myself into scrapes, and further that my indiscreet disputations about religion began to make me pointed at with horror by good people as an infidel or atheist. I determined on the point, but my father now siding with my brother, I was sensible that if I attempted to go openly, means would be used to prevent me. My friend Collins therefore undertook to manage my flight. He agreed with the captain of a New York sloop for my passage, under pretense of my being a young man of his acquaintance that had had an intrigue with a girl of bad character,ᵃ whose parents would compel me to marry her and therefore I could not appear or come away publicly. I sold some of my books to raise a little money, was taken on board the sloop privately, had a fair wind, and in three days found myself at New York, near three hundred miles from my home, at the age of seventeen, without the least recommendation to or knowledge of any person in the place, and with very little money in my pocket.

The inclination I had had for the sea was by this time done away, or I might now have gratified it. But having another profession and conceiving myself a pretty good workman, I offered my services to the printer of the place, old Mr. Wm. Bradford (who had been the first printer in Pennsylvania, but had removed thence in consequence of a quarrel with the Governor, Geo. Keith). He could give me no employment, having little to do and hands enough already. "But," says he, "my son at Philadelphia has lost his principal hand, Aquila Rose, by death. If you go thither I believe he may employ you."

Philadelphia was a hundred miles farther. I set out, however, in a boat for Amboy, leaving my chest and things to follow me round by sea. In crossing the bay we met with a squall that tore our rotten sails to pieces, prevented our getting into the kill, and drove us upon Long Island. In our way a drunken Dutchman, who was a passenger, too, fell overboard; when he was sinking, I reached through the water to his shock pate and drew him up so that we got him in again. His ducking sobered him a little, and he went to sleep, taking first out of his pocket a book which

---

ᵃ [Franklin originally wrote: "that had got a naughty girl with child."—M.F.]

he desired I would dry for him. It proved to be my old favorite author Bunyan's *Pilgrim's Progress* [10] in Dutch, finely printed on good paper with copper cuts, a dress better than I had ever seen it wear in its own language. I have since found that it has been translated into most of the languages of Europe, and suppose it has been more generally read than any other book except, perhaps, the Bible. Honest John was the first that I know of who mixes narration and dialogue, a method of writing very engaging to the reader, who in the most interesting parts finds himself, as it were, admitted into the company and present at the conversation. Defoe has imitated him successfully in his *Robinson Crusoe,* in his *Moll Flanders,* and other pieces; and Richardson [10a] has done the same in his *Pamela,* etc.

On approaching the island, we found it was in a place where there could be no landing, there being a great surf on the stony beach. So we dropped anchor and swung out our cable toward the shore. Some people came down to the water edge and hallooed to us, as we did to them, but the wind was so high and the surf so loud that we could not understand each other. There were some canoes on the shore, and we made signs and called to them to fetch us, but they either did not comprehend us or thought it impracticable, so they went off. Night approaching, we had no remedy but to have patience till the wind abated, and in the meantime the boatman and I concluded to sleep if we could, and so we crowded into the scuttle with the Dutchman, who was still wet, and the spray breaking over the head of our boat leaked through to us, so that we were soon almost as wet as he. In this manner we lay all night with very little rest; but the wind abating the next day, we made a shift to reach Amboy before night, having been thirty hours on the water without victuals or any drink but a bottle of filthy rum, the water we sailed on being salt.

In the evening I found myself very feverish and went to bed; but having read somewhere that cold water drunk plentifully was good for a fever, I followed the prescription, sweat plentifully most of the night, my fever left me, and in the morning crossing the ferry I proceeded on my journey on foot, having fifty miles to Burlington, where I was told I should find boats that would carry me the rest of the way to Philadelphia.

It rained very hard all the day, I was thoroughly soaked and by noon a good deal tired, so I stopped at a poor inn, where I stayed all night, beginning now to wish I had never left home. I made so miserable a figure, too, that I found by the questions asked me I was suspected to be some runaway servant and in danger of being taken up on that suspicion. However, I proceeded the next day, and got in the evening to an inn within eight or ten miles of Burlington, kept by one Dr. Brown.

He entered into conversation with me while I took some refreshment and, finding I had read a little, became very sociable and friendly. Our acquaintance continued all the rest of his life. He had been, I imagine, an itinerant doctor, for there was no town in England or any country in Europe of which he could not give a very particular account. He had some letters and was ingenious, but he was an infidel and wickedly undertook some years after to travesty the Bible in doggerel verse, as Cotton had done with Virgil.[11] By this means he set many of the facts in a very ridiculous light and might have done mischief with weak minds if his work had been published, but it never was. At his house I lay that night, and the next morning reached Burlington, but had the mortification to find that the regular boats were gone a little before and no other expected to go before Tuesday, this being Saturday. Wherefore, I returned to an old woman in the town of whom I had bought some gingerbread to eat on the water and asked her advice; she invited me to lodge at her house till a passage by water should offer; and being tired with my foot traveling, I accepted the invitation. Understanding I was a printer, she would have had me remain in that town and follow my business, being ignorant of the stock necessary to begin with. She was very hospitable, gave me a dinner of ox cheek with great good will, accepting only of a pot of ale in return. And I thought myself fixed till Tuesday should come. However, walking in the evening by the side of the river, a boat came by, which I found was going toward Philadelphia, with several people in her. They took me in, and as there was no wind, we rowed all the way;

and about midnight, not having yet seen the city, some of the company were confident we must have passed it and would row no farther; the others knew not where we were, so we put toward the shore, got into a creek, landed near an old fence, with the rails of which we made a fire, the night being cold in October, and there we remained till daylight. Then one of the company knew the place to be Cooper's Creek, a little above Philadelphia, which we saw as soon as we got out of the creek, and arrived there about eight or nine o'clock, on the Sunday morning, and landed at the Market Street wharf.

I have been the more particular in this description of my journey, and shall be so of my first entry into that city, that you may in your mind compare such unlikely beginnings with the figure I have since made there. I was in my working dress, my best clothes being to come round by sea. I was dirty from my journey; my pockets were stuffed out with shirts and stockings; I knew no soul, nor where to look for lodging. Fatigued with walking, rowing, and want of sleep, I was very hungry, and my whole stock of cash consisted of a Dutch dollar and about a shilling in copper coin, which I gave to the boatmen for my passage. At first they refused it on account of my having rowed, but I insisted on their taking it. A man is sometimes more generous when he has little money than when he has plenty, perhaps through fear of being thought to have but little. I walked toward the top of the street, gazing about till near Market Street, where I met a boy with bread. I have often made a meal of dry bread, and inquiring where he had bought it, I went immediately to the baker's he directed me to. I asked for biscuit, meaning such as we had in Boston, but that sort, it seems, was not made in Philadelphia. I then asked for a threepenny loaf and was told they had none such. Not knowing the different prices nor the names of the different sorts of bread, I told him to give me three pennyworth of any sort. He gave me accordingly three great puffy rolls. I was surprised at the quantity but took it, and having no room in my pockets, walked off with a roll under each arm and eating the other. Thus I went up Market Street as far as Fourth Street, passing by the door of Mr. Read, my future wife's father, when she, standing at the door, saw me and thought I made—as I certainly did—a most awkward, ridiculous appearance. Then I turned and went down Chestnut Street and part of Walnut Street, eating my roll all the way, and coming round, found myself again at Market Street wharf near the boat I came in, to which I went for a draught of the river water, and being filled with one of my rolls, gave the other two to a woman and her child that came down the river in the boat with us and were waiting to go farther. Thus refreshed, I walked again up the street, which by this time had many clean dressed people in it who were all walking the same way; I joined them, and thereby was led into the great meetinghouse of the Quakers near the market. I sat down among them, and after looking round awhile and hearing nothing said, being very drowsy through labor and want of rest the preceding night, I fell fast asleep and continued so till the meeting broke up, when someone was kind enough to rouse me. This was therefore the first house I was in or slept in, in Philadelphia.

I then walked down again toward the river, and looking in the faces of everyone, I met a young Quaker man whose countenance pleased me, and accosting him requested he would tell me where a stranger could get a lodging. We were then near the Sign of the Three Mariners. "Here," says he, "is a house where they receive strangers, but it is not a reputable one; if thee wilt walk with me, I'll show thee a better one." He conducted me to the Crooked Billet in Water Street. There I got a dinner. And while I was eating, several sly questions were asked me, as from my youth and appearance I was suspected of being a runaway. After dinner my sleepiness returned; and being shown to a bed, I lay down without undressing and slept till six in the evening, when I was called to supper. I went to bed again very early and slept soundly till next morning. Then I dressed myself as neat as I could, and went to Andrew Bradford, the printer's. I found in the shop the old man, his father, whom I had seen at New York, and who, traveling on horseback, had got to Philadelphia before me. He introduced me to his son, who received me civilly, gave me a breakfast, but told me he did not at present want a hand, being lately supplied with one. But there was another printer in town lately set up, one Keimer, who perhaps might employ me; if not, I should be welcome to lodge at his house, and he would give me a little work to do now and then till fuller business should offer.

The old gentleman said he would go with me to the new printer. And when we found him, "Neighbor," says Bradford, "I have brought to see you a young man of your business; perhaps you may want such a one." He asked me a few questions, put a composing stick in my hand to see how I worked, and then said he would employ me soon, though he had just then nothing for me to do. And taking old Bradford, whom he had never seen before, to be one of the townspeople that had a good will for him, entered into a conversation on his present undertaking and prospects; while Bradford, not discovering that he was the other printer's father, on Keimer's saying he expected soon to get the greatest part of the business into his own hands, drew him on, by artful questions and starting little doubts, to explain all his views, what influence he relied on, and in what manner he intended to proceed. I, who stood by and heard all, saw immediately that one of them was a crafty old sophister, and the other a true novice. Bradford left me with Keimer, who was greatly surprised when I told him who the old man was.

Keimer's printing house, I found, consisted of an old damaged press and a small worn-out font of English types, which he was then using himself, composing an elegy on Aquila Rose, beforementioned, an ingenious young man of excellent character, much respected in the town, secretary to the Assembly, and a pretty poet. Keimer made verses, too, but very indifferently. He could not be said to write them, for his method was to compose them in the types directly out of his head; so there being no copy but one pair of cases, and the elegy probably requiring all the letter, no one could help him. I endeavored to put his press (which he had not yet used, and of which he understood nothing) into order fit to be worked with; and promising to come and print off his elegy as soon as he should have got it ready, I returned to Bradford's, who gave me a little job to do for the present, and there I lodged and dieted. A few days after, Keimer sent for me to print off the elegy. And now he had got another pair of cases, and a pamphlet to reprint, on which he set me to work.

These two printers I found poorly qualified for their business. Bradford had not been bred to it and was very illiterate; and Keimer, though something of a scholar, was a mere compositor, knowing nothing of presswork. He had been one of the French prophets and could act their enthusiastic agitations. At this time he did not profess any particular religion, but something of all on occasion, was very ignorant of the world, and had—as I afterward found—a good deal of the knave in his composition. He did not like my lodging at Bradford's while I worked with him. He had a house, indeed, but without furniture, so he could not lodge me; but he got me a lodging at Mr. Read's, beforementioned, who was the owner of his house. And my chest and clothes being come by this time, I made rather a more respectable appearance in the eyes of Miss Read than I had done when she first happened to see me eating my roll in the street.

I began now to have some acquaintance among the young people of the town that were lovers of reading, with whom I spent my evenings very pleasantly, and gained money by my industry and frugality. I lived very contented, and forgot Boston as much as I could, and did not wish it should be known where I resided except to my friend Collins, who was in my secret and kept it when I wrote to him. At length an incident happened that sent me back again much sooner than I had intended.

I had a brother-in-law, Robert Homes, master of a sloop that traded between Boston and Delaware. He being at Newcastle, forty miles below Philadelphia, heard there of me and wrote me a letter mentioning the concern of my relations and friends in Boston at my abrupt departure, assuring me of their good will to me, and that everything would be accommodated to my mind if I would return, to which he exhorted me very earnestly. I wrote an answer to his letter, thanked him for his advice, but stated my reasons for quitting Boston so fully and in such a light as to convince him that I was not so much in the wrong as he had apprehended.

Sir William Keith, Governor of the province, was then at New-

castle, and Captain Homes happening to be in company with
him when my letter came to hand, spoke to him of me and
showed him the letter. The Governor read it, and seemed surprised when he was told my age. He said I appeared a young
man of promising parts and therefore should be encouraged. The
printers at Philadelphia were wretched ones, and if I would set
up there, he made no doubt I should succeed; for his part, he
would procure me the public business, and do me every other
service in his power. This my brother-in-law afterwards told me
in Boston. But I knew as yet nothing of it; when one day
Keimer and I being at work together near the window, we saw
the Governor and another gentleman (who proved to be Colonel
French of Newcastle), finely dressed, come directly across the
street to our house and heard them at the door. Keimer ran down
immediately, thinking it a visit to him; but the Governor inquired for me, came up, and with a condescension and politeness
I had been quite unused to, made me many compliments, desired
to be acquainted with me, blamed me kindly for not having made
myself known to him when I first came to the place, and would
have me away with him to the tavern where he was going with
Colonel French to taste, as he said, some excellent Madeira. I was
not a little surprised, and Keimer stared with astonishment.[a]
I went, however, with the Governor and Colonel French, to a
tavern the corner of Third Street, and over the Madeira he proposed my setting up my business. He stated the probabilities of
success, and both he and Colonel French assured me I should
have their interest and influence to obtain for me the public
business of both governments.[b] On my doubting whether my
father would assist me in it, Sir William said he would give me
a letter to him in which he would set forth the advantages, and
he did not doubt he should determine him to comply. So it was
concluded I should return to Boston by the first vessel with the
Governor's letter of recommendation to my father. In the meantime the intention was to be kept secret, and I went on working

---

[a] [Franklin originally wrote: "Keimer stared like a pig poisoned."
—M.F.]

[b] [Pennsylvania and Delaware.]

with Keimer as usual. The Governor sent for me now and then to dine with him, which I considered a great honor, more particularly as he conversed with me in the most affable, familiar, and friendly manner imaginable.

About the end of April, 1724, a little vessel offered for Boston. I took leave of Keimer as going to see my friends. The Governor gave me an ample letter, saying many flattering things of me to my father and strongly recommending the project of my setting up at Philadelphia as a thing that would make my fortune. We struck on a shoal in going down the bay and sprung a leak; we had a blustering time at sea and were obliged to pump almost continually, at which I took my turn. We arrived safe, however, at Boston in about a fortnight. I had been absent seven months, and my friends had heard nothing of me, for my brother Homes was not yet returned and had not written about me. My unexpected appearance surprised the family; all were, however, very glad to see me and made me welcome, except my brother. I went to see him at his printing house. I was better dressed than ever while in his service, having a genteel new suit from head to foot, a watch, and my pockets lined with near five pounds sterling in silver. He received me not very frankly, looked me all over, and turned to his work again. The journeymen were inquisitive where I had been, what sort of a country it was, and how I liked it. I praised it much and the happy life I led in it, expressing strongly my intention of returning to it; and one of them asking what kind of money we had there, I produced a handful of silver and spread it before them, which was a kind of raree show they had not been used to, paper being the money of Boston. Then I took an opportunity of letting them see my watch, and lastly (my brother still grum and sullen) I gave them a piece of eight [12] to drink and took my leave. This visit of mine offended him extremely. For when my mother sometime after spoke to him of a reconciliation, and of her wish to see us on good terms together, and that we might live for the future as brothers, he said I had insulted him in such a manner before his people that he could never forget or forgive it. In this, however, he was mistaken.

My father received the Governor's letter with some surprise but said little of it to me for some days. Captain Homes returning, he showed it to him, and asked him if he knew Keith and what kind of a man he was, adding his opinion that he must be of small discretion to think of setting a boy up in business who wanted yet three years to arrive at man's estate. Homes said what he could in favor of the project; but my father was clear in the impropriety of it, and at last gave a flat denial. Then he wrote a civil letter to Sir William, thanking him for the patronage he had so kindly offered me, and declining to assist me as yet in setting up, I being in his opinion too young to be trusted with the management of an undertaking so important, and for which the preparation required a considerable expenditure.

My old companion Collins, who was a clerk in the post office, pleased with the account I gave him of my new country, determined to go thither also. And while I waited for my father's determination, he set out before me by land to Rhode Island, leaving his books, which were a pretty collection of mathematics and natural philosophy, to come with mine and me to New York, where he proposed to wait for me.

My father, though he did not approve Sir William's proposition, was yet pleased that I had been able to obtain so advantageous a character from a person of such note where I had resided, and that I had been so industrious and careful as to equip myself so handsomely in so short a time. Therefore, seeing no prospect of an accommodation between my brother and me, he gave his consent to my returning again to Philadelphia, advised me to behave respectfully to the people there, endeavor to obtain the general esteem, and avoid lampooning and libeling, to which he thought I had too much inclination—telling me that by steady industry and a prudent parsimony I might save enough by the time I was twenty-one to set me up, and that if I came near the matter he would help me out with the rest. This was all I could obtain, except some small gifts as tokens of his and my mother's love, when I embarked again for New York, now with their approbation and their blessing. The sloop putting in at Newport, Rhode Island, I visited my brother John, who had been married and settled there some years. He received me very affectionately, for he always loved me. A friend of his, one Vernon, having some money due to him in Pennsylvania, about thirty-five pounds currency, desired I would recover it for him and keep it till I had his directions what to employ it in. Accordingly he gave me an order. This business afterwards occasioned me a good deal of uneasiness.

At Newport we took in a number of passengers—among which were two young women traveling together and a grave, sensible, matron-like Quaker lady with her servants. I had shown an obliging readiness to render her some little services, which impressed her, I suppose, with a degree of good will toward me; for when she saw a daily growing familiarity between me and the two young women, which they appeared to encourage, she took me aside and said, "Young man, I am concerned for thee, as thou hast no friend with thee and seems not to know much of the world or of the snares youth is exposed to; depend upon it, those are very bad women; I can see it by all their actions; and if thee art not upon thy guard, they will draw thee into some danger; they are strangers to thee, and I advise thee, in a friendly concern for thy welfare, to have no acquaintance with them." As I seemed at first not to think so ill of them as she did, she mentioned some things she had observed and heard that had escaped my notice, but now convinced me she was right. I thanked her for her kind advice and promised to follow it. When we arrived at New York, they told me where they lived and invited me to come and see them; but I avoided it. And it was well I did; for the next day the captain missed a silver spoon and some other things that had been taken out of his cabin; and knowing that these were a couple of strumpets, he got a warrant to search their lodgings, found the stolen goods, and had the thieves punished. So though we escaped a sunken rock which we scraped upon in the passage, I thought this escape of rather more importance to me.

At New York I found my friend Collins, who had arrived there sometime before me. We had been intimate from children and had read the same books together, but he had the advantage of more time for reading and studying and a wonderful genius for mathematical learning, in which he far outstripped me. While I lived in Boston, most of my hours of leisure for conversation were spent with him; and he continued a sober as well as an industrious lad, was much respected for his learning by several of the clergy and other gentlemen, and seemed to promise making a good figure in life. But during my absence he had acquired a habit of sotting with brandy, and I found by his own account, as well as that of others, that he had been drunk every day since his arrival at New York, and behaved himself in a very extravagant manner. He had gamed, too, and lost his money, so that I was obliged to discharge his lodgings and defray his expenses on the road and at Philadelphia—which proved a great burden to me. The then Governor of New York, Burnet,[13] son of Bishop Burnet, hearing from the captain that a young man, one of his passengers, had a great many books, desired him to bring me to see him. I waited upon him and should have taken Collins with me had he been sober. The Governor received me with great civility, showed me his library, which was a very considerable one, and we had a good deal of conversation about books and authors. This was the second governor who had done me the honor to take notice of me, and for a poor boy like me was very pleasing.

We proceeded to Philadelphia. I received on the way Vernon's money, without which we could hardly have finished our journey. Collins wished to be employed in some countinghouse; but whether they discovered his dramming by his breath or by his behavior, though he had some recommendations, he met with no success in any application and continued lodging and boarding at the same house with me and at my expense. Knowing I had that money of Vernon's, he was continually borrowing of me, still promising repayment as soon as he should be in business. At length he had got so much of it that I was distressed to think what I should do in case of being called on to remit it. His drinking continued, about which we sometimes quarreled, for when a little intoxicated he was very fractious. Once in a boat on the Delaware with some other young men, he refused to row in his turn.

"I will be rowed home," says he.

"We will not row you," says I.

"You must," says he, "or stay all night on the water, just as you please."

The others said, "Let us row; what signifies it?"

But my mind being soured with his other conduct, I continued to refuse. So he swore he would make me row or throw me overboard; and coming along stepping on the thwarts toward me, when he came up and struck at me, I clapped my hand under his crutch and rising pitched him head-foremost into the river. I knew he was a good swimmer and so was under little concern about him; but before he could get round to lay hold of the boat, we had with a few strokes pulled her out of his reach. And ever when he drew near the boat, we asked if he would row, striking a few strokes to slide her away from him. He was ready to stifle with vexation, and obstinately would not promise to row; however, seeing him at last beginning to tire, we drew him into the boat and brought him home dripping wet in the evening. We hardly exchanged a civil word after this adventure. At length a West India captain who had a commission to procure a tutor for the sons of a gentleman at Barbados, happening to meet with him, proposed to carry him thither to fill that situation. He accepted and left me, promising to remit me what he owed me out of the first money he should receive, but I never heard of him after.

The violation of my trust respecting Vernon's money was one of the first great errata of my life, and this affair showed that my father was not much out in his judgment when he supposed me too young to manage business of importance. But Sir William, on reading his letter, said he was too prudent, that there was a great difference in persons, and discretion did not always accompany years, nor was youth always without it. "And since he will not set you up," says he, "I will do it myself. Give me an inventory of the things necessary to be had from England, and I will send for them. You shall repay me when you are able; I am resolved to have a good printer here, and I am sure you must succeed." This was spoken with such an appearance of cordiality that I had not the least doubt of his meaning what he said. I had hitherto kept the proposition of my setting up a secret in Philadelphia, and I still kept it. Had it been known that I depended on the Governor, probably some friend that knew him better would have advised me not to rely on him, as I afterwards heard it as his known character to be liberal of promises which he never meant to keep. Yet unsolicited as he was by me, how could I think his generous offers insincere? I believed him one of the best men in the world.

I presented him an inventory of a little printing house, amounting by my computation to about £100 sterling. He liked it but asked me if my being on the spot in England to choose the types and see that everything was good of the kind might not be of some advantage. "Then," says he, "when there you may make acquaintances and establish correspondences in the bookselling and stationery way." I agreed that this might be advantageous. "Then," says he, "get yourself ready to go with *Annis*," which was the annual ship and the only one at that time usually passing between London and Philadelphia. But it would be some months before *Annis* sailed, so I continued working with Keimer, fretting extremely about the money Collins had got from me, and in daily apprehensions of being called upon for it by Vernon—which, however, did not happen for some years after.

I believe I have omitted mentioning that in my first voyage from Boston to Philadelphia, being becalmed off Block Island, our crew employed themselves catching cod and hauled up a great number. Till then I had stuck to my resolution to eat nothing that had had life; and on this occasion I considered, according to my Master Tryon, the taking every fish as a kind of unprovoked murder, since none of them had or ever could do us any injury that might justify this massacre. All this seemed very reasonable. But I had formerly been a great lover of fish, and when this came hot out of the frying pan, it smelled admirably well. I balanced some time between principle and inclination till I recollected that when the fish were opened, I saw smaller fish taken out of their stomachs. "Then," thought I, "if you eat one another, I don't see why we mayn't eat you." So I dined upon cod very heartily and have since continued to eat as other people, returning only now and then occasionally to a vegetable diet. So convenient a thing it is to be a *reasonable creature,* since it enables one to find or make a reason for everything one has a mind to do.

Keimer and I lived on a pretty good familiar footing and agreed tolerably well, for he suspected nothing of my setting up. He retained a great deal of his old enthusiasm and loved argumentation. We therefore had many disputations. I used to work him so with my Socratic method and had trepanned him so often by questions apparently so distant from any point we had in hand, and yet by degrees leading to the point and bringing him into difficulties and contradictions, that at last he grew ridiculously cautious and would hardly answer the most common question without asking first, "What do you intend to infer from that?" However, it gave him so high an opinion of my abilities in the confuting way that he seriously proposed my being his colleague in a project he had of setting up a new sect. He was to preach the doctrines, and I was to confound all opponents. When he came to explain with me upon the doctrines, I found several conundrums which I objected to, unless I might have my way a little, too, and introduce some of mine. Keimer wore his beard at full length, because somewhere in the Mosaic Law it is said, "Thou shalt not mar the corners of thy beard." He likewise kept the seventh day Sabbath, and these two points were essentials with him. I disliked both but agreed to admit them upon condition of his adopting the doctrine of not using animal food. "I doubt," says he, "my constitution will bear it." I assured him it would and that he would be the better for it. He was usually a great glutton, and I wished to give myself some diversion in half-starving him. He consented to try the practice if I would keep him company; I did so, and we held it for three months. Our provisions were purchased, cooked, and brought to us regularly by a woman in the neighborhood who had from me a list of forty dishes to be prepared for us at different times, in which there entered neither fish, flesh, nor fowl. This whim suited me better at this time from the cheapness of it, not costing us above

eighteen pence sterling each per week. I have since kept several
Lents most strictly, leaving the common diet for that, and that
for common, abruptly, without the least inconvenience, so that
I think there is little in the advice of making those changes
by easy gradations. I went on pleasantly, but poor Keimer suffered grievously, tired of the project, longed for the flesh pots
of Egypt, and ordered a roast pig. He invited me and two women
friends to dine with him, but it being brought too soon upon
table, he could not resist the temptation and ate it all up before
we came.

I had made some courtship during this time to Miss Read.[14]
I had a great respect and affection for her, and had some reasons
to believe she had the same for me; but as I was about to take
a long voyage and we were both very young, only a little above
eighteen, it was thought most prudent by her mother to prevent
our going too far at present, as a marriage, if it was to take place,
would be more convenient after my return, when I should be, as
I hoped, set up in my business. Perhaps, too, she thought my expectations not so well founded as I imagined them to be.

My chief acquaintances at this time were Charles Osborne,
Joseph Watson, and James Ralph [15]—all lovers of reading. The
two first were clerks to an eminent scrivener or conveyancer in
the town, Charles Brogden; the other was clerk to a merchant.
Watson was a pious, sensible young man of great integrity. The
others [were] rather more lax in their principles of religion, particularly Ralph, who as well as Collins had been unsettled by
me, for which they both made me suffer. Osborne was sensible,
candid, frank—sincere and affectionate to his friends—but in literary matters too fond of criticism. Ralph was ingenious, genteel
in his manners, and extremely eloquent; I think I never knew a
prettier talker. Both were great admirers of poetry and began to
try their hands in little pieces. Many pleasant walks we four
had together on Sundays in the woods on the banks of the
Schuylkill, when we read to one another and conferred on what
we read. Ralph was inclined to give himself up entirely to poetry,
not doubting but he might make great proficiency in it and even
make his fortune by it. He pretended that the greatest poets must,

when they first began to write, have committed as many faults as he did. Osborne endeavored to dissuade him, assured him he had no genius for poetry, and advised him to think of nothing beyond the business he was bred to: "That in the mercantile way, though he had no stock, he might by his diligence and punctuality recommend himself to employment as a factor and in time acquire wherewith to trade on his own account." I approved for my part the amusing one's self with poetry now and then, so far as to improve one's language, but no further. On this it was proposed that we should each of us at our next meeting produce a piece of our own composing in order to improve by our mutual observations, criticisms, and corrections. As language and expression was what we had in view, we excluded all considerations of invention, by agreeing that the task should be a version of the eighteenth Psalm, which describes the descent of a deity. When the time of our meeting drew nigh, Ralph called on me first and let me know his piece was ready; I told him I had been busy and, having little inclination, had done nothing. He then showed me his piece for my opinion; and I much approved it, as it appeared to have great merit. "Now," says he, "Osborne never will allow the least merit in anything of mine but makes a thousand criticisms out of mere envy. He is not so jealous of you. I wish therefore you would take this piece and produce it as yours. I will pretend not to have had time, and so produce nothing. We shall then see what he will say to it." It was agreed, and I immediately transcribed it that it might appear in my own hand. We met. Watson's performance was read; there were some beauties in it, but many defects. Osborne's was read; it was much better. Ralph did it justice, remarked some faults, but applauded the beauties. He himself had nothing to produce. I was backward, seemed desirous of being excused, had not had sufficient time to correct, etc.; but no excuse could be admitted, produce I must. It was read and repeated; Watson and Osborne gave up the contest and joined in applauding it. Ralph only made some criticisms and proposed some amendments, but I defended my text. Osborne was against Ralph, and told him he was no better able to criticize than compose verses. As these two were returning home together, Osborne expressed himself still more strongly in favor of what he thought my production, having before refrained, as he said, lest I should think he meant to flatter me. "But who would have imagined," says he, "that Franklin had been capable of such a performance—such painting, such force, such fire! He has even improved the original. In his common conversation, he seems to have no choice of words; he hesitates and blunders; and yet, good God, how he writes!" When we next met, Ralph discovered the trick we had played him, and Osborne was a little laughed at. This transaction fixed Ralph in his resolution of becoming a poet. I did all I could to dissuade him from it, but he continued scribbling verses till Pope cured him.[a] He became, however, a pretty good prose writer. More of him hereafter. But as I may not have occasion to mention the other two, I shall just remark here that Watson died in my arms a few years after, much lamented, being the best of our set. Osborne went to the West Indies, where he became an eminent lawyer and made money but died young. He and I had made a serious agreement that the one who happened first to die should, if possible, make a friendly visit to the other and acquaint him how he found things in that separate state. But he never fulfilled his promise.

The Governor, seeming to like my company, had me frequently to his house; and his setting me up was always mentioned as a fixed thing. I was to take with me letters recommendatory to a number of his friends, besides the letter of credit, to furnish me with the necessary money for purchasing the press, types, paper, etc. For these letters I was appointed to call at different times, when they were to be ready, but a future time was still named. Thus we went on till the ship (whose departure, too, had been several times postponed) was on the point of sailing. Then when I called to take my leave and receive the letters, his secretary, Dr. Bard, came out to me and said the Governor was extremely busy in writing but would be down at Newcastle before the ship, and there the letters would be delivered to me.

---

[a] "Silence ye wolves, while Ralph to Cynthia howls,
  And makes night hideous:—answer him ye owls!"
                              (Pope's *Dunciad*)

Ralph, though married and having one child, had determined to accompany me in this voyage. It was thought he intended to establish a correspondence and obtain goods to sell on commission. But I found afterwards that having some cause of discontent with his wife's relations, he proposed to leave her on their hands and never to return to America. Having taken leave of my friends and exchanged promises with Miss Read, I quitted Philadelphia in the ship, which anchored at Newcastle. The Governor was there, but when I went to his lodging, his secretary came to me from him with expressions of the greatest regret that he could not then see me, being engaged in business of the utmost importance, but that he would send the letters to me on board, wished me heartily a good voyage and a speedy return, etc. I returned on board a little puzzled but still not doubting.

Mr. Andrew Hamilton, a famous lawyer of Philadelphia, had taken passage in the same ship for himself and son, and with Mr. Denham, a Quaker merchant, and Messrs. Onion and Russel, masters of an ironwork in Maryland, had engaged the great cabin, so that Ralph and I were forced to take up with a berth in the steerage—and none on board knowing us, were considered as ordinary persons. But Mr. Hamilton and his son (it was James, since Governor) returned from Newcastle to Philadelphia, the father being recalled by a great fee to plead for a seized ship. And just before we sailed, Col. French coming on board and showing me great respect, I was more taken notice of and with my friend Ralph invited by the other gentlemen to come into the cabin, there being now room. Accordingly, we removed thither.

Understanding that Col. French had brought on board the Governor's dispatches, I asked the captain for those letters that were to be under my care. He said all were put into the bag together; and he could not then come at them, but before we landed in England I should have an opportunity of picking them out. So I was satisfied for the present, and we proceeded on our voyage. We had a sociable company in the cabin and lived uncommonly well, having the addition of all Mr. Hamilton's stores, who had laid in plentifully. In this passage, Mr. Denham contracted a friendship for me that continued during his life. The voyage was otherwise not a pleasant one, as we had a great deal of bad weather.

When we came into the channel, the captain kept his word with me and gave me an opportunity of examining the bag for the Governor's letters. I found none upon which my name was put as under my care; I picked out six or seven that by the handwriting I thought might be the promised letters, especially as one of them was addressed to Basket, the King's printer, another to some stationer. We arrived in London the 24th of December, 1724. I waited upon the stationer who came first in my way, delivering the letter as from Gov. Keith. "I don't know such a person," says he, but opening the letter, "Oh, this is from Riddlesden; I have lately found him to be a complete rascal, and I will have nothing to do with him, nor receive any letters from him." So putting the letter into my hand, he turned on his heel and left me to serve some customer. I was surprised to find these were not the Governor's letters; and after recollecting and comparing circumstances, I began to doubt his sincerity. I found my friend Denham and opened the whole affair to him. He let me into Keith's character, told me there was not the least probability that he had written any letters for me, that no one who knew him had the smallest dependence on him, and he laughed at the idea of the Governor's giving me a letter of credit, having, as he said, no credit to give. On my expressing some concern about what I should do, he advised me to endeavor getting some employment in the way of my business. "Among the printers here," says he, "you will improve yourself; and when you return to America, you will set up to greater advantage."

We both of us happened to know, as well as the stationer, that Riddlesden, the attorney, was a very knave. He had half ruined Miss Read's father by drawing him in to be bound for him. By his letter it appeared there was a secret scheme on foot to the prejudice of Mr. Hamilton (supposed to be then coming over with us) and that Keith was concerned in it with Riddlesden. Denham, who was a friend of Hamilton's, thought he ought to be acquainted with it. So when he arrived in England, which was soon after, partly from resentment and ill will to Keith and Riddlesden, and partly from good will to him, I waited on him and gave him the letter. He thanked me cordially, the information being of importance to him. And from that time he became my friend, greatly to my advantage afterwards on many occasions.

But what shall we think of a Governor playing such pitiful tricks and imposing so grossly on a poor ignorant boy! It was a habit he had acquired. He wished to please everybody; and having little to give, he gave expectations. He was otherwise an ingenious, sensible man, a pretty good writer, and a good governor for the people, though not for his constituents, the proprietaries, whose instructions he sometimes disregarded. Several of our best laws were of his planning and passed during his administration.

Ralph and I were inseparable companions. We took lodgings together in Little Britain [16] at 3 s. 6 d. per week, as much as we could then afford. He found some relations, but they were poor and unable to assist him. He now let me know his intentions of remaining in London and that he never meant to return to Philadelphia. He had brought no money with him, the whole he could muster having been expended in paying his passage. I had fifteen pistoles,[17] so he borrowed occasionally of me to subsist while he was looking out for business. He first endeavored to get into the playhouse, believing himself qualified for an actor; but Wilkes, to whom he applied, advised him candidly not to think of that employment, as it was impossible he should succeed in it. Then he proposed to Roberts, a publisher in Paternoster Row, to write for him a weekly paper like the *Spectator,* on certain conditions which Roberts did not approve. Then he endeavored to get employment as a hackney writer to copy for the stationers and lawyers about the Temple,[17a] but could find no vacancy.

For myself, I immediately got into work at Palmer's, then a famous printing house in Bartholomew Close, and here I continued near a year. I was pretty diligent, but I spent with Ralph a good deal of my earnings in going to plays and other places of amusement. We had together consumed all my pistoles, and now just rubbed on from hand to mouth. He seemed quite to have forgotten his wife and child, and I by degrees my engagements with Miss Read, to whom I never wrote more than one letter, and that was to let her know I was not likely soon to return. This was another of the great errata of my life which I should wish to correct if I were to live it over again. In fact, by our expenses, I was constantly kept unable to pay my passage.

At Palmer's I was employed in composing for the second edition of Wollaston's *Religion of Nature*.[18] Some of his reasonings not appearing to me well founded, I wrote a little metaphysical piece in which I made remarks on them. It was entitled *A Dissertation on Liberty and Necessity, Pleasure and Pain*. I inscribed it to my friend Ralph; I printed a small number. It occasioned my being more considered by Mr. Palmer as a young man of some ingenuity, though he seriously expostulated with me upon the principles of my pamphlet, which to him appeared abominable. My printing this pamphlet was another erratum.

While I lodged in Little Britain I made an acquaintance with one Wilcox, a bookseller, whose shop was next door. He had an immense collection of secondhand books. Circulating libraries were not then in use; but we agreed that on certain reasonable terms, which I have now forgotten, I might take, read, and return any of his books. This I esteemed a great advantage, and I made as much use of it as I could.

My pamphlet by some means falling into the hands of one Lyons, a surgeon, author of a book entitled *The Infallibility of Human Judgment*, it occasioned an acquaintance between us; he took great notice of me, called on me often to converse on those subjects, carried me to the Horns, a pale ale house in —— Lane, Cheapside, and introduced me to Dr. Mandeville, author of *The Fable of the Bees*,[19] who had a club there of which he was the soul, being a most facetious, entertaining companion. Lyons, too, introduced me to Dr. Pemberton[20] at Batson's Coffee House, who promised to give me an opportunity sometime or other of seeing Sir Isaac Newton, of which I was extremely desirous; but this never happened.

I had brought over a few curiosities, among which the principal was a purse made of the asbestos, which purifies by fire.

Sir Hans Sloane [21] heard of it, came to see me, and invited me
to his house in Bloomsbury Square, where he showed me all his
curiosities and persuaded me to add that to the number, for
which he paid me handsomely.

   In our house there lodged a young woman, a milliner, who,
I think, had a shop in the cloisters. She had been genteelly bred,
was sensible, lively, and of a most pleasing conversation. Ralph
read plays to her in the evenings, they grew intimate, she took
another lodging, and he followed her. They lived together some
time, but he being still out of business, and her income not sufficient to maintain them with her child, he took a resolution of
going from London, to try for a country school, which he thought
himself well qualified to undertake, as he wrote an excellent hand
and was a master of arithmetic and accounts. This, however, he
deemed a business below him, and confident of future better
fortune when he should be unwilling to have it known that
he was once so meanly employed, he changed his name and did
me the honor to assume mine. For I soon after had a letter from
him, acquainting me that he was settled in a small village in
Berkshire, I think it was, where he taught reading and writing
to ten or a dozen boys at sixpence per week, recommending
Mrs. T. to my care and desiring me to write to him, directing
for Mr. Franklin, schoolmaster at such a place. He continued to
write to me frequently, sending me large specimens of an epic
poem which he was then composing, and desiring my remarks
and corrections. These I gave him from time to time, but endeavored rather to discourage his proceeding. One of Young's satires [22]
was then just published. I copied and sent him a great part of it,
which set in a strong light the folly of pursuing the Muses with
any hope of advancement by them. All was in vain; sheets of the
poem continued to come by every post. In the meantime Mrs. T.,
having on his account lost her friends and business, was often in
distresses and used to send for me and borrow what I could spare
to help her out of them. I grew fond of her company, and being
at this time under no religious restraint, and presuming on my
importance to her, I attempted familiarities (another erratum),
which she repulsed with a proper resentment. She wrote to Ralph

and acquainted him with my conduct; this occasioned a breach between us. And when he returned to London, he let me know he considered all the obligations he had been under to me as annulled—from which I concluded I was never to expect his repaying the money I had lent him or that I had advanced for him. This, however, was of little consequence, as he was totally unable; and by the loss of his friendship I found myself relieved from a heavy burden. I now began to think of getting a little money beforehand, and expecting better employment, I left Palmer's to work at Watts' near Lincoln's Inn Fields, a still greater printing house. Here I continued all the rest of my stay in London.

At my first admission into this printing house, I took to working at press, imagining I felt a want of the bodily exercise I had been used to in America, where presswork is mixed with the composing. I drank only water; the other workmen, near fifty in number, were great guzzlers of beer. On occasion I carried up and down stairs a large form of types in each hand, when others carried but one in both hands. They wondered to see from this and several instances that the "Water-American," as they called me, was *stronger* than themselves who drank *strong* beer. We had an alehouse boy who attended always in the house to supply the workmen. My companion at the press drank every day a pint before breakfast, a pint at breakfast with his bread and cheese, a pint between breakfast and dinner, a pint at dinner, a pint in the afternoon about six o'clock, and another when he had done his day's work. I thought it a detestable custom; but it was necessary, he supposed, to drink *strong* beer that he might be *strong* to labor. I endeavored to convince him that the bodily strength afforded by beer could only be in proportion to the grain or flour of the barley dissolved in the water of which it was made, that there was more flour in a pennyworth of bread, and therefore if he would eat that with a pint of water, it would give him more strength than a quart of beer. He drank on, however, and had four or five shillings to pay out of his wages every Saturday night for that muddling liquor; an expense I was free from. And thus these poor devils keep themselves always under.

Watts after some weeks desiring to have me in the composing room, I left the pressmen. A new *bienvenu* for drink, being five shillings, was demanded of me by the compositors. I thought it an imposition, as I had paid below. The master thought so, too, and forbade my paying it. I stood out two or three weeks, was accordingly considered as an excommunicate, and had so many little pieces of private malice practiced on me by mixing my sorts, transposing my pages, breaking my matter, etc., etc., if ever I stepped out of the room—and all ascribed to the "chapel ghost," which they said ever haunted those not regularly admitted—that notwithstanding the master's protection, I found myself obliged to comply and pay the money, convinced of the folly of being on ill terms with those one is to live with continually. I was now on a fair footing with them and soon acquired considerable influence. I proposed some reasonable alterations in their chapel * laws, and carried them against all opposition. From my example, a great many of them left their muddling breakfast of beer, bread, and cheese, finding they could with me be supplied from a neighboring house with a large porringer of hot water gruel, sprinkled with pepper, crumbed with bread, and a bit of butter in it, for the price of a pint of beer, viz., three halfpence. This was a more comfortable as well as a cheaper breakfast and kept their heads clearer. Those who continued sotting with beer all day were often, by not paying, out of credit at the alehouse and used to make interest with me to get beer, their "light," as they phrased it, "being out." I watched the paytable on Saturday night, and collected what I stood engaged for them, having to pay sometimes near thirty shillings a week on their accounts. This and my being esteemed a pretty good "riggite," that is, a jocular, verbal satirist, supported my consequence in the society. My constant attendance (I never making a St. Monday [24]) recommended me to the master; and my uncommon quickness at composing occasioned my being put upon all work of dispatch, which was generally better paid. So I went on now very agreeably.

My lodging in Little Britain being too remote, I found another

---

* A printing house is always called a chapel by the workmen.[23]

in Duke Street opposite to the Romish chapel. It was up two
pair of stairs backwards, at an Italian warehouse. A widow lady
kept the house; she had a daughter and a maidservant and a
journeyman, who attended the warehouse but lodged abroad.
After sending to inquire my character at the house where I last
lodged, she agreed to take me in at the same rate, 3 s. 6 d. per
week, cheaper, as she said, from the protection she expected in
having a man lodge in the house. She was a widow, an elderly
woman, and had been bred a Protestant (being a clergyman's
daughter), but was converted to the Catholic religion by her
husband, whose memory she much revered; had lived much among
people of distinction and knew a thousand anecdotes of them as
far back as the times of Charles the Second. She was lame in her
knees with the gout and therefore seldom stirred out of her room,
so sometimes wanted company; and hers was so highly amusing
to me that I was sure to spend an evening with her whenever she
desired it. Our supper was only half an anchovy each, on a very
little slice of bread and butter, and half a pint of ale between us;
but the entertainment was in her conversation. My always keeping
good hours and giving little trouble in the family made her unwilling to part with me so that when I talked of a lodging I had
heard of nearer my business for 2 s. a week, which, intent as I
now was on saving money, made some difference, she bid me not
think of it, for she would abate me two shillings a week for the
future; so I remained with her at 1 s. 6 d. as long as I stayed in
London.

In a garret of her house there lived a maiden lady of seventy
in the most retired manner, of whom my landlady gave me
this account: that she was a Roman Catholic, had been sent
abroad when young and lodged in a nunnery with an intent of
becoming a nun; but the country not agreeing with her, she
returned to England, where, there being no nunnery, she had
vowed to lead the life of a nun as near as might be done in those
circumstances. Accordingly, she had given all her estate to
charitable uses, reserving only twelve pounds a year to live on,
and out of this sum she still gave a part in charity, living herself on water gruel only and using no fire but to boil it. She had

lived many years in that garret, being permitted to remain there gratis by successive Catholic tenants of the house below, as they deemed it a blessing to have her there. A priest visited her, to confess her every day.

"I have asked her," says my landlady, "how she, as she lived, could possibly find so much employment for a confessor."

"Oh," says she, "it is impossible to avoid *vain thoughts.*"

I was permitted once to visit her. She was cheerful and polite, and conversed pleasantly. The room was clean, but had no other furniture than a mattress, a table with a crucifix and book, a stool, which she gave me to sit on, and a picture over the chimney of St. Veronica, displaying her handkerchief with the miraculous figure of Christ's bleeding face on it, which she explained to me with great seriousness. She looked pale but was never sick, and I give it as another instance on how small an income life and health may be supported.

At Watts' printing house I contracted an acquaintance with an ingenious young man, one Wygate, who having wealthy relations, had been better educated than most printers, was a tolerable Latinist, spoke French, and loved reading. I taught him and a friend of his to swim, at twice going into the river, and they soon became good swimmers. They introduced me to some gentlemen from the country who went to Chelsea by water to see the college [25] and Don Saltero's curiosities. In our return, at the request of the company, whose curiosity Wygate had excited, I stripped and leaped into the river and swam from near Chelsea to Blackfriar's,[26] performing on the way many feats of activity, both upon and under water, that surprised and pleased those to whom they were novelties. I had from a child been ever delighted with this exercise, had studied and practiced all Thevenot's motions and positions, added some of my own, aiming at the graceful and easy as well as the useful. All these I took this occasion of exhibiting to the company and was much flattered by their admiration. And Wygate, who was desirous of becoming a master, grew more and more attached to me on that account, as well as from the similarity of our studies. He at length proposed to me traveling all over Europe together, supporting ourselves everywhere by working at our business. I was once inclined to it; but mentioning it to my good friend Mr. Denham, with whom I often spent an hour when I had leisure, he dissuaded me from it, advising me to think only of returning to Pennsylvania, which he was now about to do.

I must record one trait of this good man's character. He had formerly been in business at Bristol, but failed in debt to a number of people, compounded, and went to America. There, by a close application to business as a merchant, he acquired a plentiful fortune in a few years. Returning to England in the ship with me, he invited his old creditors to an entertainment, at which he thanked them for the easy composition they had favored him with; and when they expected nothing but the treat, every man at the first remove found under his plate an order on a banker for the full amount of the unpaid remainder with interest.

He now told me he was about to return to Philadelphia and should carry over a great quantity of goods in order to open a store there. He proposed to take me over as his clerk to keep his books (in which he would instruct me), copy his letters, and attend the store. He added that as soon as I should be acquainted with mercantile business he would promote me by sending me with a cargo of flour and bread, etc., to the West Indies, and procure me commissions from others which would be profitable, and if I managed well, would establish me handsomely. The thing pleased me, for I was grown tired of London, remembered with pleasure the happy months I had spent in Pennsylvania, and wished again to see it. Therefore, I immediately agreed on the terms of fifty pounds a year, Pennsylvania money—less, indeed, than my then present gettings as a compositor but affording a better prospect.

I now took leave of printing, as I thought, forever, and was daily employed in my new business—going about with Mr. Denham among the tradesmen to purchase various articles and see them packed up, delivering messages, calling upon workmen to dispatch, etc.; and when all was on board, I had a few days' leisure. On one of these days I was, to my surprise, sent for by a great man I knew only by name, a Sir William Wyndham,[27] and I waited upon him. He had heard by some means or other of my swimming from Chelsea to Blackfriar's and of my teaching Wygate and another young man to swim in a few hours. He had two sons about to set out on their travels; he wished to have them first taught swimming, and proposed to gratify me handsomely if I would teach them. They were not yet come to town, and my stay was uncertain, so I could not undertake it. But from this incident I thought it likely that if I were to remain in England and open a swimming school, I might get a good deal of money; and it struck me so strongly that, had the overture been made me sooner, probably I should not so soon have returned to America. After many years, you and I had something of more importance to do with one of these sons of Sir William Wyndham, become Earl of Egremont, which I shall mention in its place.

Thus I passed about eighteen months in London. Most part of the time I worked hard at my business and spent but little upon myself except in seeing plays and in books. My friend Ralph had kept me poor. He owed me about twenty-seven pounds, which I was now never likely to receive—a great sum out of my small earnings. I loved him notwithstanding, for he had many amiable qualities. I had improved my knowledge, however, though I had by no means improved my fortune. But I had made some very ingenious acquaintance, whose conversation was of great advantage to me, and I had read considerably.

We sailed from Gravesend on the 23rd of July, 1726. For the incidents of the voyage, I refer you to my Journal, where you will find them all minutely related. Perhaps the most important part of that Journal is the *plan* to be found in it, which I formed at sea, for regulating the future conduct of my life. It is the more remarkable as being formed when I was so young and yet being pretty faithfully adhered to quite through to old age.

We landed at Philadelphia the 11th of October, where I found sundry alterations. Keith was no longer Governor, being superceded by Major Gordon. I met him walking the streets as a common citizen. He seemed a little ashamed at seeing me, but passed without saying anything. I should have been as much ashamed at seeing Miss Read, had not her friends, despairing with reason of my return after the receipt of my letter, persuaded her to marry another, one Rogers, a potter, which was done in my absence. With him, however, she was never happy, and soon parted from him, refusing to cohabit with him or bear his name, it being now said he had another wife. He was a worthless fellow, though an excellent workman, which was the temptation to her friends. He got into debt and ran away in 1727 or '28, went to the West Indies, and died there. Keimer had got a better house, a shop well supplied with stationery, plenty of new types, and a number of hands, though none good, and seemed to have a great deal of business.

Mr. Denham took a store in Water Street, where we opened our goods. I attended the business diligently, studied accounts, and grew in a little time expert at selling. We lodged and boarded together; he counseled me as a father, having a sincere regard for me. I respected and loved him, and we might have gone on together very happily; but in the beginning of February, 1727, when I had just passed my twenty-first year, we both were taken ill. My distemper was a pleurisy, which very nearly carried me off. I suffered a good deal, gave up the point in my own mind, and was rather disappointed when I found myself recovering, regretting in some degree that I must now sometime or other have all that disagreeable work to go over again. I forget what Mr. Denham's distemper was; it held him a long time and at length carried him off. He left me a small legacy in a nuncupative will, as a token of his kindness for me, and he left me once more to the wide world; for the store was taken into the care of his executors, and my employment under him ended. My brother-in-law Homes, being now at Philadelphia, advised my return to my business; and Keimer tempted me with an offer of large wages by the year to come and take the management of his printing house, that he might better attend to his stationer's shop. I had heard a bad character of him in London, from his wife and her friends, and was not for having any more to do with him. I tried for further employment as a merchant's clerk, but not readily meeting with any, I closed again with Keimer.

I found in his house these hands: Hugh Meredith, a Welsh Pennsylvanian, thirty years of age, bred to country work; he was honest, sensible, a man of experience, and fond of reading, but addicted to drinking. Stephen Potts, a young countryman of full age, bred to the same, of uncommon natural parts, and great wit and humor, but a little idle. These he had agreed with at extreme low wages per week, to be raised a shilling every three months, as they would deserve by improving in their business, and the expectation of these high wages to come on hereafter was what he had drawn them in with. Meredith was to work at press, Potts at bookbinding, which he by agreement was to teach them, though he knew neither one nor t'other. John ——, a wild Irishman, brought up to no business, whose service for four years Keimer had purchased from the captain of a ship, he too was to be made a pressman. George Webb, an Oxford scholar, whose time for four years he had likewise bought, intending him for a compositor (of whom more presently) ; and David Harry, a country boy, whom he had taken apprentice.

I soon perceived that the intention of engaging me at wages so much higher than he had been used to give was to have these raw, cheap hands formed through me, and as soon as I had instructed them, then, they being all articled to him, he should be able to do without me. I went on, however, very cheerfully, put his printing house in order, which had been in great confusion, and brought his hands by degrees to mind their business and to do it better.

It was an odd thing to find an Oxford scholar in the situation of a bought servant.[28] He was not more than eighteen years of age, and he gave me this account of himself: that he was born in Gloucester, educated at grammar school there, and had been distinguished among the scholars for some apparent superiority in performing his part when they exhibited plays; belonged to the Witty Club there, and had written some pieces in prose and verse which were printed in the Gloucester newspapers; thence was sent to Oxford; there he continued about a year, but not well satisfied, wishing of all things to see London and become a player. At length receiving his quarterly allowance of fifteen guineas, instead of discharging his debts, he walked out of town, hid his gown in a furze bush, and footed it to London; where, having no friend to advise him, he fell into bad company, soon spent his guineas, found no means of being introduced among the players, grew necessitous, pawned his clothes, and wanted bread. Walking the street very hungry and not knowing what to do with himself, a crimps bill [28] was put into his hand, offering immediate entertainment and encouragement to such as would bind themselves to serve in America. He went directly, signed the indentures, was put into the ship, and came over, never writing a line to acquaint his friends what was become of him. He was lively, witty, good-natured, and a pleasant companion; but idle, thoughtless, and imprudent to the last degree.

John, the Irishman, soon ran away. With the rest I began to live very agreeably; for they all respected me, the more as they found Keimer incapable of instructing them and that from me they learned something daily. We never worked on a Saturday, that being Keimer's Sabbath. So I had two days for reading. My acquaintance with ingenious people in the town increased. Keimer himself treated me with great civility and apparent regard; and nothing now made me uneasy but my debt to Vernon, which I was yet unable to pay, being hitherto but a poor economist. He, however, kindly made no demand of it.

Our printing house often wanted sorts, and there was no letter founder in America. I had seen types cast at James's in London, but without much attention to the manner. However, I now contrived a mold, made use of the letters we had, as puncheons, struck the matrices in lead, and thus supplied in a pretty tolerable way all deficiencies. I also engraved several things on occasion. I made the ink, I was warehouse man, and in short quite a factotum.

But however serviceable I might be, I found that my services became every day of less importance as the other hands improved in the business; and when Keimer paid me a second quarter's wages, he let me know that he felt them too heavy and thought

I should make an abatement. He grew by degrees less civil, put on more the airs of master, frequently found fault, was captious, and seemed ready for an outbreaking. I went on, nevertheless, with a good deal of patience, thinking that his incumbered circumstances were partly the cause. At length a trifle snapped our connection; for a great noise happening near the courthouse, I put my head out of the window to see what was the matter. Keimer being in the street, looked up and saw me, called out to me in a loud voice and angry tone to mind my business, adding some reproachful words that nettled me the more for their publicity, all the neighbors who were looking out on the same occasion being witnesses how I was treated. He came up immediately into the printing house, continued the quarrel; high words passed on both sides, he gave me the quarter's warning we had stipulated, expressing a wish that he had not been obliged to so long a warning. I told him his wish was unnecessary for I would leave him that instant, and so taking my hat, walked out of doors, desiring Meredith, whom I saw below, to take care of some things I left, and bring them to my lodging.

Meredith came accordingly in the evening, when we talked my affair over. He had conceived a great regard for me and was very unwilling that I should leave the house while he remained in it. He dissuaded me from returning to my native country, which I began to think of. He reminded me that Keimer was in debt for all he possessed, that his creditors began to be uneasy, that he kept his shop miserably, sold often without profit for ready money, and often trusted without keeping accounts; that he must therefore fail, which would make a vacancy I might profit of. I objected my want of money. He then let me know that his father had a high opinion of me, and from some discourse that had passed between them, he was sure would advance money to set us up, if I would enter into partnership with him. "My time," says he, "will be out with Keimer in the spring; by that time we may have our press and types in from London. I am sensible I am no workman. If you like it, your skill in the business shall be set against the stock I furnish;

and we will share the profits equally." The proposal was agreeable to me, and I consented. His father was in town and approved of it—the more as he saw I had great influence with his son, had prevailed on him to abstain long from dram-drinking, and he hoped might break him of that wretched habit entirely, when we came to be so closely connected. I gave an inventory to the father, who carried it to a merchant; the things were sent for; the secret was to be kept till they should arrive, and in the meantime I was to get work if I could at the other printing house. But I found no vacancy there and so remained idle a few days, when Keimer, on a prospect of being employed to print some paper money in New Jersey which would require cuts and various types that I only could supply, and apprehending Bradford might engage me and get the job from him, sent me a very civil message that old friends should not part for a few words, the effect of sudden passion, and wishing me to return. Meredith persuaded me to comply, as it would give more opportunity for his improvement under my daily instructions. So I returned, and we went on more smoothly than for some time before. The New Jersey job was obtained. I contrived a copperplate press for it, the first that had been seen in the country. I cut several ornaments and checks for the bills. We went together to Burlington, where I executed the whole to satisfaction; and he received so large a sum for the work as to be enabled thereby to keep his head much longer above water.

At Burlington I made an acquaintance with many principal people of the province. Several of them had been appointed by the Assembly a committee to attend the press and take care that no more bills were printed than the law directed. They were therefore by turns constantly with us, and generally he who attended brought with him a friend or two for company. My mind having been much more improved by reading than Keimer's, I suppose it was for that reason my conversation seemed to be more valued. They had me to their houses, introduced me to their friends, and showed me much civility; while he, though the master, was a little neglected. In truth he was an odd fish, ignorant of common life, fond of rudely opposing received opinions, slovenly to extreme dirtiness, enthusiastic in some points of religion, and a little knavish withal.

We continued there near three months, and by that time I could reckon among my acquired friends Judge Allen, Samuel Bustill, the Secretary of the province, Isaac Pearson, Joseph Cooper, and several of the Smiths, members of the Assembly, and Isaac Decow, the Surveyor General. The latter was a shrewd, sagacious old man, who told me that he began for himself when young by wheeling clay for the brickmakers, learned to write after he was of age, carried the chain for surveyors, who taught him surveying, and he had now by his industry acquired a good estate; and says he, "I foresee that you will soon work this man out of his business and make a fortune in it at Philadelphia." He had not then the least intimation of my intention to set up there or anywhere. These friends were afterward of great use to me, as I occasionally was to some of them. They all continued their regard for me as long as they lived.

Before I enter upon my public appearance in business, it may be well to let you know the then state of my mind with regard to my principles and morals, that you may see how far those influenced the future events of my life. My parents had early given me religious impressions, and brought me through my childhood piously in the dissenting way. But I was scarce fifteen when, after doubting by turns of several points, as I found them disputed in the different books I read, I began to doubt of revelation itself. Some books against deism fell into my hands; they were said to be the substance of the sermons which had been preached at Boyle's lectures. It happened that they wrought an effect on me quite contrary to what was intended by them, for the arguments of the deists which were quoted to be refuted appeared to me much stronger than the refutations. In short, I soon became a thorough deist. My arguments perverted some others, particularly Collins and Ralph; but each of them having afterwards wronged me greatly without the least compunction, and recollecting Keith's conduct toward me (who was another freethinker) and my own towards Vernon and Miss Read (which at times gave me great trouble), I began to suspect that this doctrine, though it might be true, was not very useful. My London pamphlet, which had for its motto these lines of Dryden: [29]

> Whatever is, is right
> Though purblind man
> Sees but a part of the chain, the nearest link,
> His eyes not carrying to the equal beam,
> That poises all above.

and which from the attributes of God, his infinite wisdom, goodness, and power, concluded that nothing could possibly be wrong in the world and that vice and virtue were empty distinctions, no such things existing, appeared now not so clever a performance as I once thought it; and I doubted whether some error had not insinuated itself unperceived into my argument so as to infect all that followed, as is common in metaphysical reasonings. I grew convinced that *truth, sincerity,* and *integrity,* in dealings between man and man, were of the utmost importance to the felicity of life, and I formed written resolutions (which still remain in my Journal book) to practice them ever while I lived. Revelation had indeed no weight with me as such; but I entertained an opinion that though certain actions might not be bad *because* they were forbidden by it, or good *because* it commanded them, yet probably those actions might be forbidden *because* they were bad for us or commanded *because* they were beneficial to us, in their own natures, all the circumstances of things considered. And this persuasion, with the kind hand of Providence, or some guardian angel, or accidental favorable circumstances and situations, or all together, preserved me (through this dangerous time of youth and the hazardous situations I was sometimes in among strangers, remote from the eye and advice of my father) without any *willful* gross immorality or injustice that might have been expected from my want of religion. I say *willful* because the instances I have mentioned had something of necessity in them, from my youth, inexperience, and the knavery of others. I had, therefore, a tolerable character to begin the world with; I valued it properly and determined to preserve it.

We had not been long returned to Philadelphia, before the

new types arrived from London. We settled with Keimer and left him by his consent before he heard of it. We found a house to hire near the market and took it. To lessen the rent (which was then but £24 a year, though I have since known it let for seventy) we took in Thomas Godfrey, a glazier, and his family, who were to pay a considerable part of it to us, and we to board with them. We had scarce opened our letters and put our press in order before George House, an acquaintance of mine, brought a countryman to us whom he had met in the street inquiring for a printer. All our cash was now expended in the variety of particulars we had been obliged to procure, and this countryman's five shillings, being our first fruits and coming so seasonably, gave me more pleasure than any crown I have since earned, and from the gratitude I felt toward House, has made me often more ready than perhaps I should otherwise have been to assist young beginners.

There are croakers in every country always boding its ruin. Such a one then lived in Philadelphia, a person of note, an elderly man with a wise look and very grave manner of speaking. His name was Samuel Mickle. This gentleman, a stranger to me, stopped one day at my door and asked me if I was the young man who had lately opened a new printing house. Being answered in the affirmative, he said he was sorry for me because it was an expensive undertaking and the expense would be lost, for Philadelphia was a sinking place, the people already half bankrupts or near being so—all appearances of the contrary, such as new buildings and the rise of rents, being to his certain knowledge fallacious, for they were in fact among the things that would soon ruin us. And he gave me such a detail of misfortunes now existing, or that were soon to exist, that he left me half-melancholy. Had I known him before I engaged in this business, probably I never should have done it. This man continued to live in this decaying place and to declaim in the same strain, refusing for many years to buy a house there because all was going to destruction, and at last I had the pleasure of seeing him give five times as much for one as he might have bought it for when he first began his croaking.

I should have mentioned before that in the autumn of the preceding year I had formed most of my ingenious acquaintance into a club for mutual improvement which we called the Junto. We met on Friday evenings. The rules I drew up required that every member in his turn should produce one or more queries on any point of morals, politics, or natural philosophy, to be discussed by the company, and once in three months produce and read an essay of his own writing on any subject he pleased. Our debates were to be under the direction of a president, and to be conducted in the sincere spirit of inquiry after truth, without fondness for dispute or desire of victory; and to prevent warmth, all expressions of positiveness in opinion or of direct contradiction were after some time made contraband and prohibited under small pecuniary penalties.

The first members were: Joseph Breintnal, a copier of deeds for the scriveners, a good-natured, friendly, middle-aged man, a great lover of poetry—reading all he could meet with and writing some that was tolerable—very ingenious in many little knickknackeries, and of sensible conversation.

Thomas Godfrey, a self-taught mathematician, great in his way, and afterwards inventor of what is now called Hadley's Quadrant. But he knew little out of his way and was not a pleasing companion, as like most great mathematicians I have met with, he expected unusual precision in everything said, or was forever denying or distinguishing upon trifles to the disturbance of all conversation. He soon left us.

Nicholas Scull, a surveyor, afterwards Surveyor General, who loved books, and sometimes made a few verses.

William Parsons, bred a shoemaker, but loving reading, had acquired a considerable share of mathematics, which he first studied with a view to astrology that he afterwards laughed at. He also became Surveyor General.

William Maugridge, a joiner, but a most exquisite mechanic, and a solid, sensible man.

Hugh Meredith, Stephen Potts, and George Webb I have characterized before.

Robert Grace, a young gentleman of some fortune, generous, lively, and witty, a lover of punning and of his friends.

Lastly, William Coleman, then a merchant's clerk, about my age, who had the coolest, clearest head, the best heart, and the exactest morals of almost any man I ever met with. He became afterwards a merchant of great note, and one of our provincial judges. Our friendship continued without interruption to his death, upwards of forty years. And the club continued almost as long and was the best school of philosophy and politics that then existed in the province; for our queries, which were read the week preceding their discussion, put us on reading with attention upon the several subjects that we might speak more to the purpose; and here, too, we acquired better habits of conversation, everything being studied in our rules which might prevent our disgusting each other—from hence the long continuance of the club, which I shall have frequent occasion to speak further of hereafter. But my giving this account of it here is to show something of the interest I had, every one of these exerting themselves in recommending business to us. Breintnal particularly procured us from the Quakers the printing forty sheets of their history, the rest being to be done by Keimer; and upon this we worked exceedingly hard, for the price was low. It was a folio, *pro patria* size, in pica with long primer notes. I composed of it a sheet a day, and Meredith worked it off at press. It was often eleven at night, and sometimes later, before I had finished my distribution for the next day's work. For the little jobs sent in by our other friends now and then put us back. But so determined I was to continue doing a sheet a day of the folio, that one night when having imposed my forms I thought my day's work over, one of them by accident was broken and two pages reduced to pie, I immediately distributed and composed it over again before I went to bed. And this industry visible to our neighbors began to give us character and credit—particularly, I was told, that mention being made of the new printing office at the merchants' Every-night Club, the general opinion was that it must fail, there being already two printers in the place, Keimer and Bradford; but Doctor Baird (whom you and I saw many years after at his native place, St.

Andrew's in Scotland) gave a contrary opinion: "For the industry of that Franklin," says he, "is superior to anything I ever saw of the kind; I see him still at work when I go home from club, and he is at work again before his neighbors are out of bed." This struck the rest, and we soon after had offers from one of them to supply us with stationery; but as yet we did not choose to engage in shop business.

I mention this industry the more particularly and the more freely, though it seems to be talking in my own praise, that those of my posterity who shall read it may know the use of that virtue, when they see its effects in my favor throughout this relation.

George Webb, who had found a female friend that lent him wherewith to purchase his time of Keimer, now came to offer himself as a journeyman to us. We could not then employ him, but I foolishly let him know, as a secret, that I soon intended to begin a newspaper and might then have work for him. My hopes of success, as I told him, were founded on this: that the then only newspaper, printed by Bradford, was a paltry thing, wretchedly managed, no way entertaining, and yet was profitable to him. I therefore thought a good paper could scarcely fail of good encouragement. I requested Webb not to mention it, but he told it to Keimer, who immediately, to be beforehand with me, published proposals for printing one himself, on which Webb was to be employed. I was vexed at this, and to counteract them, not being able to commence our paper, I wrote several amusing pieces for Bradford's paper under the title of the "Busybody," which Breintnal continued some months. By this means the attention of the public was fixed on that paper, and Keimer's proposals, which we burlesqued and ridiculed, were disregarded. He began his paper, however, and after carrying it on three-quarters of a year with at most only ninety subscribers, he offered it to me for a trifle; and I, having been ready some time to go on with it, took it in hand directly, and it proved in a few years extremely profitable to me.[30]

I perceive that I am apt to speak in the singular number, though our partnership still continued; it may be that in fact the whole management of the business lay upon me. Meredith was no compositor, a poor pressman, and seldom sober. My friends lamented my connection with him, but I was to make the best of it.

Our first papers made a quite different appearance from any before in the province, a better type and better printed; but some spirited remarks of my writing on the dispute then going on between Governor Burnet and the Massachusetts Assembly struck the principal people, occasioned the paper and the manager of it to be much talked of, and in a few weeks brought them all to be our subscribers. Their example was followed by many, and our number went on growing continually. This was one of the first good effects of my having learned a little to scribble. Another was that the leading men, seeing a newspaper now in the hands of one who could also handle a pen, thought it convenient to oblige and encourage me. Bradford still printed the votes and laws and other public business. He had printed an address of the House to the Governor in a coarse blundering manner. We reprinted it elegantly and correctly, and sent one to every member. They were sensible of the difference, it strengthened the hands of our friends in the House, and they voted us their printers for the year ensuing.

Among my friends in the House I must not forget Mr. Hamilton, before-mentioned, who was then returned from England and had a seat in it. He interested himself for me strongly in that instance, as he did in many others afterwards, continuing his patronage till his death.*

Mr. Vernon, about this time, put me in mind of the debt I owed him, but did not press me. I wrote him an ingenuous letter of acknowledgments, craved his forbearance a little longer, which he allowed me; and as soon as I was able, I paid the principal with interest and many thanks; so that erratum was in some degree corrected.

But now another difficulty came upon me which I had never the least reason to expect. Mr. Meredith's father, who was to have paid for our printing house according to the expectations given me, was able to advance only one hundred pounds currency,

* I got his son once 500 £. [marg. note]

which had been paid; and a hundred more was due to the merchant, who grew impatient and sued us all. We gave bail but saw that if the money could not be raised in time, the suit must come to a judgment and execution, and our hopeful prospects must with us be ruined, as the press and letters must be sold for payment, perhaps at half price. In this distress two true friends, whose kindness I have never forgotten nor ever shall forget while I can remember anything, came to me separately, unknown to each other, and without any application from me, offered each of them to advance me all the money that should be necessary to enable me to take the whole business upon myself if that should be practicable; but they did not like my continuing the partnership with Meredith, who, as they said, was often seen drunk in the streets and playing at low games in alehouses, much to our discredit. These two friends were *William Coleman* and *Robert Grace*. I told them I could not propose a separation while any prospect remained of the Merediths fulfilling their part of our agreement, because I thought myself under great obligations to them for what they had done and would do if they could. But if they finally failed in their performance and our partnership must be dissolved, I should then think myself at liberty to accept the assistance of my friends.

Thus the matter rested for some time; when I said to my partner, "Perhaps your father is dissatisfied at the part you have undertaken in this affair of ours and is unwilling to advance for you and me what he would for you alone. If that is the case, tell me, and I will resign the whole to you and go about my business."

"No," says he, "my father has really been disappointed and is really unable; and I am unwilling to distress him further. I see this is a business I am not fit for. I was bred a farmer, and it was a folly in me to come to town and put myself at thirty years of age an apprentice to learn a new trade. Many of our Welsh people are going to settle in North Carolina, where land is cheap. I am inclined to go with them and follow my old employment. You may find friends to assist you. If you will take the debts of the company upon you, return to my father the hundred pounds he has advanced, pay my little personal debts, and give me thirty pounds and a new saddle, I will relinquish the partnership and leave the whole in your hands."

I agreed to this proposal. It was drawn up in writing, signed and sealed immediately. I gave him what he demanded, and he went soon after to Carolina, from whence he sent me next year two long letters containing the best account that had been given of that country, the climate, soil, husbandry, etc., for in those matters he was very judicious. I printed them in the papers, and they gave great satisfaction to the public.

As soon as he was gone, I recurred to my two friends; and because I would not give an unkind preference to either, I took half what each had offered and I wanted of one, and half of the other, paid off the company's debts, and went on with the business in my own name, advertising that the partnership was dissolved. I think this was in or about the year 1729.

About this time there was a cry among the people for more paper money, only £15,000 being extant in the province and that soon to be sunk. The wealthy inhabitants opposed any addition, being against all paper currency, from the apprehension that it would depreciate as it had done in New England, to the prejudice of all creditors. We had discussed this point in our Junto, where I was on the side of an addition, being persuaded that the first small sum struck in 1723 had done much good by increasing the trade, employment, and number of inhabitants in the province, since I now saw all the old houses inhabited and many new ones building where, as I remembered well that when I first walked about the streets of Philadelphia eating my roll, I saw most of the houses in Walnut Street between Second and Front Streets with bills on their doors, "To be Let," and many likewise in Chestnut Street and other streets— which made me then think the inhabitants of the city were one after another deserting it.

Our debates possessed me so fully of the subject that I wrote and printed an anonymous pamphlet on it entitled *The Nature and Necessity of a Paper Currency*. It was well received by the common people in general; but the rich men disliked it, for it increased and strengthened the clamor for more money; and they happening to have no writers among them that were able to answer it, their opposition slackened, and the point was carried by a majority in the House. My friends there, who considered I had been of some service, thought fit to reward me by employing me in printing the money—a very profitable job and a great help to me. This was another advantage gained by my being able to write.

The utility of this currency became by time and experience so evident, as never afterwards to be much disputed, so that it grew soon to £55,000 and in 1739 to £80,000, since which it arose during war to upward of £350,000—trade, building, and inhabitants all the while increasing—though I now think there are limits beyond which the quantity may be hurtful.

I soon afterwards obtained, through my friend Hamilton, the printing of the Newcastle paper money, another profitable job as I then thought it—small things appearing great to those in small circumstances—and these to me were really great advantages, as they were great encouragements. He procured me also the printing of the laws and votes of that government, which continued in my hands as long as I followed the business.

I now opened a small stationer's shop. I had in it blanks of all sorts, the correctest that ever appeared among us. I was assisted in that by my friend Breintnal. I had also paper, parchment, chapmen's books, etc. One Whitemash, a compositor I had known in London, an excellent workman, now came to me and worked with me constantly and diligently; and I took an apprentice, the son of Aquila Rose.

I began now gradually to pay off the debt I was under for the printing house. In order to secure my credit and character as a tradesman, I took care not only to be in *reality* industrious and frugal, but to avoid all *appearances* of the contrary. I dressed plain and was seen at no places of idle diversion. I never went out a fishing or shooting; a book, indeed, sometimes debauched me from my work, but that was seldom, snug, and gave no scandal; and to show that I was not above my business, I sometimes brought home the paper I purchased at the stores, through the streets on a wheelbarrow. Thus being esteemed an industrious, thriving, young man, and paying duly for what I bought, the merchants who imported stationery solicited my custom; others proposed supplying me with books, and I went on swimmingly. In the meantime Keimer's credit and business declining daily, he was at last forced to sell his printing house to satisfy his creditors. He went to Barbados and there lived some years in very poor circumstances.

His apprentice, David Harry, whom I had instructed while I worked with him, set up in his place at Philadelphia, having bought his materials. I was at first apprehensive of a powerful rival in Harry, as his friends were very able and had a good deal of interest. I therefore proposed a partnership to him, which he, fortunately for me, rejected with scorn. He was very proud, dressed like a gentleman, lived expensively, took much diversion and pleasure abroad, ran in debt, and neglected his business— upon which all business left him; and finding nothing to do, he followed Keimer to Barbados, taking the printing house with him. There this apprentice employed his former master as a journeyman. They quarreled often, Harry went continually be- hindhand and at length was forced to sell his types and return to his country work in Pennsylvania. The person who bought them employed Keimer to use them, but a few years after he died.

There remained now no other competitor with me at Philadel- phia but the old one, Bradford, who was rich and easy, did a little printing now and then by straggling hands, but was not very anxious about the business. However, as he kept the Post Office, it was imagined he had better opportunities of obtaining news, his paper was thought a better distributor of advertise- ments than mine and therefore had many more—which was a profitable thing to him and a disadvantage to me. For though I did indeed receive and send papers by the post, yet the public opinion was otherwise; for what I did send was by bribing the riders, who took them privately—Bradford being unkind enough to forbid it, which occasioned some resentment on my part; and I thought so meanly of him for it that when I afterwards came into his situation, I took care never to imitate it.

I had hitherto continued to board with Godfrey, who lived in part of my house with his wife and children, and had one side of the shop for his glazier's business, though he worked little, being always absorbed in his mathematics. Mrs. Godfrey projected a match for me with a relation's daughter, took opportunities of bringing us often together, till a serious courtship on my part ensued, the girl being in herself very deserving. The old folks encouraged me by continued invitations to supper and by leaving us together, till at length it was time to explain. Mrs. Godfrey managed our little treaty. I let her know that I expected as much money with their daughter as would pay off my remaining debt for the printing house, which I believe was not then above a hundred pounds. She brought me word they had no such sum to spare. I said they might mortgage their house in the Loan Office. The answer to this after some days was that they did not approve the match; that on inquiry of Bradford they had been informed the printing business was not a profitable one, the types would soon be worn out and more wanted; that S. Keimer and D. Harry had failed one after the other, and I should probably soon follow them; and therefore I was forbidden the house, and the daughter shut up. Whether this was a real change of sentiment or only artifice, on a supposition of our being too far engaged in affection to retract and therefore that we should steal a marriage, which would leave them at liberty to give or withhold what they pleased, I know not. But I suspected the motive, resented it, and went no more. Mrs. Godfrey brought me afterwards some more favorable accounts of their disposition and would have drawn me on again, but I declared absolutely my resolution to have nothing more to do with that family. This was resented by the Godfreys, we differed, and they removed, leaving me the whole house, and I resolved to take no more inmates. But this affair having turned my thoughts to marriage, I looked round me and made overtures of acquaintance in other places, but soon found that the business of a printer being generally thought a poor one, I was not to expect money with a wife, unless with such a one as I should not otherwise think agreeable. In the meantime that hard-to-be-governed passion of youth had hurried me frequently into intrigues with low women that fell in my way, which were attended with some expense and great inconvenience, besides a continual risk to my health by a distemper, which of all things I dreaded, though by great good luck I escaped it.

A friendly correspondence as neighbors and old acquaintances had continued between me and Miss Read's family, who all had a regard for me from the time of my first lodging in their house. I was often invited there and consulted in their affairs, wherein I sometimes was of service. I pitied poor Miss Read's unfortunate situation, who was generally dejected, seldom cheerful, and avoided company. I considered my giddiness and inconstancy when in London as in a great degree the cause of her unhappiness, though the mother was good enough to think the fault more her own than mine, as she had prevented our marrying before I went thither and persuaded the match in my absence. Our mutual affection was revived, but there were now great objections to our union. That match was indeed looked upon as invalid, a preceding wife being said to be living in England; but this could not easily be proved because of the distance. And though there was a report of his death, it was not certain. Then, though it should be true, he had left many debts which his successor might be called upon to pay. We ventured, however, over all these difficulties, and I took her to wife, Sept. 1, 1730. None of the inconveniences happened that we had apprehended; she proved a good and faithful helpmate, assisted me much by attending the shop; we throve together and ever mutually endeavored to make each other happy. Thus I corrected that great erratum as well as I could.

About this time our club meeting, not at a tavern, but in a little room of Mr. Grace's set apart for that purpose, a proposition was made by me that since our books were often referred to in our disquisitions upon the queries, it might be convenient to us to have them all together where we met, that upon occasion they might be consulted; and by thus clubbing our books to a common library, we should, while we liked to keep them together, have each of us the advantage of using the books of all the other members, which would be nearly as beneficial as if each owned the whole. It was liked and agreed to, and we filled one end of the room with such books as we could best spare. The number was not so great as we expected; and though they had been of great use, yet some inconveniences occurring for want of due care of them, the collection after about a year was separated, and each took his books home again.

And now I set on foot my first project of a public nature, that for a subscription library. I drew up the proposals, got them put into form by our great scrivener, Brockden, and by the help of my friends in the Junto, procured fifty subscribers of forty shillings each to begin with, and ten shillings a year for fifty years —the term our company was to continue. We afterwards obtained a charter, the company being increased to one hundred. This was the mother of all the North American subscription libraries, now so numerous. It is become a great thing itself and continually increasing. These libraries have improved the general conversation of the Americans, made the common tradesmen and farmers as intelligent as most gentlemen from other countries, and perhaps have contributed in some degree to the stand so generally made throughout the Colonies in defense of their privileges.

*Memo:* Thus far was written with the intention expressed in the beginning and therefore contains several little family anecdotes of no importance to others. What follows was written many years after, in compliance with the advice contained in these letters, and accordingly intended for the public. The affairs of the Revolution occasioned the interruption.

[*Ten years and more had passed since the writing of the first part of the* Autobiography. *Franklin had returned to America in 1775, and the following year was sent as one of a commission of three to negotiate a treaty with France. He was living at Passy, near Paris, where toward the close of 1782, or early in 1783, he received the following letter.—M.F.*]

My dear and honored friend:

I have often been desirous of writing to thee, but could not be reconciled to the thoughts that the letter might fall into the hands of the British, lest some printer or busybody should publish some part of the contents and give our friends pain and myself censure.

Sometime since there fell into my hands to my great joy about twenty-three sheets in thy own handwriting containing an account of the parentage and life of thyself, directed to thy son, ending in the year 1730, with which there were notes likewise in thy writing, a copy of which I enclose in hopes it may be a means, if thou continued it up to a later period, that the first and latter part may be put together; and if it is not yet continued, I hope thou wilt not delay it. Life is uncertain, as the preacher tells us, and what will the world say if kind, humane, and benevolent Ben Franklin should leave his friends and the world deprived of so pleasing and profitable a work, a work which would be useful and entertaining not only to a few but to millions?

The influence writings under that class have on the minds of youth is very great and has nowhere appeared so plain as in our public friend's Journal. It almost insensibly leads the youth into the resolution of endeavoring to become as good and as eminent as the journalist. Should thine, for instance, when published—and I think it could not fail of it—lead the youth to equal the industry and temperance of thy early youth, what a blessing with that class would such a work be! I know of no character living, nor many of them put together, who has so much in his power as thyself to promote a greater spirit of industry and early attention to business, frugality, and temperance with the American youth. Not that I think the work would have no other merit and use in the world—far from it—but the first is of such vast importance, and I know nothing that can equal it. . . .

I trust I need make no apology to my good friend for mentioning to him these matters, believing he continues a relish for every exertion of the sort, in confidence of which I rest with great truth and perfect esteem his

> Very affectionate friend,
> (Signed)   Abel James [20a]

The foregoing letter and the minutes accompanying it being shown to a friend, I received from him the following:

Paris, January 31, 1783.

My dearest sir:

When I had read over your sheets of minutes of the principal incidents of your life, recovered for you by your Quaker acquaintance, I told you I would send you a letter expressing my reasons why I thought it would be useful to complete and publish it as he desired. Various concerns have for sometime past prevented this letter being written, and I do not know whether it was worth any expectation; happening to be at leisure, however, at present, I shall by writing at least interest and instruct myself; but as the terms I am inclined to use may tend to offend a person of your manners, I shall only tell you how I would address any other person who was as good and as great as yourself but less diffident. I would say to him, sir, I solicit the history of your life from the following motives: Your history is so remarkable that if you do not give it, somebody else will certainly give it; and perhaps so as nearly to do as much harm as your own management of the thing might do good. It will, moreover, present a table of the internal circumstances of your country which will very much tend to invite to it settlers of virtuous and manly minds. And considering the eagerness with which such information is sought by them, and the extent of your reputation, I do not know of a more efficacious advertisement than your biography would give. All that has happened to you is also connected with the detail of the manners and situation of a rising people; and in this respect I do not think that the writings of Caesar and Tacitus can be more interesting to a true judge of human nature and society. But these, sir, are small reasons, in my opinion, compared with the chance which your life will give for the forming of future great men; and in conjunction with your Art of Virtue (which you design to publish) of improving the features of private character, and consequently of aiding all happiness, both public and domestic. The two works I allude to, sir, will in particular give a noble rule and example of self-education. School and other education constantly proceed upon false principles and show a clumsy apparatus pointed at a false mark; but your apparatus is simple and the mark a true one; and while parents and young persons are left destitute of other just means of estimating and becoming prepared for a reasonable course in life, your discovery that the thing is in many a man's private power will be invaluable! Influence upon the private character, late in life, is not only an influence late in life, but a weak influence. It is in youth that we plant our chief habits and prejudices; it is in youth that we take our party as to profession, pursuits, and matrimony. In youth, therefore, the turn is given; in youth the education even of the next generation is given; in youth the private and public character is determined; and the term of life extending but from youth to age, life ought to begin well from youth, and more especially before we take our party as to our principal objects. But your biography will not merely teach self-education, but the education of a wise man; and the wisest man will receive lights and improve his progress, by seeing detailed the conduct of another wise man. And why are weaker men to be deprived of such helps, when we see our race has been blundering on in the dark, almost without a guide in this particular, from the farthest trace of time? Show then, sir, how much is to be done, both to sons and fathers; and invite all wise men to become like yourself, and other men to become wise. When we see how cruel statesmen and warriors can be to the human race, and how absurd distinguished men can be to their acquaintance, it will be instructive to observe the instances multiply of pacific, acquiescing manners; and to find how compatible it is to be great and domestic, enviable and yet good-humored.

The little private incidents which you will also have to relate will have considerable use, as we want, above all things, rules of prudence in ordinary affairs; and it will be curious to see how you have acted in these. It will be so far a sort of key to life, and explain many things that all men ought to have once explained to them, to give them a chance of becoming wise by foresight. The nearest thing to having experience of one's own is to have other people's affairs brought before us in a shape that is interesting; this is sure to happen from your pen; our affairs and management will have an air of simplicity or importance that will not fail to strike; and I am convinced you have conducted them with as much originality as if you had been conducting discussions in politics or philosophy; and what more worthy of experiments and system (its importance and its errors considered) than human life?

Some men have been virtuous blindly, others have speculated fantastically, and others have been shrewd to bad purposes; but you, sir, I am sure, will give under your hand nothing but what is at the same moment wise, practical, and good. Your account of yourself (for I suppose the parallel I am drawing for Dr. Franklin will hold not only in point of character but of private history) will show that you are ashamed of no origin—a thing the more important as you prove how little necessary all origin is to happiness, virtue, or greatness. As no end likewise happens without a means, so we shall find, sir, that even you yourself framed a plan by which you became considerable; but at the same time we may see that though the event is flattering, the means are as simple as wisdom could make them; that is, depending upon nature, virtue, thought, and habit. Another thing demonstrated will be the propriety of every man's waiting for his time for appearing upon the stage of the world. Our sensations being very much fixed to the moment, we are apt to forget that more moments are to follow the first, and consequently that man should arrange his conduct so as to suit the whole of life. Your attribution appears to have been applied to your life, and the passing moments of it have been enlivened with content and enjoyment, instead of being tormented with foolish impatience or regrets. Such a conduct is easy for those who make virtue and themselves in countenance by examples of other truly great men, of whom patience is so often the characteristic. Your Quaker correspondent, sir (for here again I will suppose the subject of my letter resembling Dr. Franklin), praised your frugality, diligence, and temperance, which he considered as a pattern for all youth; but it is singular that he should have forgotten your modesty and your disinterestedness, without which you never could have waited for your advancement or found your situation in the meantime comfortable—which is a strong lesson to show the poverty of glory and the importance of regulating our minds. If this corre-

spondent had known the nature of your reputation as well as I
do, he would have said, Your former writings and measures would
secure attention to your Biography and Art of Virtue; and your
Biography and Art of Virtue, in return, would secure attention
to them. This is an advantage attendant upon a various character, and which brings all that belongs to it into greater play;
and it is the more useful, as perhaps more persons are at a loss
for the means of improving their minds and characters than they
are for the time or the inclination to do it. But there is one
concluding reflection, sir, that will show the use of your life as
a mere piece of biography. This style of writing seems a little
gone out of vogue, and yet it is a very useful one; and your
specimen of it may be particularly serviceable as it will make a
subject of comparison with the lives of various public cutthroats
and intriguers, and with absurd monastic self-tormentors or vain
literary triflers. If it encourages more writings of the same kind
with your own and induces more men to spend lives fit to be
written, it will be worth all Plutarch's *Lives* put together. But
being tired of figuring to myself a character of which every fea-
ture suits only one man in the world, without giving him the
praise of it, I shall end my letter, my dear Dr. Franklin, with
a personal application to your proper self. I am earnestly desirous
then, my dear sir, that you should let the world into the traits of
your genuine character, as civil broils may otherwise tend to
disguise or traduce it. Considering your great age, the caution of
your character, and your peculiar style of thinking, it is not
likely that any one besides yourself can be sufficiently master of
the facts of your life or the intentions of your mind. Besides all
this, the immense Revolution of the present period will necessarily turn our attention toward the author of it, and when
virtuous principles have been pretended in it, it will be highly
important to show that such have really influenced; and, as your
own character will be the principal one to receive a scrutiny, it
is proper (even for its effects upon your vast and rising country,
as well as upon England and upon Europe) that it should stand
respectable and eternal. For the furtherance of human happiness
I have always maintained that it is necessary to prove that man

is not even at present a vicious and detestable animal, and still more to prove that good management may greatly amend him; and it is for much the same reason that I am anxious to see the opinion established that there are fair characters existing among the individuals of the race; for the moment that all men, without exception, shall be conceived abandoned, good people will cease efforts deemed to be hopeless, and perhaps think of taking their share in the scramble of life, or at least of making it comfortable principally for themselves. Take then, my dear sir, this work most speedily into hand: show yourself good as you are good; temperate as you are temperate; and above all things, prove yourself as one who from your infancy have loved justice, liberty, and concord in a way that has made it natural and consistent for you to have acted as we have seen you act in the last seventeen years of your life. Let Englishmen be made not only to respect, but even to love you. When they think well of individuals in your native country, they will go nearer to thinking well of your country; and when your countrymen see themselves well thought of by Englishmen, they will go nearer to thinking well of England. Extend your views even further; do not stop at those who speak the English tongue, but after having settled so many points in nature and politics, think of bettering the whole race of men. As I have not read any part of the life in question, but know only the character that lived it, I write somewhat at hazard. I am sure, however, that the life and the treatise I allude to (on the Art of Virtue) will necessarily fulfill the chief of my expectations, and still more so if you take up the measure of suiting these performances to the several views above stated. Should they even prove unsuccessful in all that a sanguine admirer of yours hopes from them, you will at least have framed pieces to interest the human mind; and whoever gives a feeling of pleasure that is innocent to man has added so much to the fair side of a life otherwise too much darkened by anxiety and too much injured by pain. In the hope, therefore, that you will listen to the prayer addressed to you in this letter, I beg to subscribe myself, my dearest sir, etc., etc.

(Signed)   Benj. Vaughan [30b]

## CONTINUATION OF THE ACCOUNT OF MY LIFE.
### BEGUN AT PASSY, 1784

It is some time since I received the above letters, but I have been too busy till now to think of complying with the request they contain. It might, too, be much better done if I were at home among my papers, which would aid my memory and help to ascertain dates; but my return being uncertain, and having just now a little leisure, I will endeavor to recollect and write what I can. If I live to get home, it may there be corrected and improved.

Not having any copy here of what is already written, I know not whether an account is given of the means I used to establish the Philadelphia Public Library, which from a small beginning is now become so considerable, though I remember to have come down to near the time of that transaction, 1730. I will therefore begin here with an account of it, which may be struck out if found to have been already given.

At the time I established myself in Pennsylvania, there was not a good bookseller's shop in any of the Colonies to the southward of Boston. In New York and Philadelphia the printers were indeed stationers; they sold only paper, etc., almanacs, ballads, and a few common schoolbooks. Those who loved reading were obliged to send for their books from England. The members of the Junto had each a few. We had left the alehouse where we first met and hired a room to hold our club in. I proposed that we should all of us bring our books to that room, where they would not only be ready to consult in our conferences but become a common benefit, each of us being at liberty to borrow such as he wished to read at home. This was accordingly done and for some time contented us. Finding the advantage of this little collection, I proposed to render the benefit from books more common by commencing a public subscription library. I drew a sketch of the plan and rules that would be necessary, and got a skillful conveyancer, Mr. Charles Brockden, to put the whole in form of articles of agreement to be subscribed, by which each subscriber engaged to pay a certain sum down for the first purchase of books and an annual contribution for increasing them. So few were the readers at that time in Philadelphia and the majority of us so poor that I was not able with great industry to find more than fifty persons, mostly young tradesmen, willing to pay down for this purpose forty shillings each and ten shillings per annum. With this little fund we began. The books were imported. The library was open one day in the week for lending them to the subscribers, on their promissory notes to pay double the value if not duly returned. The institution soon manifested its utility, was imitated by other towns and in other provinces; the libraries were augmented by donations; reading became fashionable; and our people, having no public amusements to divert their attention from study, became better acquainted with books, and in a few years were observed by strangers to be better instructed and more intelligent than people of the same rank generally are in other countries.

When we were about to sign the above-mentioned articles, which were to be binding on us, our heirs, etc., for fifty years, Mr. Brockden, the scrivener, said to us, "You are young men, but it is scarce probable that any of you will live to see the expiration of the term fixed in this instrument." A number of us, however, are yet living; but the instrument was after a few years rendered null by a charter that incorporated and gave perpetuity to the company.

The objections and reluctances I met with in soliciting the subscriptions made me soon feel the impropriety of presenting one's self as the proposer of any useful project that might be supposed to raise one's reputation in the smallest degree above that of one's neighbors when one has need of their assistance to accomplish that project. I therefore put myself as much as I could out of sight, and stated it as a scheme of a "number of friends" who had requested me to go about and propose it to such as they thought lovers of reading. In this way my affair went on more smoothly, and I ever after practiced it on such occasions, and from my frequent successes can heartily recommend it. The present little sacrifice of your vanity will afterwards be amply repaid.

If it remains a while uncertain to whom the merit belongs, some-one more vain than yourself will be encouraged to claim it, and then even envy will be disposed to do you justice by plucking those assumed feathers and restoring them to their right owner.

This library afforded me the means of improvement by con-stant study, for which I set apart an hour or two each day, and thus repaired in some degree the loss of the learned education my father once intended for me. Reading was the only amuse-ment I allowed myself. I spent no time in taverns, games, or frolics of any kind. And my industry in my business continued as indefatigable as it was necessary. I was in debt for my printing house, I had a young family coming on to be educated, and I had two competitors to contend with for business, who were estab-lished in the place before me. My circumstances, however, grew daily easier—my original habits of frugality continuing, and my father having among his instructions to me when a boy frequently repeated a proverb of Solomon, "Seest thou a man diligent in his calling, he shall stand before kings, he shall not stand before mean men." I from thence considered industry as a means of ob-taining wealth and distinction, which encouraged me, though I did not think that I should ever literally stand before kings, which, however, has since happened; for I have stood before five, and even had the honor of sitting down with one, the king of Denmark, to dinner.

We have an English proverb that says,

> He that would thrive
> Must ask his wife.

It was lucky for me that I had one as much disposed to industry and frugality as myself. She assisted me cheerfully in my busi-ness, folding and stitching pamphlets, tending shop, purchasing old linen rags for the papermakers, etc. We kept no idle servants, our table was plain and simple, our furniture of the cheapest. For instance, my breakfast was for a long time bread and milk, (no tea), and I ate it out of a twopenny earthen porringer with a pewter spoon. But mark how luxury will enter families and make a progress, in spite of principle. Being called one morning to breakfast, I found it in a china bowl, with a spoon of silver. They had been bought for me without my knowledge by my wife, and had cost her the enormous sum of twenty-three shillings, for which she had no other excuse or apology to make but that she thought *her* husband deserved a silver spoon and china bowl as well as any of his neighbors. This was the first appearance of plate and china in our house, which afterwards in a course of years, as our wealth increased, augmented gradually to several hundred pounds in value.

I had been religiously educated as a Presbyterian; and though some of the dogmas of that persuasion, such as the eternal decrees of God, election, reprobation, etc., appeared to me unintelligible, others doubtful, and I early absented myself from the public assemblies of the sect, Sunday being my studying day, I never was without some religious principles. I never doubted, for instance, the existence of the Deity, that he made the world and governed it by his providence, that the most acceptable service of God was the doing good to man, that our souls are immortal, and that all crime will be punished and virtue rewarded either here or hereafter. These I esteemed the essentials of every religion, and being to be found in all the religions we had in our country, I respected them all, though with different degrees of respect as I found them more or less mixed with other articles which without any tendency to inspire, promote, or confirm morality, served principally to divide us and make us unfriendly to one another. This respect to all, with an opinion that the worst had some good effects, induced me to avoid all discourse that might tend to lessen the good opinion another might have of his own religion; and as our province increased in people and new places of worship were continually wanted and generally erected by voluntary contribution, my mite for such purpose, whatever might be the sect, was never refused.

Though I seldom attended any public worship, I had still an opinion of its propriety and of its utility when rightly conducted, and I regularly paid my annual subscription for the support of the only Presbyterian minister or meeting we had in Philadelphia. He used to visit me sometimes as a friend and admonish me to attend his administrations, and I was now and then prevailed on to do so, once for five Sundays successively. Had he been, *in my opinion,* a good preacher, perhaps I might have continued, notwithstanding the occasion I had for the Sunday's leisure in my course of study; but his discourses were chiefly either polemic arguments or explications of the peculiar doctrines of our sect, and were all to me very dry( uninteresting, and unedifying since not a single moral principle was inculcated or enforced, their aim seeming to be rather to make us Presbyterians than good citizens.) At length he took for his text that verse of the fourth chapter of Philippians, "Finally, brethren, whatsoever things are true, honest, just, pure, lovely, or of good report, if there be any virtue, or any praise, think on these things"; and I imagined, in a sermon on such a text, we could not miss of having some morality. But he confined himself to five points only as meant by the apostle; viz., 1. Keeping holy the Sabbath day, 2. Being diligent in reading the Holy Scriptures, 3. Attending duly the public worship, 4. Partaking of the sacrament, 5. Paying a due respect to God's ministers. These might be all good things, but as they were not the kind of good things that I expected from that text, I despaired of ever meeting with them from any other, was disgusted, and attended his preaching no more. I had some years before composed a little liturgy or form of prayer for my own private use; viz., in 1728, entitled "Articles of Belief and Acts of Religion." I returned to the use of this and went no more to the public assemblies. My conduct might be blamable, but I leave it without attempting further to excuse it, my present purpose being to relate facts and not to make apologies for them.

It was about this time I conceived the bold and arduous project of arriving at moral perfection. I wished to live without committing any fault at any time; I would conquer all that either natural inclination, custom, or company might lead me into. As I knew, or thought I knew, what was right and wrong, I did not see why I might not *always* do the one and avoid the other. But I soon found I had undertaken a task of more difficulty than I had imagined. While my attention was taken up and care employed in guarding against one fault, I was often surprised by another.

Habit took the advantage of inattention. Inclination was sometimes too strong for reason. I concluded at length that the mere speculative conviction that it was our interest to be completely virtuous was not sufficient to prevent our slipping, and that the contrary habits must be broken and good ones acquired and established before we can have any dependence on a steady, uniform rectitude of conduct. For this purpose I therefore contrived the following method:

In the various enumerations of the moral virtues I had met with in my reading, I found the catalogue more or less numerous, as different writers included more or fewer ideas under the same name. Temperance, for example, was by some confined to eating and drinking, while by others it was extended to mean the moderating every other pleasure, appetite, inclination, or passion—bodily or mental, even to our avarice and ambition. I proposed to myself, for the sake of clearness, to use rather more names with fewer ideas annexed to each than a few names with more ideas; and I included under thirteen names of virtues all that at that time occurred to me as necessary or desirable, and annexed to each a short precept which fully expressed the extent I gave to its meaning.

These names of virtues with their precepts were:

### 1. Temperance

Eat not to dullness. Drink not to elevation.

### 2. Silence

Speak not but what may benefit others or yourself. Avoid trifling conversation.

### 3. Order

Let all your things have their places. Let each part of your business have its time.

### 4. Resolution

Resolve to perform what you ought. Perform without fail what you resolve.

## 5. Frugality

Make no expense but to do good to others or yourself; i.e., waste nothing.

## 6. Industry

Lose no time. Be always employed in something useful. Cut off all unnecessary actions.

## 7. Sincerity

Use no hurtful deceit. Think innocently and justly; and, if you speak, speak accordingly.

## 8. Justice

Wrong none by doing injuries or omitting the benefits that are your duty.

## 9. Moderation

Avoid extremes. Forbear resenting injuries so much as you think they deserve.

## 10. Cleanliness

Tolerate no uncleanliness in body, clothes, or habitation.

## 11. Tranquillity

Be not disturbed at trifles or at accidents common or unavoidable.

## 12. Chastity

Rarely use venery but for health or offspring—never to dullness, weakness, or the injury of your own or another's peace or reputation.

## 13. Humility

Imitate Jesus and Socrates.

My intention being to acquire the *habitude* of all these virtues, I judged it would be well not to distract my attention by attempting the whole at once but to fix it on one of them at a time, and when I should be master of that, then to proceed to another, and so on till I should have gone through the thirteen. And as the previous acquisition of some might facilitate the acquisition of certain others, I arranged them with that view as they stand above. *Temperance* first, as it tends to procure that coolness and clearness of head, which is so necessary where constant vigilance was to be kept up, and guard maintained, against the unremitting attraction of ancient habits and the force of perpetual temptations. This being acquired and established, *Silence* would be more easy; and my desire being to gain knowledge at the same time that I improved in virtue, and considering that in conversation it was obtained rather by the use of the ear than of the tongue, and therefore wishing to break a habit I was getting into of prattling, punning, and joking, which only made me acceptable to trifling company, I gave *Silence* the second place. This and the next, *Order*, I expected would allow me more time for attending to my project and my studies. *Resolution,* once become habitual, would keep me firm in my endeavors to obtain all the subsequent virtues; *Frugality* and *Industry,* freeing me from my remaining debt and, producing affluence and independence, would make more easy the practice of *Sincerity* and *Justice,* etc., etc. Conceiving then that agreeable to the advice of Pythagoras in his golden verses, daily examination would be necessary, I contrived the following method for conducting that examination.

I made a little book in which I allotted a page for each of the virtues. I ruled each page with red ink so as to have seven columns, one for each day of the week, marking each column with a letter for the day. I crossed these columns with thirteen red lines, marking the beginning of each line with the first letter of one of the virtues, on which line and in its proper column I might mark by a little black spot every fault I found upon examination to have been committed respecting that virtue upon that day.

I determined to give a week's strict attention to each of the virtues successively. Thus in the first week my great guard was to avoid even the least offense against temperance, leaving the other virtues to their ordinary chance, only marking every evening the faults of the day. Thus if in the first week I could keep my first line marked "T." clear of spots, I supposed the habit of that virtue so much strengthened and its opposite weakened that I might venture extending my attention to include the next, and for the following week keep both lines clear of spots. Proceeding thus to the last, I could go through a course complete in thirteen weeks, and four courses in a year. And like him who, having a garden to weed, does not attempt to eradicate all the bad herbs at once, which would exceed his reach and his strength, but works on one of the beds at a time, and having accomplished the first, proceeds to a second; so I should have (I hoped) the encouraging pleasure of seeing on my pages the progress I made in virtue by clearing successively my lines of their spots, till in the end by a number of courses, I should be happy in viewing a clean book after a thirteen weeks' daily examination.

[The form of the page appears
on the opposite page.]

This my little book had for its motto these lines from Addison's *Cato:* [31]

Here will I hold: if there is a power above us,
(And that there is, all Nature cries aloud
Through all her works) he must delight in virtue,
And that which he delights in must be happy.

Another from Cicero:

*O vitae philosophia dux! O virtutum indagatrix, expultrixque vitiorum! Unus dies bene et ex preceptis tuis actus, peccanti immortalitati est anteponendus.* [32]

## TEMPERANCE

*Eat not to dulness.*

*Drink not to elevation.*

|      | S   | M | T | W | T | F | S |
|------|-----|---|---|---|---|---|---|
| T    |     |   |   |   |   |   |   |
| S    | √ √ | √ |   | √ |   | √ |   |
| O    | √   | √ | √ |   | √ | √ | √ |
| R    |     |   | √ |   |   | √ |   |
| F    |     | √ |   |   | √ |   |   |
| I    |     |   | √ |   |   |   |   |
| S    |     |   |   |   |   |   |   |
| J    |     |   |   |   |   |   |   |
| M    |     |   |   |   |   |   |   |
| Cl.  |     |   |   |   |   |   |   |
| T    |     |   |   |   |   |   |   |
| Ch   |     |   |   |   |   |   |   |
| H    |     |   |   |   |   |   |   |
|      |     |   |   |   |   |   |   |

Another from the proverbs of Solomon speaking of wisdom or virtue:

Length of days is in her right hand, and in her left hand riches and honours; her ways are ways of pleasantness, and all her paths are peace (III, 16, 17).

And conceiving God to be the fountain of wisdom, I thought it right and necessary to solicit his assistance for obtaining it; to this end I formed the following little prayer, which was prefixed to my tables of examination, for daily use:

O powerful Goodness, bountiful Father, merciful Guide! Increase in me that wisdom which discovers my truest interests; strengthen my resolutions to perform what that wisdom dictates. Accept my kind offices to thy other children, as the only return in my power for thy continual favors to me.

I used also sometimes a little prayer which I took from Thomson's *Poems:* [33] viz.,

Father of light and life, thou Good supreme,
Oh, teach me what is good, teach me thy self!
Save me from folly, vanity and vice,
From every low pursuit, and fill my soul
With knowledge, conscious peace, and virtue pure,
Sacred, substantial, never-fading bliss!

The precept of *Order* requiring that *"every part of my business should have its allotted time,"* one page in my little book contained the following scheme of employment for the twenty-four hours of a natural day.

[The form of the page appears
on the opposite page.]

I entered upon the execution of this plan for self-examination and continued it with occasional intermissions for some time. I

| | | |
|---|---|---|
| The morning question, What good shall I do this day? | 5 6 7 | Rise, wash, and address *Powerful Goodness;* contrive day's business and take the resolution of the day; prosecute the present study; and breakfast. |
| | 8 9 10 11 | Work. |
| | 12 1 | Read or overlook my accounts, and dine. |
| | 2 3 4 5 | Work |
| | 6 7 8 9 | Put things in their places, supper, music, or diversion, or conversation; examination of the day |
| Evening question, What good have I done today? | 10 11 12 1 2 3 4 | Sleep. |

was surprised to find myself so much fuller of faults than I had imagined, but I had the satisfaction of seeing them diminish. To avoid the trouble of renewing now and then my little book, which by scraping out the marks on the paper of old faults to make room for new ones in a new course became full of holes, I transferred my tables and precepts to the ivory leaves of a memorandum book on which the lines were drawn with red ink that made a durable stain, and on those lines I marked my faults with a black lead pencil, which marks I could easily wipe out with a wet sponge. After a while I went through one course only in a year, and afterwards only one in several years, till at length I omitted them entirely, being employed in voyages and business abroad with a multiplicity of affairs that interfered; but I always carried my little book with me. My scheme of *Order* gave me the most trouble, and I found that though it might be practicable where a man's business was such as to leave him the disposition of his time, that of a journeyman printer for instance, it was not possible to be exactly observed by a master, who must mix with the world and often receive people of business at their own hours. Order, too, with regard to places for things, papers, etc., I found extremely difficult to acquire. I had not been early accustomed to *method*, and having an exceeding good memory, I was not so sensible of the inconvenience attending want of method. This article therefore cost me so much painful attention, and my faults in it vexed me so much, and I made so little progress in amendment and had such frequent relapses, that I was almost ready to give up the attempt and content myself with the faulty character in that respect. Like the man who in buying an ax of a smith, my neighbor, desired to have the whole of its surface as bright as the edge; the smith consented to grind it bright for him if he would turn the wheel. He turned while the smith pressed the broad face of the ax hard and heavily on the stone, which made the turning of it very fatiguing. The man came every now and then from the wheel to see how the work went on; and at length would take his ax as it was, without further grinding. "No," says the smith, "turn on, turn on; we shall have it bright

by and by; as yet 'tis only speckled." "Yes," says the man, "but
I think I like a speckled ax best." And I believe this may have
been the case with many who having, for want of some such
means as I employed, found the difficulty of obtaining good and
breaking bad habits in other points of vice and virtue, have given
up the struggle and concluded that "a speckled ax was best."
For something that pretended to be reason was every now and
then suggesting to me that such extreme nicety as I exacted of
myself might be a kind of foppery in morals, which if it were
known would make me ridiculous; that a perfect character might
be attended with the inconvenience of being envied and hated;
and that a benevolent man should allow a few faults in himself,
to keep his friends in countenance. In truth, I found myself incor-
rigible with respect to *Order;* and now I am grown old and my
memory bad, I feel very sensibly the want of it. But on the whole,
though I never arrived at the perfection I had been so ambitious
of obtaining but fell far short of it, yet I was by the endeavor a
better and a happier man than I otherwise should have been if I
had not attempted it; as those who aim at perfect writing by
imitating the engraved copies, though they never reach the wished-
for excellence of those copies, their hand is mended by the endeavor and is tolerable while it continues fair and legible.

It may be well my posterity should be informed that to this
little artifice, with the blessing of God, their ancestor owed the
constant felicity of his life down to his seventy-ninth year, in
which this is written. What reverses may attend the remainder is
in the hand of providence; but if they arrive, the reflection on
past happiness enjoyed ought to help his bearing them with more
resignation. To *Temperance* he ascribes his long-continued health
and what is still left to him of a good constitution; to *Industry*
and *Frugality,* the early easiness of his circumstances and acquisition of his fortune, with all that knowledge which enabled him
to be a useful citizen and obtained for him some degree of reputation among the learned. To *Sincerity* and *Justice,* the confidence
of his country and the honorable employs it conferred upon him;
and to the joint influence of the whole mass of the virtues, even

in the imperfect state he was able to acquire them, all that evenness of temper and that cheerfulness in conversation which makes his company still sought for and agreeable even to his younger acquaintance. I hope, therefore, that some of my descendants may follow the example and reap the benefit.

It will be remarked that, though my scheme was not wholly without religion, there was in it no mark of any of the distinguishing tenets of any particular sect. I had purposely avoided them; for being fully persuaded of the utility and excellence of my method, and that it might be serviceable to people in all religions, and intending sometime or other to publish it, I would not have anything in it that should prejudice anyone of any sect against it. I purposed writing a little comment on each virtue, in which I would have shown the advantages of possessing it and the mischiefs attending its opposite vice; I should have called my book *The Art of Virtue* ᵃ because it would have shown the means and manner of obtaining virtue, which would have distinguished it from the mere exhortation to be good, that does not instruct and indicate the means, but is like the apostle's man of verbal charity, who only, without showing to the naked and hungry how or where they might get clothes or victuals, exhorted them to be fed and clothed (*James* II: 15, 16).

But it so happened that my intention of writing and publishing this comment was never fulfilled. I did, indeed, from time to time put down short hints of the sentiments, reasonings, etc., to be made use of in it, some of which I have still by me; but the necessary close attention to private business in the earlier part of life and public business since have occasioned my postponing it. For it being connected in my mind with *a great and extensive project* that required the whole man to execute, and which an unforeseen succession of employs prevented my attending to, it has hitherto remained unfinished.

In this piece it was my design to explain and enforce this doctrine: That vicious actions are not hurtful because they are forbidden, but forbidden because they are hurtful, the nature of

---

ᵃ Nothing so likely to make a man's fortune as virtue. [marg. note]

man alone considered; that it was therefore everyone's interest to be virtuous who wished to be happy even in this world. And I should from this circumstance, there being always in the world a number of rich merchants, nobility, states, and princes who have need of honest instruments for the management of their affairs, and such being so rare, have endeavored to convince young persons that no qualities are so likely to make a poor man's fortune as those of probity and integrity.

My list of virtues contained at first but twelve. But a Quaker friend having kindly informed me that I was generally thought proud, that my pride showed itself frequently in conversation, that I was not content with being in the right when discussing any point, but was overbearing and rather insolent—of which he convinced me by mentioning several instances—I determined endeavoring to cure myself if I could of this vice or folly among the rest, and I added *Humility* to my list, giving an extensive meaning to the word. I cannot boast of much success in acquiring the *reality* of this virtue, but I had a good deal with regard to the *appearance* of it. I made it a rule to forbear all direct contradiction to the sentiments of others and all positive assertion of my own. I even forbade myself, agreeable to the old laws of our Junto, the use of every word or expression in the language that imported a fixed opinion, such as "certainly," "undoubtedly," etc.; and I adopted instead of them, "I conceive," "I apprehend," or "I imagine" a thing to be so or so, or "It so appears to me at present." When another asserted something that I thought an error, I denied myself the pleasure of contradicting him abruptly and of showing immediately some absurdity in his proposition; and in answering I began by observing that in certain cases or circumstances his opinion would be right, but that in the present case there "appeared" or "seemed to me" some difference, etc. I soon found the advantage of this change in my manners: The conversations I engaged in went on more pleasantly; the modest way in which I proposed my opinions procured them a readier reception and less contradiction; I had less mortification when I was found to be in the wrong, and I more easily prevailed with others to give up their mistakes and join with me when I happened to be in the right. And this mode, which I at first put on with some violence to natural inclination, became at length so easy and so habitual to me that perhaps for these fifty years past no one has ever heard a dogmatical expression escape me. And to this habit (after my character of integrity) I think it principally owing that I had early so much weight with my fellow citizens when I proposed new institutions, or alterations in the old, and so much influence in public councils when I became a member. For I was but a bad speaker, never eloquent, subject to much hesitation in my choice of words, hardly correct in language, and yet I generally carried my point.

In reality there is perhaps no one of our natural passions so hard to subdue as *pride;* disguise it, struggle with it, beat it down, stifle it, mortify it as much as one pleases, it is still alive and will every now and then peep out and show itself. You will see it perhaps often in this history. For even if I could conceive that I had completely overcome it, I should probably be proud of my humility.

[Thus far written at Passy, 1784.] [a]

*I am now about to write at home (Philadelphia), August 1788, but cannot have the help expected from my papers, many of them being lost in the war. I have, however, found the following:* [b]

Having mentioned *a great and extensive project* which I had conceived, it seems proper that some account should be here given of that project and its object. Its first rise in my mind appears in the following little paper, accidentally preserved, viz.,

---

[a] [Square brackets are Franklin's.—M.F.]
[b] [The italicized paragraph is a marginal note in the original manuscript.]

Observations on my Reading History in Library,
May 9, 1731.

"That the great affairs of the world, the wars, revolutions, etc., are carried on and effected by parties.

"That the view of these parties is their present general interest, or what they take to be such.

"That the different views of these different parties occasion all confusion.

"That while a party is carrying on a general design, each man has his particular private interest in view.

"That as soon as a party has gained its general point, each member becomes intent upon his particular interest, which, thwarting others, breaks that party into divisions and occasions more confusion.

"That few in public affairs act from a mere view of the good of their country, whatever they may pretend; and though their actings bring real good to their country, yet men primarily considered that their own and their country's interest was united and did not act from a principle of benevolence.

"That fewer still in public affairs act with a view to the good of mankind.

"There seems to me at present to be great occasion for raising a united party for virtue, by forming the virtuous and good men of all nations into a regular body, to be governed by suitable good and wise rules, which good and wise men may probably be more unanimous in their obedience to than common people are to common laws.

"I at present think that whoever attempts this aright and is well qualified, cannot fail of pleasing God and of meeting with success.

B.F."

Revolving this project in my mind, as to be undertaken hereafter when my circumstances should afford me the necessary leisure, I put down from time to time on pieces of paper such thoughts as occurred to me respecting it. Most of these are lost, but I find one purporting to be the substance of an intended creed, containing, as I thought, the essentials of every known religion and being free of everything that might shock the professors of any religion. It is expressed in these words, viz.,

"That there is one God who made all things.

"That he governs the world by his providence.

"That he ought to be worshipped by adoration, prayer, and thanksgiving.

"But that the most acceptable service to God is doing good to man.

"That the soul is immortal.

"And that God will certainly reward virtue and punish vice, either here or hereafter."

My ideas at that time were that the sect should be begun and spread at first among young and single men only; that each person to be initiated should not only declare his assent to such creed but should have exercised himself with the thirteen weeks' examination and practice of the virtues, as in the before-mentioned model; that the existence of such a society should be kept a secret till it was become considerable, to prevent solicitations for the admission of improper persons; but that the members should each of them search among his acquaintance for ingenuous, well-disposed youths to whom, with prudent caution, the scheme should be gradually communicated; that the members should engage to afford their advice, assistance, and support to each other in promoting one another's interest, business, and advancement in life; that for distinction we should be called the Society of the Free and Easy: free, as being by the general practice and habit of the virtues, free from the dominion of vice; and particularly by the practice of industry and frugality, free from debt, which exposes a man to confinement and a species of slavery to his creditors. This is as much as I can now recollect of the project, except that I communicated it in part to two young men who adopted it with some enthusiasm. But my then narrow circumstances and the necessity I was under of sticking close to my business occasioned my postponing the further prosecution of it at that time, and my multifarious occupations public and private induced me to continue postponing, so that it has been omitted till I have no longer strength or activity left sufficient for such an enterprise, though I am still of opinion that it was a practicable scheme and might have been very useful by forming a great number of good citizens. And I was not discouraged by the seeming magnitude of the undertaking, as I have always thought that one man of tolerable abilities may work great changes and accomplish great affairs among mankind if he first forms a good plan, and, cutting off all amusements or other employments that would divert his attention, makes the execution of that same plan his sole study and business.

In 1732 I first published my *Almanack,* under the name of Richard Saunders; it was continued by me about twenty-five years, commonly called *Poor Richard's Almanack.*[34] I endeavored to make it both entertaining and useful, and it accordingly came to be in such demand that I reaped considerable profit from it, vending annually near ten thousand. And observing that it was generally read, scarce any neighborhood in the province being without it, I considered it as a proper vehicle for conveying instruction among the common people, who bought scarce any other books. I therefore filled all the little spaces that occurred between the remarkable days in the calendar with proverbial sentences, chiefly such as inculcated industry and frugality as the means of procuring wealth and thereby securing virtue—it being more difficult for a man in want to act always honestly, as (to use here one of those proverbs) "it is hard for an empty sack to stand upright." These proverbs, which contained the wisdom of many ages and nations, I assembled and formed into a connected discourse prefixed to the *Almanack* of 1757,[a] as the harangue of a wise old man to the people attending an auction. The bringing all these scattered counsels thus into a focus enabled them to make greater impression. The piece, being universally approved, was copied in all the newspapers of the Continent, reprinted in Britain on a broadside to be stuck up in houses, two translations were

---

[a] [See page 202: "The Way to Wealth."]

made of it in French, and great numbers bought by the clergy and gentry to distribute gratis among their poor parishioners and tenants. In Pennsylvania, as it discouraged useless expense in foreign superfluities, some thought it had its share of influence in producing that growing plenty of money which was observable for several years after its publication.

I considered my newspaper also as another means of communicating instruction, and in that view frequently reprinted in it extracts from the *Spectator* and other moral writers, and sometimes published little pieces of my own which had been first composed for reading in our Junto. Of these are a Socratic dialogue tending to prove that whatever might be his parts and abilities, a vicious man could not properly be called a man of sense; [35] (and a discourse on self-denial showing that virtue was not secure till its practice became a habitude and was free from the opposition of contrary inclinations.) These may be found in the papers about the beginning of 1735. In the conduct of my newspaper I carefully excluded all libeling and personal abuse, which is of late years become so disgraceful to our country. Whenever I was solicited to insert anything of that kind and the writers pleaded, as they generally did, the liberty of the press and that a newspaper was like a stagecoach in which any one who would pay had a right to a place, my answer was that I would print the piece separately if desired, and the author might have as many copies as he pleased to distribute himself, but that I would not take upon me to spread his detraction, and that having contracted with my subscribers to furnish them with what might be either useful or entertaining, I could not fill their papers with private altercation in which they had no concern without doing them manifest injustice. Now many of our printers make no scruple of gratifying the malice of individuals by false accusations of the fairest characters among ourselves, augmenting animosity even to the producing of duels, and are moreover so indiscreet as to print scurrilous reflections on the government of neighboring states and even on the conduct of our best national allies, which may be attended with the most pernicious consequences. These things I mention as a caution to young printers, that they may be encouraged not to pollute their presses and disgrace their profession by such infamous practices but refuse steadily, as they may see by my example that such a course of conduct will not on the whole be injurious to their interests.

In 1733 I sent one of my journeymen to Charlestown, South Carolina, where a printer was wanting. I furnished him with a press and letters on an agreement of partnership, by which I was to receive one-third of the profits of the business, paying one-third of the expense. He was a man of learning and honest, but ignorant in matters of account; and though he sometimes made me remittances, I could get no account from him nor any satisfactory state of our partnership while he lived. On his decease, the business was continued by his widow, who being born and bred in Holland, where, as I have been informed, the knowledge of accounts makes a part of female education, she not only sent me as clear a state as she could find of the transactions past, but continued to account with the greatest regularity and exactitude every quarter afterwards, and managed the business with such success that she not only brought up reputably a family of children but at the expiration of the term was able to purchase of me the printing house and establish her son in it. I mention this affair chiefly for the sake of recommending that branch of education for our young females as likely to be of more use to them and their children in case of widowhood than either music or dancing, by preserving them from losses by imposition of crafty men, and enabling them to continue perhaps a profitable mercantile house with established correspondence till a son is grown up fit to undertake and go on with it, to the lasting advantage and enriching of the family.

About the year 1734 there arrived among us from Ireland a young Presbyterian preacher named Hemphill, who delivered with a good voice, and apparently extempore, most excellent discourses, which drew together considerable numbers of different persuasions, who joined in admiring them. Among the rest I became one of his constant hearers, his sermons pleasing me as they had little of the dogmatical kind but inculcated strongly the practice of virtue, or what in the religious style are called "good works." Those, however, of our congregation who considered themselves as ortho-

dox Presbyterians disapproved his doctrine and were joined by
most of the old clergy, who arraigned him of heterodoxy before
the synod in order to have him silenced. I became his zealous
partisan and contributed all I could to raise a party in his favor,
and we combatted for him a while with some hopes of success.
There was much scribbling pro and con upon the occasion; and
finding that, though an elegant preacher, he was but a poor writer,
I lent him my pen and wrote for him two or three pamphlets,
and one piece in the *Gazette* of April 1735. Those pamphlets, as
is generally the case with controversial writings, though eagerly
read at the time, were soon out of vogue, and I question whether
a single copy of them now exists.

During the contest an unlucky occurrence hurt his cause exceedingly. One of our adversaries, having heard him preach a
sermon that was much admired, thought he had somewhere read
that sermon before, or at least a part of it. On search he found
that part quoted at length in one of the British reviews, from a
discourse of Dr. Foster's. This detection gave many of our party
disgust, who accordingly abandoned his cause and occasioned our
more speedy discomfiture in the synod. I stuck by him, however,
as I rather approved his giving us good sermons composed by
others than bad ones of his own manufacture, though the latter
was the practice of our common teachers. He afterwards acknowledged to me that none of those he preached were his own, adding
that his memory was such as enabled him to retain and repeat any
sermon after one reading only. On our defeat he left us in search
elsewhere of better fortune, and I quitted the congregation, never
joining it after, though I continued many years my subscription
for the support of its ministers.

I had begun in 1733 to study languages. I soon made myself so
much a master of the French as to be able to read the books
with ease. I then undertook the Italian. An acquaintance who was
also learning it used often to tempt me to play chess with him.
Finding this took up too much of the time I had to spare for
study, I at length refused to play any more unless on this condition—that the victor in every game should have a right to impose
a task, either in parts of the grammar to be got by heart, or in

translation, etc., which tasks the vanquished was to perform upon honor before our next meeting. As we played pretty equally, we thus beat one another into that language. I afterwards with a little painstaking acquired as much of the Spanish as to read their books also. I have already mentioned that I had only one year's instruction in a Latin school, and that when very young, after which I neglected that language entirely. But when I had attained an acquaintance with the French, Italian, and Spanish, I was surprised to find, on looking over a Latin Testament, that I understood so much more of that language than I had imagined—which encouraged me to apply myself again to the study of it; and I met with the more success, as those preceding languages had greatly smoothed my way. From these circumstances I have thought that there is some inconsistency in our common mode of teaching languages. We are told that it is proper to begin first with the Latin, and having acquired that, it will be more easy to attain those modern languages which are derived from it; and yet we do not begin with the Greek in order more easily to acquire the Latin. It is true that if you can clamber and get to the top of a staircase without using the steps, you will more easily gain them in descending; but certainly if you begin with the lowest, you will with more ease ascend to the top. And I would therefore offer it to the consideration of those who superintend the educating of our youth, whether, since many of those who begin with the Latin quit the same after spending some years without having made any great proficiency, and what they have learned becomes almost useless so that their time has been lost, it would not have been better to have begun them with the French, proceeding to the Italian, etc., for though after spending the same time they should quit the study of languages and never arrive at the Latin, they would, however, have acquired another tongue or two that being in modern use might be serviceable to them in common life.

After ten years' absence from Boston and having become more easy in my circumstances, I made a journey thither to visit my relations, which I could not sooner well afford. In returning I called at Newport to see my brother, then settled there with his printing house. Our former differences were forgotten, and our meeting was very cordial and affectionate. He was fast declining in his health and requested of me that in case of his death, which he apprehended not far distant, I would take home his son, then but ten years of age, and bring him up to the printing business. This I accordingly performed, sending him a few years to school before I took him into the office. His mother carried on the business till he was grown up, when I assisted him with an assortment of new types, those of his father being in a manner worn out. Thus it was that I made my brother ample amends for the service I had deprived him of by leaving him so early.

In 1736, I lost one of my sons, a fine boy of four years old, by the smallpox taken in the common way. I long regretted bitterly, and still regret, that I had not given it to him by inoculation. This I mention for the sake of parents who omit that operation, on the supposition that they should never forgive themselves if a child died under it—my example showing that the regret may be the same either way, and that therefore the safer should be chosen.

Our club, the Junto, was found so useful and afforded such satisfaction to the members that several were desirous of introducing their friends, which could not well be done without exceeding what we had settled as a convenient number, viz., twelve. We had from the beginning made it a rule to keep our institution a secret, which was pretty well observed. The intention was to avoid applications of improper persons for admittance, some of whom perhaps we might find it difficult to refuse. I was one of those who were against any addition to our number, but instead of it made in writing a proposal that every member separately should endeavor to form a subordinate club with the same rules respecting queries, etc., and without informing them of the connection with the Junto. The advantages proposed were the improvement of so many more young citizens by the use of our institutions; our better acquaintance with the general sentiments of the inhabitants on any occasion, as the Junto member might propose what queries we should desire and was to report to the Junto what passed in his separate club; the promotion of our particular interests in business by more extensive recommendations; and the increase of our influence in public affairs and our power of doing good by spreading through the several clubs the sentiments of the Junto. The project was approved, and every member undertook to form his club, but they did not all succeed. Five or six only were completed, which were called by different names, as the Vine, the Union, the Band, etc. They were useful to themselves, and afforded us a good deal of amusement, information, and instruction, besides answering in some considerable degree our views of influencing the public opinion on particular occasions, of which I shall give some instances in course of time as they happened.

My first promotion was my being chosen in 1736 clerk of the General Assembly. The choice was made that year without opposition; but the year following when I was again proposed (the choice, like that of the members, being annual), a new member made a long speech against me in order to favor some other candidate. I was, however, chosen, which was the more agreeable to me, as, besides the pay for immediate service as clerk, the place gave me a better opportunity of keeping up an interest among the members, which secured to me the business of printing the votes, laws, paper money, and other occasional jobs for the public, that, on the whole, were very profitable. I therefore did not like the opposition of this new member, who was a gentleman of fortune and education with talents that were likely to give him in time great influence in the House, which, indeed, afterward happened. I did not, however, aim at gaining his favor by paying any servile respect to him, but after some time took this other method. Having heard that he had in his library a certain very scarce and curious book, I wrote a note to him expressing my desire of perusing that book and requesting he would do me the favor of lending it to me for a few days. He sent it immediately; and I returned it in about a week with another note expressing strongly my sense of the favor. When we next met in the House, he spoke to me (which he had never done before), and with great civility. And he ever afterwards manifested a readiness to serve me on all occasions, so that we became great friends, and our friendship continued to his death. This is another instance of the truth of an old maxim I had learned, which says, "He that has once done you a kindness will be more ready to do you another than he whom you yourself have obliged." And it shows how much more profitable it is prudently to remove, than to resent, return, and continue inimical proceedings.

In 1737, Col. Spotswood, late Governor of Virginia, and then Postmaster General, being dissatisfied with the conduct of his deputy at Philadelphia respecting some negligence in rendering and want of exactness in framing his accounts, took from him the commission and offered it to me. I accepted it readily and found it of great advantage; for though the salary was small, it facilitated the correspondence that improved my newspaper, increased the number demanded as well as the advertisements to be inserted, so that it came to afford me a considerable income. My old competitor's newspaper declined proportionately, and I was satisfied without retaliating his refusal, while Postmaster, to permit my papers being carried by the riders. Thus he suffered greatly from his neglect in due accounting; and I mention it as a lesson to those young men who may be employed in managing affairs for others that they should always render accounts with great clearness and punctuality. The character of observing such a conduct is the most powerful of all recommendations to new employments and increase of business.

I began now to turn my thoughts a little to public affairs, beginning, however, with small matters. The city watch was one of the first things that I conceived to want regulation. It was managed by the constables of the respective wards in turn; the constable warned a number of housekeepers to attend him for the night. Those who chose never to attend paid him six shillings a year to be excused, which was supposed to be for hiring substitutes, but was in reality much more than was necessary for that purpose and made the constableship a place of profit; and the constable for a little drink often got such ragamuffins about him as a watch that respectable housekeepers did not choose to mix with. Walking the rounds, too, was often neglected, and most of the nights spent in tippling. I thereupon wrote a paper to be read in Junto representing these irregularities but insisting more particularly on the inequality of this six-shilling tax of the constables, respecting the circumstances of those who paid it, since a poor widow housekeeper, all whose property to be guarded by the watch did not, perhaps, exceed the value of fifty pounds, paid as much as the wealthiest merchant who had thousands of pounds' worth of goods in his stores. On the whole, I proposed as a more effectual watch the hiring of proper men to serve constantly in that business; and, as a more equitable way of supporting the charge, the levying a tax that should be proportioned to the property. This idea, being approved by the Junto, was communicated to the other clubs, but as arising in each of them. And though the plan was not immediately carried into execution, yet by preparing the minds of people for the change, it paved the way for the law obtained a few years after, when the members of our clubs were grown into more influence.

About this time I wrote a paper (first to be read in Junto, but it was afterwards published) on the different accidents and carelessnesses by which houses were set on fire, with cautions against them and means proposed of avoiding them. This was much spoken of as a useful piece, and gave rise to a project which soon followed it of forming a company for the more ready extinguishing of fires, and mutual assistance in removing and securing of goods when in danger. Associates in this scheme were presently found amounting to thirty. Our articles of agreement obliged every member to keep always in good order and fit for use a certain number of leather buckets with strong bags and baskets (for packing and transporting of goods) which were to be brought to every fire; and we agreed to meet once a month and spend a social evening together in discoursing and communicating such ideas as occurred to us upon the subject of fires as might be useful in our conduct on such occasions. The utility of this institution soon appeared, and many more desiring to be admitted than we thought convenient for one company, they were advised to form another, which was accordingly done. And this went on, one new company being formed after another till they became so numerous as to include most of the inhabitants who were men of

property; and now at the time of my writing this, though upwards of fifty years since its establishment, that which I first
formed, called the Union Fire Company,[36] still subsists and flourishes, though the first members are all deceased but myself and
one who is older by a year than I am. The small fines that have
been paid by members for absence at the monthly meetings have
been applied to the purchase of fire engines, ladders, firehooks,
and other useful implements for each company, so that I question
whether there is a city in the world better provided with the
means of putting a stop to beginning conflagrations; and in fact,
since those institutions, the city has never lost by fire more than
one or two houses at a time, and the flames have often been
extinguished before the house in which they began has been half
consumed.

In 1739 arrived among us from England the Rev. Mr. Whitfield,[37] who had made himself remarkable there as an itinerant
preacher. He was at first permitted to preach in some of our
churches; but the clergy, taking a dislike to him, soon refused
him their pulpits, and he was obliged to preach in the fields. The
multitudes of all sects and denominations that attended his sermons were enormous, and it was matter of speculation to me,
who was one of the number, to observe the extraordinary influence of his oratory on his hearers and how much they admired
and respected him, notwithstanding his common abuse of them,
by assuring them they were naturally "half beasts and half
devils." It was wonderful to see the change soon made in the
manners of our inhabitants; from being thoughtless or indifferent
about religion, it seemed as if all the world were growing religious,
so that one could not walk through the town in an evening without hearing psalms sung in different families of every street. And
it being found inconvenient to assemble in the open air subject
to its inclemencies, the building of a house to meet in was no
sooner proposed and persons appointed to receive contributions,
but sufficient sums were soon received to procure the ground and
erect the building, which was one hundred feet long and seventy
broad, about the size of Westminster Hall; and the work was
carried on with such spirit as to be finished in a much shorter

time than could have been expected. Both house and ground were vested in trustees expressly for the use of any preacher of any religious persuasion who might desire to say something to the people of Philadelphia, the design in building not being to accommodate any particular sect but the inhabitants in general, so that even if the Mufti of Constantinople were to send a missionary to preach Mahometanism to us, he would find a pulpit at his service.

Mr. Whitfield, in leaving us, went preaching all the way through the Colonies to Georgia. The settlement of that province had lately been begun; but instead of being made with hardy, industrious husbandmen accustomed to labor, the only people fit for such an enterprise, it was with families of broken shopkeepers and other insolvent debtors, many of indolent and idle habits, taken out of the jails—who, being set down in the woods, unqualified for clearing land and unable to endure the hardships of a new settlement, perished in numbers, leaving many helpless children unprovided for. The sight of their miserable situation inspired the benevolent heart of Mr. Whitfield with the idea of building an orphan house there in which they might be supported and educated. Returning northward he preached up this charity and made large collections; for his eloquence had a wonderful power over the hearts and purses of his hearers, of which I myself was an instance. I did not disapprove of the design, but as Georgia was then destitute of materials and workmen and it was proposed to send them from Philadelphia at a great expense, I thought it would have been better to have built the house here and brought the children to it. This I advised, but he was resolute in his first project and rejected my counsel, and I thereupon refused to contribute. I happened soon after to attend one of his sermons, in the course of which I perceived he intended to finish with a collection, and I silently resolved he should get nothing from me. I had in my pocket a handful of copper money, three or four silver dollars, and five pistoles in gold. As he proceeded, I began to soften and concluded to give the coppers. Another stroke of his oratory made me ashamed of that and determined me to give the silver; and he finished so admirably that I emptied my pocket wholly into the collector's dish, gold and all. At this sermon there was also one of our club, who being of my sentiments respecting the building in Georgia and suspecting a collection might be intended, had by precaution emptied his pockets before he came from home; toward the conclusion of the discourse, however, he felt a strong desire to give and applied to a neighbor who stood near him to borrow some money for the purpose. The application was unfortunately made to perhaps the only man in the company who had the firmness not to be affected by the preacher. His answer was, "At any other time, Friend Hopkinson, I would lend to thee freely, but not now; for thee seems to be out of thy right senses."

Some of Mr. Whitfield's enemies affected to suppose that he would apply these collections to his own private emolument, but I who was intimately acquainted with him (being employed in printing his sermons and journals, etc.) never had the least suspicion of his integrity, but am to this day decidedly of opinion that he was in all his conduct a perfectly *honest man*. And methinks my testimony in his favor ought to have the more weight as we had no religious connection. He used, indeed, sometimes to pray for my conversion but never had the satisfaction of believing that his prayers were heard. Ours was a mere civil friendship, sincere on both sides, and lasted to his death.

The following instance will show something of the terms on which we stood. Upon one of his arrivals from England at Boston, he wrote to me that he should come soon to Philadelphia but knew not where he could lodge when there, as he understood his old, kind host, Mr. Benezet,[38] was removed to Germantown. My answer was, "You know my house; if you can make shift with its scanty accommodations, you will be most heartily welcome." He replied that if I made that kind offer for Christ's sake, I should not miss of a reward. And I returned, "Don't let me be mistaken; it was not for Christ's sake but for your sake." One of our common acquaintance jocosely remarked that knowing it to be the custom of the saints when they received any favor to shift the burden of the obligation from off their own shoulders and place it in Heaven, I had contrived to fix it on earth.

The last time I saw Mr. Whitfield was in London, when he

consulted me about his orphan house concern and his purpose of appropriating it to the establishment of a college.

He had a loud and clear voice, and articulated his words and sentences so perfectly that he might be heard and understood at a great distance, especially as his auditories, however numerous, observed the most exact silence. He preached one evening from the top of the courthouse steps, which are in the middle of Market Street and on the west side of Second Street, which crosses it at right angles. Both streets were filled with his hearers to a considerable distance. Being among the hindmost in Market Street, I had the curiosity to learn how far he could be heard by retiring backwards down the street toward the river, and I found his voice distinct till I came near Front Street, when some noise in that street obscured it. Imagining then a semicircle, of which my distance should be the radius, and that it were filled with auditors, to each of whom I allowed two square feet, I computed that he might well be heard by more than thirty thousand. This reconciled me to the newspaper accounts of his having preached to twenty-five thousand people in the fields, and to the ancient histories of generals haranguing whole armies, of which I had sometimes doubted.

By hearing him often I came to distinguish easily between sermons newly composed and those which he had often preached in the course of his travels. His delivery of the latter was so improved by frequent repetitions that every accent, every emphasis, every modulation of voice was so perfectly well turned and well placed that, without being interested in the subject, one could not help being pleased with the discourse, a pleasure of much the same kind with that received from an excellent piece of music. This is an advantage itinerant preachers have over those who are stationary, as the latter cannot well improve their delivery of a sermon by so many rehearsals.

His writing and printing from time to time gave great advantage to his enemies. Unguarded expressions and even erroneous opinions delivered in preaching might have been afterwards explained or qualified by supposing others that might have accompanied them, or they might have been denied, but *litera scripta manet*. Critics attacked his writings violently and with so much appearance of reason as to diminish the number of his votaries and prevent their increase; so that I am of opinion if he had never written anything, he would have left behind him a much more numerous and important sect. And his reputation might in that case have been still growing, even after his death; as there being nothing of his writing on which to found a censure and give him a lower character, his proselytes would be left at liberty to feign for him as great a variety of excellences as their enthusiastic admiration might wish him to have possessed.

My business was now continually augmenting and my circumstances growing daily easier, my newspaper having become very profitable, as being for a time almost the only one in this and the neighboring provinces. I experienced, too, the truth of the observation that "after getting the first hundred pounds, it is more easy to get the second"—money itself being of a prolific nature.

The partnership at Carolina having succeeded, I was encouraged to engage in others and to promote several of my workmen who had behaved well, by establishing them with printing houses in different colonies on the same terms with that in Carolina. Most of them did well, being enabled at the end of our term, six years, to purchase the types of me and go on working for themselves, by which means several families were raised. Partnerships often finish in quarrels, but I was happy in this, that mine were all carried on and ended amicably, owing, I think, a good deal to the precaution of having very explicitly settled in our articles everything to be done by or expected from each partner, so that there was nothing to dispute—which precaution I would therefore recommend to all who enter into partnerships, for whatever esteem partners may have for and confidence in each other at the time of the contract, little jealousies and disgusts may arise, with ideas of inequality in the care and burden of the business, etc., which are attended often with breach of friendship and of the connection, perhaps with lawsuits and other disagreeable consequences.

I had on the whole abundant reason to be satisfied with my being established in Pennsylvania. There were, however, two things that I regretted: there being no provision for defense nor for a complete education of youth; no militia nor any college. I therefore in 1743 drew up a proposal for establishing an academy; and at that time thinking the Reverend Mr. Peters, who was out of employ, a fit person to superintend such an institution, I communicated the project to him. But he, having more profitable views in the service of the proprietors, which succeeded, declined the undertaking. And not knowing another at that time suitable for such a trust, I let the scheme lie awhile dormant. I succeeded better the next year, 1744, in proposing and establishing a philosophical society.[39] The paper I wrote for that purpose will be found among my writings when collected.

With respect to defense, Spain having been several years at war against Britain and being at length joined by France, which brought us into greater danger, and the labored and long-continued endeavors of our Governor Thomas to prevail with our Quaker Assembly to pass a militia law and make other provisions for the security of the province having proved abortive, I determined to try what might be done by a voluntary association of the people. To promote this, I first wrote and published a pamphlet, entitled *Plain Truth,* in which I stated our defenseless situation in strong lights, with the necessity of union and discipline for our defense, and promised to propose in a few days an association to be generally signed for that purpose. The pamphlet had a sudden and surprising effect. I was called upon for the instrument of association; and having settled the draft of it with a few friends, I appointed a meeting of the citizens in the large building beforementioned. The house was pretty full. I had prepared a number of printed copies, and provided pens and ink dispersed all over the room. I harangued them a little on the subject, read the paper, and explained it, and then distributed the copies, which were eagerly signed, not the least objection being made. When the company separated and the papers were collected, we found about twelve hundred hands; and other copies being dispersed in the country, the subscribers amounted at length to upward of ten thousand. These all furnished themselves as soon as they could with arms, formed themselves into companies and regiments, chose their own officers, and met every week to be instructed in the manual exercise and other parts of military discipline. The women, by subscriptions among themselves, provided silk colors, which they presented to the companies, painted with different devices and mottos which I supplied. The officers of the companies composing the Philadelphia regiment being met, chose me for their colonel; but conceiving myself unfit, I declined that station and recommended Mr. Lawrence, a fine person and man of influence, who was accordingly appointed. I then proposed a lottery to defray the expense of building a battery below the town and furnishing it with cannon. It filled expeditiously, and the battery was soon erected, the merlons being framed of logs and filled with earth. We bought some old cannon from Boston, but these not being sufficient, we wrote to England for more, soliciting at the same time our proprietaries for some assistance, though without much expectation of obtaining it. Meanwhile Colonel Lawrence, William Allen, Abraham Taylor, Esquires, and myself were sent to New York by the associators, commissioned to borrow some cannon of Governor Clinton. He at first refused us peremptorily; but at a dinner with his council where there was great drinking of Madeira wine, as the custom at that place then was, he softened by degrees and said he would lend us six. After a few more bumpers he advanced to ten. And at length he very good-naturedly conceded eighteen. They were fine cannon, eighteen-pounders, with their carriages, which we soon transported and mounted on our battery, where the associators kept a nightly guard while the war lasted. And among the rest I regularly took my turn of duty there as a common soldier.

My activity in these operations was agreeable to the Governor and Council; they took me into confidence, and I was consulted by them in every measure wherein their concurrence was thought useful to the association. Calling in the aid of religion, I proposed to them the proclaiming a fast to promote reformation and implore the blessing of Heaven on our undertaking. They embraced the motion, but as it was the first fast ever thought of in the province, the Secretary had no precedent from which to draw the proclamation. My education in New England, where a fast is proclaimed every year, was here of some advantage. I drew it in the accustomed style; it was translated into German, printed in both languages, and circulated through the province. This gave the clergy of the different sects an opportunity of influencing their congregations to join in the association; and it would probably have been general among all but Quakers if the peace had not soon intervened.

It was thought by some of my friends that by my activity in these affairs I should offend that sect and thereby lose my interest in the Assembly, where they were a great majority. A young gentleman who had likewise some friends in the House and wished to succeed me as their clerk, acquainted me that it was decided to displace me at the next election, and he therefore in good will advised me to resign, as more consistent with my honor than being turned out. My answer to him was that I had read or heard of some public man who made it a rule never to ask for an office and never to refuse one when offered to him. "I approve," say I, "of his rule and will practice it with a small addition; I shall never *ask*, never *refuse*, nor ever *resign* an office. If they will have my office of clerk to dispose of to another, they shall take it from me. I will not, by giving it up, lose my right of sometime or other making reprisals on my adversaries." I heard, however, no more of this. I was chosen again, unanimously as usual, at the next election. Possibly as they disliked my late intimacy with the members of Council who had joined the governors in all the disputes about military preparations with which the House had long been harassed, they might have been pleased if I would voluntarily have left them; but they did not care to displace me on account merely of my zeal for the association, and they could not well give another reason. Indeed, I had some cause to believe that the defense of the country was not disagreeable to any of them, provided they were not required to assist in it. And I found that a much greater number of them than I could have imagined, though against offensive war, were clearly for the defensive. Many pamphlets pro and con were published on the subject, and some by good Quakers in favor of defense, which I believe convinced most of their younger people. A transaction in our fire company gave me some insight into their prevailing sentiments. It had been proposed that we should encourage the scheme for building a battery by laying out the present stock, then about sixty pounds, in tickets of the lottery. By our rules no money could be disposed of till the next meeting after the proposal. The company consisted of thirty members, of which twenty-two were Quakers, and eight only of other persuasions. We eight punctually attended the meeting; but though we thought that some of the Quakers would join us, we were by no means sure of a majority. Only one Quaker, Mr. James Morris, appeared to oppose the measure. He expressed much sorrow that it had ever been proposed, as he said "Friends" were all against it, and it would create such discord as might break up the company. We told him that we saw no reason for that; we were the minority, and if "Friends" were against the measure and outvoted us, we must and should, agreeable to the usage of all societies, submit. When the hour for business arrived, it was moved to put the vote. He allowed we might then do it by the rules, but as he could assure us that a number of members intended to be present for the purpose of opposing it, it would be but candid to allow a little time for their appearing. While we were disputing this, a waiter came to tell me two gentlemen below desired to speak with me. I went down and found they were two of our Quaker members. They told me there were eight of them assembled at a tavern just by; that they were determined to come and vote with us if there should be occasion, which they hoped would not be the case; and desired we would not call for their assistance if we could do without it, as their voting for such a measure might embroil them with their elders and friends. Being thus secure of a majority, I went up and, after a little seeming hesitation, agreed to a delay of another hour. This Mr. Morris allowed to be extremely fair. Not one of his opposing friends appeared, at which he expressed great surprise; and at the expiration of the hour, we carried the resolution eight to one; and as of the twenty-two Quakers, eight were ready to vote with us and thirteen by their absence manifested that they were not inclined to oppose the measure, I afterwards estimated the proportion of Quakers sincerely against defense as one to twenty-one only. For these were all regular members of that society, and in good reputation among them, and had due notice of what was proposed at that meeting.

The honorable and learned Mr. Logan,[40] who had always been of that sect, was one who wrote an address to them declaring his approbation of defensive war and supporting his opinion by many strong arguments. He put into my hands sixty pounds to be laid out in lottery tickets for the battery, with directions to apply what prizes might be drawn wholly to that service. He told me the following anecdote of his old master William Penn,[41] respecting defense. He came over from England when a young man with that proprietary, and as his secretary. It was wartime, and their ship was chased by an armed vessel supposed to be an enemy. Their captain prepared for defense, but told William Penn and his company of Quakers that he did not expect their assistance and they might retire into the cabin, which they did, except James Logan, who chose to stay upon deck and was quartered to a gun. The supposed enemy proved a friend, so there was no fighting. But when the secretary went down to communicate the intelligence, William Penn rebuked him severely for staying upon deck and undertaking to assist in defending the vessel contrary to the principles of Friends, especially as it had not been required by the captain. This reproof, being before all the company, piqued the secretary, who answered: "I being thy servant, why did thee not order me to come down? But thee was willing enough that I should stay and help to fight the ship when thee thought there was danger."

My being many years in the Assembly, the majority of which were constantly Quakers, gave me frequent opportunities of seeing the embarrassment given them by their principle against war whenever application was made to them by order of the Crown to grant aids for military purposes. They were unwilling to offend government, on the one hand, by a direct refusal and their Friends, the body of Quakers, on the other, by a compliance contrary to their principles—hence a variety of evasions to avoid complying and modes of disguising the compliance when it became unavoidable. The common mode at last was to grant money under the phrase of its being "for the King's use," and never to inquire how it was applied. But if the demand was not directly from the Crown, that phrase was found not so proper, and some other was to be invented. As when powder was wanting (I think it was for the garrison at Louisburg) and the government of New England solicited a grant of some from Pennsylvania (which was much urged on the House by Governor Thomas), they could not grant money to buy powder because that was an ingredient of war, but they voted an aid to New England of three thousand pounds, to be put into the hands of the Governor, and appropriated it for the purchasing of bread, flour, wheat, "or other grain." Some of the Council, desirous of giving the House still further embarrassment, advised the Governor not to accept provision, as not being the thing he had demanded. But he replied, "I shall take the money, for I understand very well their meaning; 'other grain' is gunpowder"—which he accordingly bought, and they never objected to it. It was in allusion to this fact that when in our fire company we feared the success of our proposal in favor of the lottery and I had said to my friend Mr. Syng, one of our members, "If we fail, let us move the purchase of a fire engine with the money; the Quakers can have no objection to that. And then if you nominate me, and I you, as a committee for that purpose, we will buy a great gun, which is certainly a 'fire engine.' " "I see," says he, "you have improved by being so long in the Assembly; your equivocal project would be just a match for their wheat 'or other grain.' "

These embarrassments that the Quakers suffered from having established and published it as one of their principles that no kind of war was lawful, and which being once published, they could not afterward, however they might change their minds, easily get rid of, reminds me of what I think a more prudent conduct in another sect among us, that of the Dunkers.[42] I was acquainted with one of its founders, Michael Welfare, soon after it appeared. He complained to me that they were grievously calumniated by the zealots of other persuasions, and charged with abominable principles and practices to which they were utter strangers. I told him this had always been the case with new

sects and that to put a stop to such abuse, I imagined it might
be well to publish the articles of their belief and the rules of
their discipline. He said that it had been proposed among them,
but not agreed to for this reason: "When we were first drawn
together as a society," says he, "it had pleased God to enlighten
our minds so far as to see that some doctrines which we once
esteemed truths were errors, and that others which we had esteemed errors were real truths. From time to time He has been
pleased to afford us further light, and our principles have been
improving and our errors diminishing. Now we are not sure
that we are arrived at the end of this progression and at the
perfection of spiritual or theological knowledge; and we fear that
if we should once print our confession of faith, we should feel
ourselves as if bound and confined by it, and perhaps be unwilling to receive further improvement, and our successors still more
so, as conceiving what their elders and founders had done to be
something sacred, never to be departed from." This modesty in a
sect is perhaps a singular instance in the history of mankind,
every other sect supposing itself in possession of all truth, and
that those who differ are so far in the wrong—like a man traveling
in foggy weather: Those at some distance before him on the road
he sees wrapped up in the fog, as well as those behind him, and
also the people in the fields on each side; but near him all appears
clear, though in truth he is as much in the fog as any of them.
To avoid this kind of embarrassment, the Quakers have of late
years been gradually declining the public service in the Assembly and in the magistracy, choosing rather to quit their power
than their principle.

In order of time, I should have mentioned before that, having
in 1742 invented an open stove for the better warming of rooms
and at the same time saving fuel, as the fresh air admitted was
warmed in entering, I made a present of the model to Mr. Robert
Grace, one of my early friends, who having an iron furnace,
found the casting of the plates for these stoves a profitable thing,
as they were growing in demand. To promote that demand, I
wrote and published a pamphlet entitled, *An Account of the
New-Invented Pennsylvania Fireplaces: Wherein Their Construc-*

*tion and Manner of Operation is Particularly Explained, Their Advantages above Every Other Method of Warming Rooms Demonstrated; and All Objections That Have Been Raised against the Use of Them Answered and Obviated, etc.* This pamphlet had a good effect. Governor Thomas was so pleased with the construction of this stove as described in it that he offered to give me a patent for the sole vending of them for a term of years; but I declined it from a principle which has ever weighed with me on such occasions; viz., "that as we enjoy great advantages from the inventions of others, we should be glad of an opportunity to serve others by any invention of ours, and this we should do freely and generously." An ironmonger in London, however, after assuming a good deal of my pamphlet, and working it up into his own, and making some small changes in the machine, which rather hurt its operation, got a patent for it there, and made, as I was told, a little fortune by it. And this is not the only instance of patents taken out for my inventions by others, though not always with the same success, which I never contested, as having no desire of profiting by patents myself and hating disputes. The use of these fireplaces in very many houses both of this and the neighboring colonies has been and is a great saving of wood to the inhabitants.

Peace being concluded and the association business therefore at an end, I turned my thoughts again to the affair of establishing an academy. The first step I took was to associate in the design a number of active friends, of whom the Junto furnished a good part, the next was to write and publish a pamphlet entitled *Proposals Relating to the Education of Youth in Pennsylvania.* This I distributed among the principal inhabitants gratis; and as soon as I could suppose their minds a little prepared by the perusal of it, I set on foot a subscription for opening and supporting an academy; it was to be paid in quotas yearly for five years; by so dividing it I judged the subscription might be larger, and I believe it was so, amounting to no less, if I remember right, than five thousand pounds.

In the introduction to these proposals, I stated their publication not as an act of mine, but of some "public-spirited gentleman"; avoiding as much as I could, according to my usual rule, the presenting myself to the public as the author of any scheme for their benefit.

The subscribers, to carry the project into immediate execution, chose out of their number twenty-four trustees and appointed Mr. Francis, then Attorney General, and myself to draw up constitutions for the government of the academy, which being done and signed, a house was hired, masters engaged, and the schools opened, I think, in the same year, 1749.

The scholars increasing fast, the house was soon found too small, and we were looking out for a piece of ground properly situated, with intention to build, when Providence threw into our way a large house ready built, which with a few alterations might well serve our purpose. This was the building before-mentioned, erected by the hearers of Mr. Whitfield, and was obtained for us in the following manner.

It is to be noted that the contributions to this building being made by people of different sects, care was taken in the nomination of trustees, in whom the building and ground were to be vested, that a predominance should not be given to any sect, lest in time that predominance might be a means of appropriating the whole to the use of such sect contrary to the original intention; it was for this reason that one of each sect was appointed, viz., one Church of England man, one Presbyterian, one Baptist, one Moravian, etc.; those in case of vacancy by death were to fill it by election from among the contributors. The Moravian happened not to please his colleagues, and on his death they resolved to have no other of that sect. The difficulty then was, how to avoid having two of some other sect by means of the new choice. Several persons were named and for that reason not agreed to. At length one mentioned me, with the observation that I was merely an honest man, and of *no sect* at all—which prevailed with them to choose me. The enthusiasm which existed when the house was built had long since abated, and its trustees had not been able to procure fresh contributions for paying the ground rent and discharging some other debts the building had occasioned, which embarrassed them greatly. Being now a member of both boards of trustees, that for the building and that for the academy, I had a good opportunity of negotiating with both, and brought them finally to an agreement by which the trustees for the building were to cede it to those of the academy, the latter undertaking to discharge the debt, to keep forever open in the building a large hall for occasional preachers according to the original intention, and maintain a free school for the instruction of poor children. Writings were accordingly drawn, and on paying the debts the trustees of the academy were put in possession of the premises, and by dividing the great and lofty hall into stories, and different rooms above and below for the several schools, and purchasing some additional ground, the whole was soon made fit for our purpose, and the scholars removed into the building. The care and trouble of agreeing with the workmen, purchasing materials, and superintending the work fell upon me, and I went through it the more cheerfully as it did not then interfere with my private business, having the year before taken a very able, industrious, and honest partner, Mr. David Hall, with whose character I was well acquainted, as he had worked for me four years. He took off my hands all care of the printing office, paying me punctually my share of the profits. This partnership continued eighteen years, successfully for us both.

The trustees of the academy after a while were incorporated by a charter from the Governor; their funds were increased by contributions in Britain and grants of land from the proprietaries, to which the Assembly has since made considerable addition, and thus was established the present University of Philadelphia.[43] I have been continued one of its trustees from the beginning, now near forty years, and have had the very great pleasure of seeing a number of the youth who have received their education in it distinguished by their improved abilities, serviceable in public stations, and ornaments to their country.

When I disengaged myself, as above mentioned, from private business, I flattered myself that, by the sufficient though moderate fortune I had acquired, I had secured leisure during the rest of my life for philosophical studies and amusements; I purchased all Dr. Spence's apparatus, who had come from England to lecture here; and I proceeded in my electrical experiments with great alacrity; but the public now considering me as a man of leisure, laid hold of me for their purposes—every part of our civil government, and almost at the same time, imposing some duty upon me. The Governor put me into the commission of the peace; the corporation of the city chose me of the common council and soon after an alderman; and the citizens at large elected me a burgess to represent them in Assembly. This latter station was the more agreeable to me, as I was at length tired with sitting there to hear debates in which as clerk I could take no part, and which were often so uninteresting that I was induced to amuse myself with making magic squares [44] or circles or anything to avoid weariness. And I conceived my becoming a member would enlarge my power of doing good. I would not, however, insinuate that my ambition was not flattered by all these promotions. It certainly was. For considering my low beginning they were great things to me. And they were still more pleasing as being so many spontaneous testimonies of the public's good opinion, and by me entirely unsolicited.

The office of justice of the peace I tried a little, by attending a few courts and sitting on the bench to hear causes. But finding that more knowledge of the common law than I possessed was necessary to act in that station with credit, I gradually withdrew from it, excusing myself by my being obliged to attend the higher duties of a legislator in the Assembly. My election to this trust was repeated every year for ten years without my ever asking any elector for his vote or signifying either directly or indirectly any desire of being chosen. On taking my seat in the House, my son was appointed their clerk.

The year following, a treaty being to be held with the Indians at Carlisle, the Governor sent a message to the House proposing that they should nominate some of their members to be joined with some members of Council as commissioners for that purpose. The House named the Speaker (Mr. Norris) and myself; and being commissioned, we went to Carlisle and met the Indians accordingly. As those people are extremely apt to get drunk and when so are very quarrelsome and disorderly, we strictly forbade the selling any liquor to them; and when they complained of this restriction, we told them that if they would continue sober during the treaty, we would give them plenty of rum when business was over. They promised this, and they kept their promise because they could get no liquor, and the treaty was conducted very orderly and concluded to mutual satisfaction. They then claimed and received the rum. This was in the afternoon. They were near one hundred men, women, and children, and were lodged in temporary cabins built in the form of a square, just without the town. In the evening, hearing a great noise among them, the commissioners walked out to see what was the matter. We found they had made a great bonfire in the middle of the square. They were all drunk, men and women, quarreling and fighting. Their dark-colored bodies, half-naked, seen only by the gloomy light of the bonfire, running after and beating one another with firebrands, accompanied by their horrid yellings, formed a scene the most resembling our ideas of hell that could well be imagined. There was no appeasing the tumult, and we retired to our lodging. At midnight a number of them came thundering at our door demanding more rum—of which we took no notice. The next day, sensible they had misbehaved in giving us that disturbance, they sent three of their old counselors to make their apology. The orator acknowledged the fault, but laid it upon the rum, and then endeavored to excuse the rum by saying, "The Great Spirit who made all things made everything for some use, and whatever use he designed anything for, that use it should always be put to. Now, when he made rum, he said, 'Let this be for Indians to get drunk with.' And it must be so." And indeed if it be the design of Providence to extirpate these savages in order to make room for cultivators of the earth, it seems not improbable that rum may be the appointed means. It has already annihilated all the tribes who formerly inhabited the seacoast.

In 1751 Dr. Thomas Bond, a particular friend of mine, conceived the idea of establishing a hospital in Philadelphia for the reception and cure of poor, sick persons, whether inhabitants of the province or strangers—a very beneficent design, which has been ascribed to me but was originally his. He was zealous and

active in endeavoring to procure subscriptions for it; but the
proposal being a novelty in America and at first not well understood, he met with small success. At length he came to me with
the compliment that he found there was no such thing as carrying
a public-spirited project through without my being concerned in
it. "For," says he, "I am often asked by those to whom I propose
subscribing, 'Have you consulted Franklin upon this business,
and what does he think of it?' And when I tell them that I have
not (supposing it rather out of your line), they do not subscribe
but say they will consider of it." I inquired into the nature and
probable utility of his scheme, and receiving from him a very
satisfactory explanation, I not only subscribed to it myself but
engaged heartily in the design of procuring subscriptions from
others. Previous, however, to the solicitation, I endeavored to
prepare the minds of the people by writing on the subject in the
newspapers, which was my usual custom in such cases, but which
he had omitted. The subscriptions afterwards were more free and
generous, but beginning to flag, I saw they would be insufficient
without some assistance from the Assembly and therefore proposed to petition for it, which was done. The country members
did not at first relish the project. They objected that it could only
be serviceable to the city, and therefore the citizens should alone
be at the expense of it; and they doubted whether the citizens
themselves generally approved of it. My allegation on the contrary that it met with such approbation as to leave no doubt of
our being able to raise £2000 by voluntary donations, they considered as a most extravagant supposition and utterly impossible.
On this I formed my plan; and asking leave to bring in a bill for
incorporating the contributors according to the prayer of their
petition and granting them a blank sum of money, which leave
was obtained chiefly on the consideration that the House could
throw the bill out if they did not like it, I drew it so as to make
the important clause a conditional one; viz., "And be it enacted
by the authority aforesaid that when the said contributors shall
have met and chosen their managers and treasurer, *and shall have
raised by their contributions a capital stock of £2000 value* (the
yearly interest of which is to be applied to the accommodating

of the sick poor in the said hospital, free of charge for diet, attendance, advice, and medicines) and *shall make the same appear to the satisfaction of the Speaker of the Assembly* for the time being, that *then* it shall and may be lawful for the said Speaker, and he is hereby required, to sign an order on the provincial treasurer for the payment of £2000 in two yearly payments, to the treasurer of the said hospital, to be applied to the founding, building, and finishing of the same." This condition carried the bill through; for the members who had opposed the grant and now conceived they might have the credit of being charitable without the expense, agreed to its passage; and then in soliciting subscriptions among the people, we urged the conditional promise of the law as an additional motive to give, since every man's donation would be doubled. Thus the clause worked both ways. The subscriptions accordingly soon exceeded the requisite sum, and we claimed and received the public gift, which enabled us to carry the design into execution. A convenient and handsome building was soon erected, the institution has by constant experience been found useful and flourishes to this day.[45] And I do not remember any of my political maneuvers the success of which gave me at the time more pleasure; or that in after-thinking of it, I more easily excused myself for having made use of cunning.

It was about this time that another projector, the Rev. Gilbert Tennent, came to me with a request that I would assist him in procuring a subscription for erecting a new meetinghouse.[46] It was to be for the use of a congregation he had gathered among the Presbyterians who were originally disciples of Mr. Whitfield. Unwilling to make myself disagreeable to my fellow citizens by too frequently soliciting their contributions, I absolutely refused. He then desired I would furnish him with a list of the names of persons I knew by experience to be generous and public-spirited. I thought it would be unbecoming in me, after their kind compliance with my solicitations, to mark them out to be worried by other beggars, and therefore refused also to give such a list. He then desired I would at least give him my advice. "That I will readily do," said I, "and, in the first place, I advise you to apply to all those who you know will give something; next, to those who you are uncertain whether they will give anything or not, and show them the list of those who have given; and lastly, do not neglect those who you are sure will give nothing, for in some of them you may be mistaken." He laughed and thanked me, and said he would take my advice. He did so, for he asked of *everybody;* and he obtained a much larger sum than he expected, with which he erected the capacious and very elegant meetinghouse that stands in Arch Street.

Our city, though laid out with a beautiful regularity, the streets large, straight, and crossing each other at right angles, had the disgrace of suffering those streets to remain long unpaved; and in wet weather the wheels of heavy carriages ploughed them into a quagmire so that it was difficult to cross them. And in dry weather the dust was offensive. I had lived near what was called the Jersey Market and saw with pain the inhabitants wading in mud while purchasing their provisions. A strip of ground down the middle of that market was at length paved with brick so that being once in the market they had firm footing, but were often over shoes in dirt to get there. By talking and writing on the subject, I was at length instrumental in getting the street paved with stone between the market and the bricked foot pavement that was on each side next the houses. This for some time gave an easy access to the market, dry-shod. But the rest of the street not being paved, whenever a carriage came out of the mud upon this pavement, it shook off and left its dirt upon it, and it was soon covered with mire, which was not removed, the city as yet having no scavengers. After some inquiry I found a poor, industrious man who was willing to undertake keeping the pavement clean by sweeping it twice a week and carrying off the dirt from before all the neighbors' doors, for the sum of sixpence per month, to be paid by each house. I then wrote and printed a paper, setting forth the advantages to the neighborhood that might be obtained by this small expense: the greater ease in keeping our houses clean, so much dirt not being brought in by people's feet; the benefit to the shops by more custom, as buyers could more easily get at them, and by not having in windy weather the dust blown in upon their goods, etc., etc. I sent one of these papers

to each house and in a day or two went round to see who would
subscribe an agreement to pay these sixpences. It was unanimously signed and for a time well executed. All the inhabitants of
the city were delighted with the cleanliness of the pavement that
surrounded the market, it being a convenience to all; and this
raised a general desire to have all the streets paved, and made
the people more willing to submit to a tax for that purpose.
After some time I drew a bill for paving the city and brought it
into the Assembly. It was just before I went to England in 1757
and did not pass till I was gone, and then with an alteration in
the mode of assessment, which I thought not for the better, but
with an additional provision for lighting as well as paving the
streets, which was a great improvement. It was by a private person, the late Mr. John Clifton, giving a sample of the utility of
lamps by placing one at his door that the people were first impressed with the idea of lighting all the city. The honor of this
public benefit has also been ascribed to me, but it belongs truly
to that gentleman. I did but follow his example and have only
some merit to claim respecting the form of our lamps as differing
from the globe lamps we at first were supplied with from London. Those we found inconvenient in these respects: They admitted no air below; the smoke therefore did not readily go out
above, but circulated in the globe, lodged on its inside, and soon
obstructed the light they were intended to afford, giving, besides,
the daily trouble of wiping them clean; and an accidental stroke
on one of them would demolish it and render it totally useless. I
therefore suggested the composing them of four flat panes, with
a long funnel above, to draw up the smoke, and crevices admitting
air below, to facilitate the ascent of the smoke. By this means
they were kept clean, and did not grow dark in a few hours as
the London lamps do, but continued bright till morning; and an
accidental stroke would generally break but a single pane, easily
repaired.[47] I have sometimes wondered that the Londoners did
not, from the effect holes in the bottom of the globe lamps used
at Vauxhall have in keeping them clean, learn to have such holes
in their street lamps. But those holes being made for another
purpose, viz., to communicate flame more suddenly to the wick by

a little flax hanging down through them, the other use of letting in air seems not to have been thought of. And therefore, after the lamps have been lit a few hours, the streets of London are very poorly illuminated.

The mention of these improvements puts me in mind of one I proposed when in London to Dr. Fothergill,[48] who was among the best men I have known and a great promoter of useful projects. I had observed that the streets when dry were never swept and the light dust carried away, but it was suffered to accumulate till wet weather reduced it to mud; and then after lying some days so deep on the pavement that there was no crossing but in paths kept clean by poor people with brooms, it was with great labor raked together and thrown up into carts open above, the sides of which suffered some of the slush at every jolt on the pavement to shake out and fall, sometimes to the annoyance of foot passengers. The reason given for not sweeping the dusty streets was that the dust would fly into the windows of shops and houses. An accidental occurrence had instructed me how much sweeping might be done in a little time. I found at my door in Craven Street one morning a poor woman sweeping my pavement with a birch broom. She appeared very pale and feeble as just come out of a fit of sickness. I asked who employed her to sweep there. She said, "Nobody. But I am very poor and in distress, and I sweeps before gentlefolkses' doors and hopes they will give me something." I bid her sweep the whole street clean and I would give her a shilling. This was at nine o'clock. At twelve she came for the shilling. From the slowness I saw at first in her working, I could scarce believe that the work was done so soon and sent my servant to examine it, who reported that the whole street was swept perfectly clean and all the dust placed in the gutter which was in the middle; and the next rain washed it quite away so that the pavement and even the kennel were perfectly clean. I then judged that if that feeble woman could sweep such a street in three hours, a strong, active man might have done it in half the time. And here let me remark the convenience of having but one gutter in such a narrow street running down its middle instead of two, one on each side near the footway. For where all the rain that falls on a street runs from the sides and meets in the middle, it forms there a current strong enough to wash away all the mud it meets with. But when divided into two channels, it is often too weak to cleanse either and only makes the mud it finds more fluid so that the wheels of carriages and feet of horses throw and dash it up on the foot pavement, which is thereby rendered foul and slippery, and sometimes splash it upon those who are walking. My proposal communicated to the good doctor was as follows:

"For the more effectual cleaning and keeping clean the streets of London and Westminster, it is proposed that the several watchmen be contracted with to have the dust swept up in dry seasons and the mud raked up at other times, each in the several streets and lanes of his round; that they be furnished with brooms and other proper instruments for these purposes, to be kept at their respective stands, ready to furnish the poor people they may employ in the service.

"That in the dry summer months the dust be all swept up into heaps at proper distances before the shops and windows of houses are usually opened, when the scavengers with close-covered carts shall also carry it all away.

"That the mud when raked up be not left in heaps to be spread abroad again by the wheels of carriages and trampling of horses; but that the scavengers be provided with bodies of carts, not placed high upon wheels, but low upon sliders, with lattice bottoms, which, being covered with straw, will retain the mud thrown into them and permit the water to drain from it, whereby it will become much lighter, water making the greatest part of its weight—these bodies of carts to be placed at convenient distances and the mud brought to them in wheelbarrows, they remaining where placed till the mud is drained, and then horses brought to draw them away."

I have since had doubts of the practicability of the latter part of this proposal, on account of the narrowness of some streets and the difficulty of placing the draining sleds so as not to encumber too much the passage. But I am still of opinion that the former, requiring the dust to be swept up and carried away before the shops are open, is very practicable in the summer when the days are long; for in walking through the Strand and Fleet Street one morning at seven o'clock, I observed there was not one shop open, though it had been daylight and the sun up above three hours—the inhabitants of London choosing voluntarily to live much by candlelight and sleep by sunshine, and yet often complaining a little absurdly of the duty on candles and the high price of tallow.

Some may think these trifling matters not worth minding or relating. But when they consider that though dust blown into the eyes of a single person or into a single shop on a windy day is but of small importance, yet the great number of the instances in a populous city and its frequent repetitions give it weight and consequence; perhaps they will not censure very severely those who bestow some attention to affairs of this seemingly low nature. Human felicity is produced not so much by great pieces of good fortune that seldom happen as by little advantages that occur every day. Thus, if you teach a poor young man to shave himself and keep his razor in order, you may contribute more to the happiness of his life than in giving him a thousand guineas. The money may be soon spent, the regret only remaining of having foolishly consumed it. But in the other case he escapes the frequent vexation of waiting for barbers and of their sometimes dirty fingers, offensive breaths, and dull razors. He shaves when most convenient to him and enjoys daily the pleasure of its being done with a good instrument. With these sentiments I have hazarded the few preceding pages, hoping they may afford hints which sometime or other may be useful to a city I love, having lived many years in it very happily—and perhaps to some of our towns in America.

Having been for some time employed by the Postmaster General of America as his comptroller, in regulating the several offices and bringing the officers to account, I was upon his death in 1753 appointed jointly with Mr. William Hunter to succeed him by a commission from the Postmaster General in England. The American office had never hitherto paid anything to that of Britain. We were to have £600 a year between us if we could make that sum out of the profits of the office. To do this, a variety of improvements were necessary; some of these were inevitably at first expensive, so that in the first four years the office became above £900 in debt to us. But it soon after began to repay us, and before I was displaced by a freak of the ministers, of which I shall speak hereafter, we had brought it to yield *three times* as much clear revenue to the Crown as the Post Office of Ireland. Since that imprudent transaction they have received from it—not one farthing.

The business of the Post Office occasioned my taking a journey this year to New England, where the College of Cambridge, of their own motion, presented me with the degree of Master of Arts. Yale College in Connecticut had before made me a similar compliment. Thus without studying in any college I came to partake of their honors. They were conferred in consideration of my improvements and discoveries in the electric branch of natural philosophy.

In 1754 war with France being again apprehended, a congress of commissioners from the different Colonies was by an order of the Lords of Trade to be assembled at Albany, there to confer with the chiefs of the six nations concerning the means of defending both their country and ours. Governor Hamilton having received this order, acquainted the House with it, requesting they would furnish proper presents for the Indians to be given on this occasion, and naming the Speaker (Mr. Norris) and myself to join Mr. Thomas Penn and Mr. Secretary Peters as commissioners to act for Pennsylvania. The House approved the nomination and provided the goods for the presents, though they did not much like treating out of the province, and we met the other commissioners at Albany about the middle of June. In our way thither, I projected and drew up a plan for the union of all the Colonies under one government, so far as might be necessary for defense and other important general purposes.[a] As we passed through New York, I had there shown my project to Mr. James Alexander and Mr. Kennedy, two gentlemen of great knowledge in public affairs;

---

[a] [Franklin's *Papers Relating to a Plan of Union of the Colonies* (1754) are printed in Smyth: *Life and Writings of Benjamin Franklin*, III, pp. 197-226.]

and being fortified by their approbation, I ventured to lay it before the Congress. It then appeared that several of the commissioners had formed plans of the same kind. A previous question was first taken whether a union should be established, which passed in the affirmative unanimously. A committee was then appointed, one member from each colony, to consider the several plans and report. Mine happened to be preferred, and with a few amendments was accordingly reported. By this plan the general government was to be administered by a president-general appointed and supported by the Crown and a grand council to be chosen by the representatives of the people of the several Colonies met in their respective Assemblies. The debates upon it in Congress went on daily hand in hand with the Indian business. Many objections and difficulties were started, but at length they were all overcome, and the plan was unanimously agreed to, and copies ordered to be transmitted to the Board of Trade and to the Assemblies of the several provinces. Its fate was singular. The Assemblies did not adopt it, as they all thought there was too much *prerogative* in it; and in England it was judged to have too much of the *democratic*. The Board of Trade therefore did not approve of it, nor recommend it for the approbation of His Majesty; but another scheme was formed, supposed better to answer the same purpose, whereby the Governors of the provinces with some members of their respective Councils were to meet and order the raising of troops, building of forts, etc., and to draw on the Treasury of Great Britain for the expense, which was afterwards to be refunded by an act of Parliament laying a tax on America. My plan, with my reasons in support of it, is to be found among my political papers that are printed. Being the winter following in Boston, I had much conversation with Governor Shirley upon both the plans. Part of what passed between us on the occasion may also be seen among those papers. The different and contrary reasons of dislike to my plan make me suspect that it was really the true medium; and I am still of opinion it would have been happy for both sides [of] the water if it had been adopted. The Colonies so united would have been sufficiently strong to have defended themselves; there would then have been

no need of troops from England; of course the subsequent pretense for taxing America and the bloody contest it occasioned
would have been avoided. But such mistakes are not new; history
is full of the errors of states and princes.

> Look round the habitable world, how few
> Know their own good, or knowing it pursue.

Those who govern, having much business on their hands, do
not generally like to take the trouble of considering and carrying
into execution new projects. The best public measures are therefore seldom *adopted from previous wisdom, but forced by the
occasion.*

The Governor of Pennsylvania, in sending it down to the Assembly, expressed his approbation of the plan "as appearing to
him to be drawn up with great clearness and strength of judgment, and therefore recommended it as well worthy their closest
and most serious attention." The House, however, by the management of a certain member, took it up when I happened to be
absent, which I thought not very fair, and reprobated it without
paying any attention to it at all, to my no small mortification.

In my journey to Boston this year, I met at New York with
our new Governor, Mr. Morris, just arrived there from England,
with whom I had been before intimately acquainted. He brought
a commission to supersede Mr. Hamilton, who, tired with the
disputes his proprietary instructions subjected him to, had re-
signed. Mr. Morris asked me if I thought he must expect as un-
comfortable an administration.

I said, "No, you may on the contrary have a very comfortable
one, if you will only take care not to enter into any dispute with
the Assembly."

"My dear friend," says he pleasantly, "how can you advise my
avoiding disputes? You know I love disputing; it is one of my
greatest pleasures. However, to show the regard I have for your
counsel, I promise you I will, if possible, avoid them." He had
some reason for loving to dispute, being eloquent, an acute
sophister, and therefore generally successful in argumentative
conversation. He had been brought up to it from a boy, his father,

as I have heard, accustoming his children to dispute with one another for his diversion while sitting at table after dinner. But I think the practice was not wise, for in the course of my observation, these disputing, contradicting, and confuting people are generally unfortunate in their affairs. They get victory sometimes, but they never get good will, which would be of more use to them. We parted, he going to Philadelphia, and I to Boston. In returning I met at New York with the votes of the Assembly, by which it appeared that notwithstanding his promise to me, he and the House were already in high contention, and it was a continual battle between them as long as he retained the government. I had my share of it, for as soon as I got back to my seat in the Assembly I was put on every committee for answering his speeches and messages, and by the committees always desired to make the drafts. Our answers as well as his messages were often tart, and sometimes indecently abusive. And as he knew I wrote for the Assembly, one might have imagined that when we met we could hardly avoid cutting throats. But he was so good-natured a man that no personal difference between him and me was occasioned by the contest, and we often dined together. One afternoon, in the height of this public quarrel, we met in the street. "Franklin," says he, "you must go home with me and spend the evening. I am to have some company that you will like"; and taking me by the arm, he led me to his house. In gay conversation over our wine after supper he told us jokingly that he much admired the idea of Sancho Panza, who, when it was proposed to give him a government, requested it might be a government of *blacks*, as then, if he could not agree with his people, he might sell them. One of his friends who sat next me says, "Franklin, why do you continue to side with these damned Quakers? Had not you better sell them? The Proprietor would give you a good price." "The Governor," say I, "has not yet *blacked* them enough." He had indeed labored hard to blacken the Assembly in all his messages, but they wiped off his coloring as fast as he laid it on, and placed it in return thick upon his own face; so that finding he was likely to be negrofied himself, he, as well as Mr. Hamilton, grew tired of the contest and quitted the government.

These public quarrels were all at bottom owing to the proprietaries, our hereditary governors,[a] who when any expense was
to be incurred for the defense of their province, with incredible
meanness instructed their deputies to pass no act for levying the
necessary taxes unless their vast estates were in the same act
expressly excused; and they had even taken bonds of those
deputies to observe such instructions. The Assemblies for three
years held out against this injustice, though constrained to bend
at last. At length Captain Denny, who was Governor Morris's
successor, ventured to disobey those instructions; how that was
brought about I shall show hereafter.

But I am got forward too fast with my story; there are still
some transactions to be mentioned that happened during the
administration of Governor Morris.

War being in a manner commenced with France,[b] the government of Massachusetts Bay projected an attack upon Crown
Point, and sent Mr. Quincy to Pennsylvania and Mr. Pownall,
afterwards Governor Pownall, to New York to solicit assistance.
As I was in the Assembly, knew its temper, and was Mr. Quincy's
countryman, he applied to me for my influence and assistance.
I dictated his address to them, which was well received. They
voted an aid of £10,000, to be laid out in provisions. But the
Governor refusing his assent to their bill (which included this
with other sums granted for the use of the Crown) unless a clause
were inserted exempting the proprietary estate from bearing any
part of the tax that would be necessary, the Assembly, though
very desirous of making their grant to New England effectual,
were at a loss how to accomplish it. Mr. Quincy labored hard with
the Governor to obtain his assent, but he was obstinate. I then
suggested a method of doing the business without the Governor,
by orders on the Trustees of the Loan Office, which by law the
Assembly had the right of drawing. There was indeed little or no
money at that time in the office, and therefore I proposed that the
orders should be payable in a year and to bear an interest of 5

---

[a] My acts in Morris's time, military, etc. [marg. note]
[b] [The French and Indian War (1754-1763).]

per cent. With these orders I supposed the provisions might easily be purchased. The Assembly with very little hesitation adopted the proposal. The orders were immediately printed, and I was one of the committee directed to sign and dispose of them. The fund for paying them was the interest of all the paper currency then extant in the province upon loan, together with the revenue arising from the excise, which being known to be more than sufficient, they obtained instant credit, and were not only received in payment for the provisions, but many moneyed people who had cash lying by them vested it in those orders, which they found advantageous as they bore interest while upon hand and might on any occasion be used as money, so that they were eagerly all bought up, and in a few weeks none of them were to be seen. Thus this important affair was by my means completed. Mr. Quincy returned thanks to the Assembly in a handsome memorial, went home highly pleased with the success of his embassy, and ever after bore for me the most cordial and affectionate friendship.

The British government, not choosing to permit the union of the Colonies as proposed at Albany and to trust that union with their defense, lest they should thereby grow too military and feel their own strength, suspicions, and jealousies at this time being entertained of them, sent over General Braddock with two regiments of regular English troops for that purpose. He landed at Alexandria in Virginia and thence marched to Frederick [a] in Maryland, where he halted for carriages. Our Assembly apprehending, from some information, that he had conceived violent prejudices against them, as averse to the service, wished me to wait upon him, not as from them, but as Postmaster General, under the guise of proposing to settle with him the mode of conducting with most celerity and certainty the dispatches between him and the Governors of the several provinces, with whom he must necessarily have continual correspondence, and of which they proposed to pay the expense. My son accompanied me on this journey. We found the General at Frederick, waiting impatiently for the return of those he had sent through the back parts of Maryland and Vir-

---

[a] [Franklin originally wrote: "Frederic Town."—M.F.]

ginia to collect wagons. I stayed with him several days, dined with him daily, and had full opportunity of removing all his prejudices by the information of what the Assembly had before his arrival actually done and were still willing to do to facilitate his operations. When I was about to depart, the returns of wagons to be obtained were brought in, by which it appeared that they amounted only to twenty-five, and not all of those were in serviceable condition. The General and all the officers were surprised, declared the expedition was then at an end, being impossible, and exclaimed against the ministers for ignorantly landing them in a country destitute of the means of conveying their stores, baggage, etc., not less than 150 wagons being necessary. I happened to say I thought it was pity they had not been landed rather in Pennsylvania, as in that country almost every farmer had his wagon. The General eagerly laid hold of my words and said, "Then you, sir, who are a man of interest there, can probably procure them for us; and I beg you will undertake it." I asked what terms were to be offered the owners of the wagons, and I was desired to put on paper the terms that appeared to me necessary. This I did, and they were agreed to, and a commission and instructions accordingly prepared immediately. What those terms were will appear in the advertisement I published as soon as I arrived at Lancaster; which being, from the great and sudden effect it produced, a piece of some curiosity, I shall insert it at length, as follows:

## ADVERTISEMENT

Lancaster, April 26, 1753

Whereas, 150 wagons, with 4 horses to each wagon, and 1,500 saddle or pack horses are wanted for the service of His Majesty's forces, now about to rendezvous at Wills's Creek, and His Excellency, General Braddock, having been pleased to empower me to contract for the hire of the same; I hereby give notice that I shall attend for that purpose at Lancaster from this day to next Wednesday evening, and at York from next Thursday morning till Friday evening, where I shall be ready to agree for wagons and teams, or single horses, on the following terms; viz., 1. That there shall be paid for each wagon with 4 good horses and a driver, fifteen shillings per diem. And for each able horse with a packsaddle or other saddle and furniture, two shillings per diem. And for each able horse without a saddle, eighteen pence per diem. 2. That the pay commence from the time of their joining the forces at Wills's Creek (which must be on or before the 20th May ensuing) and that a reasonable allowance be paid over and above for the time necessary for their traveling to Wills's Creek and home again after their discharge. 3. Each wagon and team, and every saddle or pack horse is to be valued by indifferent persons chosen between me and the owner; and in case of the loss of any wagon, team, or other horse in the service, the price according to such valuation is to be allowed and paid. 4. Seven days' pay is to be advanced and paid in hand by me to the owner of each wagon and team, or horse, at the time of contracting, if required; and the remainder to be paid by General Braddock or by the paymaster of the army at the time of their discharge, or from time to time as it shall be demanded. 5. No drivers of wagons or persons taking care of the hired horses are on any account to be called upon to do the duty of soldiers, or be otherwise employed than in conducting or taking care of their carriages or horses. 6. All oats, Indian corn, or other forage that wagons or horses bring to the camp, more than is necessary for the subsistence of the horses, are to be taken for the use of the army, and a reasonable price paid for the same.

Note—My son, William Franklin, is empowered to enter into like contracts with any person in Cumberland County.

B. Franklin.

*To the inhabitants of the Counties of Lancaster, York, and Cumberland*

FRIENDS AND COUNTRYMEN,

Being occasionally at the camp at Frederick, a few days since, I found the General and officers extremely exasperated on account of their not being supplied with horses and carriages, which had been expected from this province as most able to furnish them;

but through the dissensions between our Governor and Assembly, money had not been provided, nor any steps taken for that purpose.

It was proposed to send an armed force immediately into these counties to seize as many of the best carriages and horses as should be wanted and compel as many persons into the service as would be necessary to drive and take care of them.

I apprehended that the progress of British soldiers through these counties on such an occasion (especially considering the temper they are in and their resentment against us) would be attended with many and great inconveniences to the inhabitants, and therefore more willingly took the trouble of trying first what might be done by fair and equitable means. The people of these back counties have lately complained to the Assembly that a sufficient currency was wanting; you have an opportunity of receiving and dividing among you a very considerable sum; for if the service of this expedition should continue (as it is more than probable it will) for 120 days, the hire of these wagons and horses will amount to upward of £30,000, which will be paid you in silver and gold of the King's money.

The service will be light and easy, for the army will scarce march above twelve miles per day, and the wagons and baggage horses, as they carry those things that are absolutely necessary to the welfare of the army, must march with the army and no faster, and are, for the army's sake, always placed where they can be most secure, whether in a march or in a camp.

If you are really, as I believe you are, good and loyal subjects to His Majesty, you may now do a most acceptable service and make it easy to yourselves; for three or four of such as cannot separately spare from the business of their plantations a wagon and four horses and a driver may do it together—one furnishing the wagon, another one or two horses, and another the driver—and divide the pay proportionately between you. But if you do not this service to your King and country voluntarily when such good pay and reasonable terms are offered to you, your loyalty will be strongly suspected. The King's business must be done; so many brave troops, come so far for your defense, must not stand idle through your backwardness to do what may be reasonably expected from you; wagons and horses must be had, violent measures will probably be used; and you will be left to seek for a recompense where you can find it, and your case perhaps be little pitied or regarded.

I have no particular interest in this affair, as (except the satisaction of endeavoring to do good) I shall have only my labor for my pains. If this method of obtaining the wagons and horses is not likely to succeed, I am obliged to send word to the General in fourteen days; and I suppose Sir John St. Clair, the hussar, with a body of soldiers, will immediately enter the province for the purpose—which I shall be sorry to hear because I am very sincerely and truly

Your friend and well-wisher,<br>B. Franklin

I received of the General about £800 to be disbursed in advance money to the wagon owners, etc.; but that sum being insufficient, I advanced upward of £200 more, and in two weeks the 150 wagons with 259 carrying horses were on their march for the camp. The advertisement promised payment according to the valuation in case any wagon or horse should be lost. The owners, however, alleging they did not know General Braddock, or what dependence might be had on his promise, insisted on my bond for the performance, which I accordingly gave them.

While I was at the camp supping one evening with the officers of Col. Dunbar's regiment, he represented to me his concern for the subalterns, who he said were generally not in affluence, and could ill afford in this dear country to lay in the stores that might be necessary in so long a march through a wilderness where nothing was to be purchased. I commiserated their case and resolved to endeavor procuring them some relief. I said nothing, however, to him of my intention, but wrote the next morning to the Committee of Assembly, who had the disposition of some public money, warmly recommending the case of these officers to their consideration and proposing that a present should be sent them of necessaries and refreshments. My son, who had had some experience of a camp life and of its wants, drew up a list for me, which I enclosed in my letter. The Committee approved and used such diligence that, conducted by my son, the stores arrived at the camp as soon as the wagons. They consisted of twenty parcels, each containing

        6 lb. loaf sugar
        6 lb. good muscovado do
        1 lb. good green tea
        1 lb. good bohea do
        6 lb. good ground coffee
        6 lb. chocolate
        ½ cwt. best white biscuit
        ½ lb. pepper
        1 quart best white wine vinegar
        1 Gloucester cheese
        1 keg containing 20 lb. good butter
        2 doz. old Madeira wine
        2 gallons Jamaica spirits
        1 bottle flour of mustard
        2 well-cured hams
        ½ doz. dried tongues
        6 lb. rice
        6 lb. raisins

These twenty parcels, well packed, were placed on as many horses, each parcel with the horse being intended as a present for one officer. They were very thankfully received and the kindness acknowledged by letters to me from the colonels of both regiments in the most grateful terms. The General, too, was highly satisfied with my conduct in procuring him the wagons, etc., etc., and readily paid my account of disbursements, thanking me repeatedly and requesting my further assistance in sending provisions after him. I undertook this also and was busily employed in it till we heard of his defeat, advancing, for the service, of my own money upward of £1,000 sterling, of which I sent him an account. It came to his hands, luckily for me, a few days before the battle, and he returned me immediately an order on the paymaster for the round sum of £1,000, leaving the remainder to the next account. I consider this payment as good luck, having never been able to obtain that remainder—of which more hereafter.

This General was, I think, a brave man, and might probably have made a figure as a good officer in some European war. But he had too much self-confidence, too high an opinion of the validity of regular troops, and too mean a one of both Americans and Indians. George Croghan, our Indian interpreter, joined him on his march with one hundred of those people, who might have been of great use to his army as guides, scouts, etc., if he had treated them kindly; but he slighted and neglected them, and they gradually left him. In conversation with him one day, he was giving me some account of his intended progress. "After taking Fort Duquesne," says he, "I am to proceed to Niagara, and having taken that, to Frontenac, if the season will allow time, and I suppose it will; for Duquesne can hardly detain me above three or four days; and then I see nothing that can obstruct my march to Niagara." Having before revolved in my mind the long line his army must make in their march by a very narrow road to be cut for them through the woods and bushes, and also what I had read of a former defeat of 1,500 French who invaded the Iroquois country, I had conceived some doubts and some fears for the event of the campaign. But I ventured only to say, "To be sure, sir, if you arrive well before Duquesne with these fine troops so well provided with artillery, that place, not yet completely fortified and, as we hear, with no very strong garrison, can probably make but a short resistance. The only danger I apprehend of obstruction to your march is from the ambuscades of Indians, who by constant practice are dextrous in laying and executing them. And the slender line, near four miles long, which your army must make, may expose it to be attacked by surprise in its flanks, and to be cut like a thread into several pieces, which from their distance cannot come up in time to support each other." He smiled at my ignorance and replied, "These savages may indeed be a formidable enemy to your raw American militia; but upon the King's regular and disciplined troops, sir, it is impossible they should make any impression." I was conscious of an impropriety in my disputing with a military man in matters of his profession and said no more. The enemy, however, did not take the advantage of his army which I apprehended its long line of march exposed it to, but let it advance without interruption till within nine miles of the place; and then when more in a body (for it had just passed a river, where the front had halted till all were come over) and in a more open part of the woods than any it had passed, attacked its advance guard by a heavy fire from behind trees and bushes—which was the first intelligence the General had of an enemy's being near him. This guard being disordered, the General hurried the troops up to their assistance, which was done in great confusion through wagons, baggage, and cattle. And presently the fire came upon their flank; the officers, being on horseback, were more easily distinguished, picked out as marks, and fell very fast; and the soldiers were crowded together in a huddle, having or hearing no orders, and standing to be shot at till two-thirds of them were killed, and then being seized with a panic the whole fled with precipitation. The wagoners took each a horse out of his team and scampered; their example was immediately followed by others so that all the wagons, provisions, artillery, and stores were left to the enemy. The General, being wounded, was brought off with difficulty; his secretary, Mr. Shirley, was killed by his side; and out of 86 officers, 63 were killed or wounded, and 714 men killed out of 1,100. These 1,100 had been picked men from the whole army; the rest had been left behind with Col. Dunbar, who was to follow with the heavier part of the stores, provisions, and baggage. The flyers, not being pursued, arrived at Dunbar's camp, and the panic they brought with them instantly seized him and all his people. And though he had now above 1,000 men and the enemy who had beaten Braddock did not at most exceed 400 Indians and French together, instead of proceeding and endeavoring to recover some of the lost honor, he ordered all the stores, ammunition, etc., to be destroyed that he might have more horses to assist his flight toward the settlements and less lumber to remove. He was there met with requests from the governors of Virginia, Maryland, and Pennsylvania that he would post his troops on the frontiers so as to afford some protection to the inhabitants; but he continued his hasty march through all the country, not thinking himself safe till he arrived at Philadelphia, where the inhabitants could protect him. This whole transaction gave us Americans the first suspicion that our exalted ideas of the prowess of British regulars had not been well founded.

In their first march, too, from their landing till they got beyond the settlements, they had plundered and stripped the inhabitants, totally ruining some poor families, besides insulting, abusing, and confining the people if they remonstrated. This was enough to put us out of conceit of such defenders if we had really wanted any. How different was the conduct of our French friends [49] in 1781, who during a march through the most inhabited part of our country from Rhode Island to Virginia, near seven hundred miles, occasioned not the smallest complaint for the loss of a pig, a chicken, or even an apple!

Captain Orme, who was one of the General's aides-de-camp and, being grievously wounded, was brought off with him and continued with him to his death, which happened in a few days, told me that he was totally silent all the first day and at night only said, "Who would have thought it?"; that he was silent again the following day, only saying at last, "We shall better know how to deal with them another time," and died a few minutes after.

The secretary's papers with all the General's orders, instructions, and correspondence falling into the enemy's hands, they selected and translated into French a number of the articles, which they printed to prove the hostile intentions of the British court before the declaration of war. Among these I saw some letters of the General to the ministry speaking highly of the great service I had rendered the army and recommending me to their notice. David Hume,[50] too, who was some years after secretary to Lord Hertford when Minister in France and afterwards to General Conway when Secretary of State, told me he had seen among the papers in that office letters from Braddock highly recommending me. But the expedition having been unfortunate, my service, it seems, was not thought of much value, for those recommendations were never of any use to me. As to rewards from himself, I asked only one, which was that he would give orders to his officers not to enlist any more of our bought servants and that he would discharge such as had been already enlisted. This he readily granted, and several were accordingly returned to their masters on my application. Dunbar, when the command devolved on him, was not so generous. He being at Philadelphia on his retreat, or rather flight, I applied to him for the discharge of the servants of three poor farmers of Lancaster County that he had enlisted, reminding him of the late General's orders on that head. He promised me that if the masters would come to him at Trenton, where he should be in a few days on his march to New York, he would there deliver their men to them. They accordingly were at the expense and trouble of going to Trenton, and there he refused to perform his promise, to their great loss and disappointment.

As soon as the loss of the wagons and horses was generally known, all the owners came upon me for the valuation which I had given bond to pay. Their demands gave me a great deal of trouble. I acquainted them that the money was ready in the pay-master's hands, but that orders for paying it must first be obtained from General Shirley, and that I had applied for it; but he being at a distance, an answer could not soon be received, and they must have patience. All this was not sufficient to satisfy, and some began to sue me. General Shirley at length relieved me from this terrible situation by appointing commissioners to examine the claims and ordering payment. They amounted to near £20,000, which to pay would have ruined me.

Before we had the news of this defeat, the two Doctors Bond came to me with a subscription paper for raising money to defray the expense of a grand firework, which it was intended to exhibit at a rejoicing on receipt of the news of our taking Fort Duquesne. I looked grave and said it would, I thought, be time enough to prepare for the rejoicing when we knew we should have occasion to rejoice. They seemed surprised that I did not immediately comply with their proposal. "Why, the devil," says one of them, "you surely don't suppose that the fort will not be taken?" "I don't know that it will not be taken; but I know that the events of war are subject to great uncertainty." I gave them the reasons of my doubting. The subscription was dropped and the projectors thereby missed the mortification they would have undergone if the firework had been prepared. Dr. Bond on some other occasions afterwards said that he did not like Franklin's forebodings.

Governor Morris, who had continually worried the Assembly with message after message, before the defeat of Braddock, to beat them into the making of acts to raise money for the defense of the province without taxing, among others, the proprietary estates, and had rejected all their bills for not having such an exempting clause, now redoubled his attacks, with more hope of success, the danger and necessity being greater. The Assembly, however, continued firm, believing they had justice on their side and that it would be giving up an essential right if they suffered the Governor to amend their money bills. In one of the last, indeed, which was for granting £50,000, his proposed amendment was only of a single word: the bill expressed that all estates real and personal were to be taxed, those of the proprietaries *not* excepted. His amendment was, for "not" read "only"—a small but very material alteration! However, when the news of this disaster reached England, our friends there whom we had taken care to furnish with all the Assembly's answers to the Governor's messages, raised a clamor against the proprietaries for their meanness and injustice in giving their Governor such instructions, some going so far as to say that by obstructing the defense of their province, they forfeited their right to it. They were intimidated by this, and sent orders to their receiver general to add £5,000 of their money to whatever sum might be given by the Assembly for such purpose. This, being notified to the House, was accepted in lieu of their share of a general tax, and a new bill was formed with an exempting clause which passed accordingly. By this act I was appointed one of the commissioners for disposing of the money, £60,000. I had been active in modeling it and procuring its passage, and had at the same time drawn a bill for establishing and disciplining a voluntary militia, which I carried through the House without much difficulty, as care was taken in it to leave the Quakers at their liberty. To promote the association necessary to form the militia, I wrote a dialogue * stating and answering all the objections I could think of to such a militia, which was printed and had, as I thought, great effect. While the several companies in the city and country were forming and learning their exercise, the Governor prevailed with me to take charge of our northwestern frontier, which was infested by the enemy, and provide for the defense of the inhabitants by raising troops and building a line of forts. I undertook this military business, though I did not conceive myself well qualified for it. He gave me a commission with full powers and a parcel of blank commissions for officers, to be given to whom I thought fit. I had but little difficulty in raising men, having soon 560 under my command. My son, who had in the preceding war been an officer in the army raised against Canada, was my aide-de-camp, and of great use to me. The Indians had burned Gnadenhut,[51] a village settled by the Moravians, and massacred the inhabitants, but the place was thought a good situation for one of the forts. In order to march thither, I assembled the companies at Bethlehem,[52] the chief establishment of those people. I was surprised to find it in so good a posture of defense. The destruction of Gnadenhut had made them apprehend danger. The principal buildings were defended by a stockade. They had purchased a quantity of arm. and ammunition from New York, and had even placed quantities of small paving stones between the windows of their high stone houses, for their women to throw down upon the heads of any Indians that should attempt to force into them. The armed brethren, too, kept watch, and relieved as methodically as in any garrison town. In conversation with Bishop Spangenberg I mentioned my surprise; for knowing they had obtained an act of Parliament exempting them from military duties in the Colonies, I had supposed they were conscientiously scrupulous of bearing arms. He answered me that it was not one of their established principles, but that at the time of their obtaining that act it was thought to be a principle with many of their people. On this

---

* [This dialogue and the Militia Act are in the *Gentleman's Magazine* for February and March 1756.—M. F.]

occasion, however, they to their surprise found it adopted by but a few. It seems they were either deceived in themselves or deceived the Parliament. But common sense, aided by present danger, will sometimes be too strong for whimsical opinions.

It was the beginning of January when we set out upon this business of building forts. I sent one detachment toward the Minisinks, with instructions to erect one for the security of that upper part of the country; and another to the lower part, with similar instructions. And I concluded to go myself with the rest of my force to Gnadenhut, where a fort was thought more immediately necessary. The Moravians procured me five wagons for our tools, stores, baggage, etc. Just before we left Bethlehem, eleven farmers who had been driven from their plantations by the Indians came to me requesting a supply of firearms, that they might go back and fetch off their cattle. I gave them each a gun with suitable ammunition. We had not marched many miles before it began to rain, and it continued raining all day. There were no habitations on the road to shelter us till we arrived near night at the house of a German, where, and in his barn, we were all huddled together as wet as water could make us. It was well we were not attacked in our march, for our arms were of the most ordinary sort and our men could not keep their gunlocks dry. The Indians are dextrous in contrivances for that purpose, which we had not. They met that day the eleven poor farmers above mentioned and killed ten of them. The one who escaped informed us that his and his companions' guns would not go off, the priming being wet with the rain. The next day being fair, we continued our march and arrived at the desolated Gnadenhut. There was a sawmill near, round which were left several piles of boards, with which we soon hutted ourselves—an operation the more necessary at that inclement season as we had no tents. Our first work was to bury more effectually the dead we found there, who had been half interred by the country people. The next morning our fort was planned and marked out, the circumference measuring 455 feet, which would require as many palisades to be made of trees, one with another of a foot diameter each. Our axes, of which we had seventy, were immediately set to work to cut down trees; and our men being dextrous in the use of them, great dispatch was made. Seeing the trees fall so fast, I had the curiosity to look at my watch when two men began to cut at a pine. In six minutes they had it upon the ground, and I found it of fourteen inches diameter. Each pine made three palisades of eighteen feet long, pointed at one end. While these were preparing, our other men dug a trench all round of three feet deep in which the palisades were to be planted, and the bodies being taken off our wagons and the fore and hind wheels separated by taking out the pin which united the two parts of the perch, we had ten carriages with two horses each, to bring the palisades from the woods to the spot. When they were set up, our carpenters built a stage of boards all round within, about six feet high, for the men to stand on when to fire through the loopholes. We had one swivel gun which we mounted on one of the angles and fired it as soon as fixed, to let the Indians know, if any were within hearing, that we had such pieces; and thus our fort (if such a magnificent name may be given to so miserable a stockade) was finished in a week, though it rained so hard every other day that the men could not work.

This gave me occasion to observe that when men are employed they are best contented. For on the days they worked they were good-natured and cheerful, and with the consciousness of having done a good day's work they spent the evenings jollily; but on the idle days they were mutinous and quarrelsome, finding fault with their pork, the bread, etc., and in continual ill-humor—which put me in mind of a sea captain whose rule it was to keep his men constantly at work; and when his mate once told him that they had done everything and there was nothing further to employ them about, "Oh," says he, "make them scour the anchor."

This kind of fort, however contemptible, is a sufficient defense against Indians who have no cannon. Finding ourselves now posted securely and having a place to retreat to on occasion, we ventured out in parties to scour the adjacent country. We met with no Indians, but we found the places on the neighboring hills where they had lain to watch our proceedings. There was an art in their contrivance of those places that seems worth mention. It being winter, a fire was necessary for them. But a common fire on the surface of the ground would by its light have discovered their position at a distance. They had therefore dug holes in the ground about three feet in diameter and somewhat deeper. We saw where they had with their hatchets cut off the charcoal from the sides of burnt logs lying in the woods. With these coals they had made small fires in the bottom of the holes, and we observed among the weeds and grass the prints of their bodies made by their laying all round with their legs hanging down in the holes to keep their feet warm, which with them is an essential point. This kind of fire, so managed, could not discover them either by its light, flame, sparks, or even smoke. It appeared that their number was not great, and it seems they saw we were too many to be attacked by them with prospect of advantage.

We had for our chaplain a zealous Presbyterian minister, Mr. Beatty, who complained to me that the men did not generally attend his prayers and exhortations. When they enlisted, they were promised, besides pay and provisions, a gill of rum a day, which was punctually served out to them half in the morning and the other half in the evening, and I observed they were as punctual in attending to receive it. Upon which I said to Mr. Beatty, "It is perhaps below the dignity of your profession to act as steward of the rum. But if you were to deal it out, and only just after prayers, you would have them all about you." He liked the thought, undertook the office, and with the help of a few hands to measure out the liquor executed it to satisfaction; and never were prayers more generally and more punctually attended—so that I thought this method preferable to the punishments inflicted by some military laws for non-attendance on divine service.

I had hardly finished this business and got my fort well stored with provisions when I received a letter from the Governor, acquainting me that he had called the Assembly and wished my attendance there, if the posture of affairs on the frontiers was such that my remaining there was no longer necessary. My friends, too, of the Assembly pressing me by their letters to be, if possible, at the meeting, and my three intended forts being now completed, and the inhabitants contented to remain on their

farms under that protection, I resolved to return—the more willingly as a New England officer, Col. Clapham, experienced in
Indian war, being on a visit to our establishment, consented to
accept the command. I gave him a commission, and, parading the
garrison, had it read before them, and introduced him to them
as an officer who from his skill in military affairs was much more
fit to command them than myself, and giving them a little exhortation took my leave. I was escorted as far as Bethlehem, where
I rested a few days to recover from the fatigue I had undergone.
The first night being in a good bed, I could hardly sleep, it was
so different from my hard lodging on the floor of our hut at
Gnadenhut, wrapped only in a blanket or two.

While at Bethlehem, I inquired a little into the practices of the
Moravians. Some of them had accompanied me, and all were
very kind to me. I found they worked for a common stock, ate
at common tables, and slept in common dormitories, great numbers together. In the dormitories I observed loopholes at certain
distances all along just under the ceiling, which I thought judiciously placed for change of air. I was at their church, where
I was entertained with good music, the organ being accompanied
with violins, hautboys, flutes, clarinets, etc. I understood that
their sermons were not usually preached to mixed congregations
of men, women, and children, as is our common practice; but
that they assembled sometimes the married men, at other times
their wives, then the young men, the young women, and the
little children, each division by itself. The sermon I heard was
to the latter, who came in and were placed in rows on benches,
the boys under the conduct of a young man, their tutor, and the
girls conducted by a young woman. The discourse seemed well
adapted to their capacities and was delivered in a pleasing, familiar manner, coaxing them, as it were, to be good. They behaved
very orderly, but looked pale and unhealthy, which made me
suspect they were kept too much within-doors or not allowed
sufficient exercise. I inquired concerning the Moravian marriages,
whether the report was true that they were by lot. I was told
that lots were used only in particular cases; that generally when
a young man found himself disposed to marry, he informed the

elders of his class, who consulted the elder ladies that governed the young women. As these elders of the different sexes were well acquainted with the tempers and dispositions of their respective pupils, they could best judge what matches were suitable, and their judgments were generally acquiesced in. But if, for example, it should happen that two or three young women were found to be equally proper for the young man, the lot was then recurred to. I objected, "If the matches are not made by the mutual choice of the parties, some of them may chance to be very unhappy." "And so they may," answered my informer, "if you let the parties choose for themselves"—which, indeed, I could not deny.

Being returned to Philadelphia, I found the association went on swimmingly, the inhabitants that were not Quakers having pretty generally come into it, formed themselves into companies, and [had] chosen their captains, lieutenants, and ensigns according to the new law. Dr. Bond visited me and gave me an account of the pains he had taken to spread a general good liking to the law, and ascribed much to those endeavors. I had had the vanity to ascribe all to my dialogue; however, not knowing but that he might be in the right, I let him enjoy his opinion, which I take to be generally the best way in such cases. The officers' meeting chose me to be colonel of the regiment, which I this time accepted. I forget how many companies we had, but we paraded about 1,200 well-looking men, with a company of artillery who had been furnished with six brass fieldpieces, which they had become so expert in the use of as to fire twelve times in a minute. The first time I reviewed my regiment, they accompanied me to my house and would salute me with some rounds fired before my door, which shook down and broke several glasses of my electrical apparatus. And my new honor proved not much less brittle, for all our commissions were soon after broken by a repeal of the law in England.

During the short time of my colonelship, being about to set out on a journey to Virginia, the officers of my regiment took it into their heads that it would be proper for them to escort me out of town as far as the lower ferry. Just as I was getting on horseback, they came to my door, between thirty and forty, mounted, and all in their uniforms. I had not been previously acquainted with the project or I should have prevented it, being naturally averse to the assuming of state on any occasion, and I was a good deal chagrined at their appearance as I could not avoid their accompanying me. What made it worse was that as soon as we began to move, they drew their swords and rode with them naked all the way. Somebody wrote an account of this to the Proprietor, and it gave him great offense. No such honor had been paid him when in the province, nor to any of his governors; and he said it was only proper to princes of the blood royal—which may be true for aught I know, who was, and still am, ignorant of the etiquette in such cases. This silly affair, however, greatly increased his rancor against me, which was before not a little on account of my conduct in the Assembly respecting the exemption of his estate from taxation, which I had always opposed very warmly, and not without severe reflections on his meanness and injustice in contending for it. He accused me to the ministry as being the great obstacle to the King's service, preventing by my influence in the House the proper form of the bills for raising money; and he instanced this parade with my officers as a proof of my having an intention to take the government of the province out of his hands by force. He also applied to Sir Everard Fauckener, the Postmaster General, to deprive me of my office. But it had no other effect than to procure from Sir Everard a gentle admonition.

Notwithstanding the continual wrangle between the Governor and the House, in which I as a member had so large a share, there still subsisted a civil intercourse between that gentleman and myself, and we never had any personal difference. I have sometimes since thought that his little or no resentment against me for the answers it was known I drew up to his messages might be the effect of professional habit, and that, being bred a lawyer, he might consider us both as merely advocates for contending clients in a suit, he for the proprietaries and I for the Assembly. He would therefore sometimes call in a friendly way to advise with me on difficult points and sometimes, though not often, take my advice. We acted in concert to supply Braddock's army with provisions, and when the shocking news arrived of his defeat, the Governor sent in haste for me to consult with him on measures for preventing the desertion of the back counties. I forget now the advice I gave, but I think it was that Dunbar should be written to and prevailed with, if possible, to post his troops on the frontiers for their protection, till by reinforcements from the Colonies he might be able to proceed on the expedition. And after my return from the frontier, he would have had me undertake the conduct of such an expedition with provincial troops for the reduction of Fort Duquesne, Dunbar and his men being otherwise employed; and he proposed to commission me as general. I had not so good an opinion of my military abilities as he professed to have, and I believe his professions must have exceeded his real sentiments. But probably he might think that my popularity would facilitate the raising of the men and my influence in Assembly the grant of money to pay them, and that, perhaps, without taxing the proprietary estate. Finding me not so forward to engage as he expected, the project was dropped; and he soon after left the government, being superseded by Capt. Denny.

Before I proceed in relating the part I had in public affairs under this new Governor's administration, it may not be amiss here to give some account of the rise and progress of my philosophical reputation.

In 1746, being at Boston, I met there with a Dr. Spence, who was lately arrived from Scotland and showed me some electric experiments. They were imperfectly performed, as he was not very expert; but being on a subject quite new to me, they equally surprised and pleased me. Soon after my return to Philadelphia, our library company received from Mr. Peter Colinson,[53] F.R.S., of London, a present of a glass tube,[54] with some account of the use of it in making such experiments. I eagerly seized the opportunity of repeating what I had seen at Boston, and by much practice acquired great readiness in performing those also which we had an account of from England, adding a number of new ones. I say much practice, for my house was continually full for some time with people who came to see these new wonders. To divide a little this incumbrance among my friends, I caused a number of similar tubes to be blown at our glass house, with which they furnished themselves, so that we had at length several performers. Among these the principal was Mr. Kinnersley, an ingenious neighbor, who, being out of business, I encouraged to undertake showing the experiments for money, and drew up for him two lectures in which the experiments were ranged in such order and accompanied with explanations in such method as that the foregoing should assist in comprehending the following. He procured an elegant apparatus for the purpose, in which all the little machines that I had roughly made for myself were nicely formed by instrument makers. His lectures were well attended and gave great satisfaction, and after some time he went through the Colonies exhibiting them in every capital town and picked up some money. In the West India Islands, indeed, it was with difficulty the experiments could be made, from the general moisture of the air.

Obliged as we were to Mr. Colinson for his present of the tube, etc., I thought it right he should be informed of our success in using it and wrote him several letters containing accounts of our experiments. He got them read in the Royal Society, where they were not at first thought worth so much notice as to be printed in their transactions. One paper which I wrote for Mr. Kinnersley, on the sameness of lightning with electricity, I sent to Dr. Mitchell, an acquaintance of mine and one of the members also of that Society, who wrote me word that it had been read but was laughed at by the connoisseurs. The papers, however, being shown to Dr. Fothergill, he thought them of too much value to be stifled and advised the printing of them. Mr. Colinson then gave them to Cave for publication in his *Gentleman's Magazine;* but he chose to print them separately in a pamphlet, and Dr. Fothergill wrote the preface. Cave, it seems, judged rightly for his profit; for by the additions that arrived afterwards, they swelled to a quarto volume, which has had five editions and cost him nothing for copy money.

It was, however, some time before those papers were much taken notice of in England. A copy of them happening to fall into the hands of the Count de Buffon, a philosopher deservedly of great reputation in France and indeed all over Europe, he prevailed with M. Dalibard to translate them into French, and they were printed at Paris. The publication offended the Abbé Nollet, preceptor in natural philosophy to the royal family, and an able experimenter who had formed and published a theory of electricity which then had the general vogue. He could not at first believe that such a work came from America and said it must have been fabricated by his enemies at Paris to decry his system. Afterwards having been assured that there really existed such a person as Franklin of Philadelphia, which he had doubted, he wrote and published a volume of letters, chiefly addressed to me, defending his theory and denying the verity of my experiments and of the positions deduced from them. I once purposed answering the Abbé and actually began the answer. But on consideration that my writings contained only a description of experiments which anyone might repeat and verify, and, if not to be verified, could not be defended; or of observations offered as conjectures and not delivered dogmatically, therefore not laying me under any obligation to defend them; and reflecting that a dispute between two persons writing in different languages might be lengthened greatly by mistranslations, and thence misconceptions, of one another's meaning—much of one of the Abbé's letters being founded on an error in the translation; I concluded to let my papers shift for themselves, believing it was better to spend what time I could spare from public business in making new experiments than in disputing about those already made. I therefore never answered M. Nollet, and the event gave me no cause to repent my silence, for my friend M. le Roy of the Royal Academy of Sciences took up my cause and refuted him; my book was translated into the Italian, German, and Latin languages; and the doctrine it contained was by degrees universally adopted by the philosophers of Europe in preference to that of the Abbé, so that he lived to see himself the last of his sect—except Mr. B——, his *élève* and immediate disciple.

What gave my book the more sudden and general celebrity was the success of one of its proposed experiments, made by Messrs. Dalibard and Delor at Marly, for drawing lightning from the clouds. This engaged the public attention everywhere. M. Delor, who had an apparatus for experimental philosophy and lectured in that branch of science, undertook to repeat what he called the "Philadelphia Experiments," and after they were performed before the King and court, all the curious of Paris flocked to see them. I will not swell this narrative with an account of that capital experiment, nor of the infinite pleasure I received in the success of a similar one I made soon after with a kite at Philadelphia, as both are to be found in the histories of electricity.[55] Dr. Wright, an English physician then at Paris, wrote to a friend who was of the Royal Society an account of the high esteem my experiments were in among the learned abroad, and of their wonder that my writings had been so little noticed in England. The Society on this resumed the consideration of the letters that had been read to them, and the celebrated Dr. Watson drew up a summary account of them and of all I had afterwards sent to England on the subject, which he accompanied with some praise of the writer. This summary was then printed in their transactions. And some members of the Society in London, particularly the very ingenious Mr. Canton, having verified the experiment of procuring lightning from the clouds by a pointed rod and acquainting them with the success, they soon made me more than amends for the slight with which they had before treated me. Without my having made any application for that honor, they chose me a member and voted that I should be excused the customary payments, which would have amounted to twenty-five guineas, and ever since have given me their transactions gratis. They also presented me with the gold medal of Sir Godfrey Copley for the year 1753, the delivery of which was accompanied by a very handsome speech of the president, Lord Macclesfield, wherein I was highly honored.

Our new Governor, Capt. Denny, brought over for me the before-mentioned medal from the Royal Society, which he presented to me at an entertainment given him by the city. He accompanied it with very polite expressions of his esteem for me, having, as he said, been long acquainted with my character. After dinner, when the company, as was customary at that time, were engaged in drinking, he took me aside into another room and acquainted me that he had been advised by his friends in England to cultivate a friendship with me, as one who was capable of giving him the best advice and of contributing most effectually to the making his administration easy, that he therefore desired of all things to have a good understanding with me; and he begged me to be assured of his readiness on all occasions to render me every service that might be in his power. He said much to me also of the Proprietor's good dispositions toward the province and of the advantage it might be to us all, and to me in particular, if the opposition that had been so long continued to his measures were dropped and harmony restored between him and the people, in effecting which it was thought no one could be more serviceable than myself, and I might depend on adequate acknowledgments and recompenses, etc., etc. The drinkers, finding we did not return immediately to the table, sent us a decanter of Madeira, which the Governor made liberal use of, and in proportion became more profuse of his solicitations and promises. My answers were to this purpose: that my circumstances, thanks to God, were such as to make proprietary favors unnecessary to me; and that being a member of the Assembly, I could not possibly accept of any; that, however, I had no personal enmity to the Proprietary; and that whenever the public measures he proposed should appear to be for the good of the people, no one should espouse and forward them more zealously than myself, my past opposition having been founded on this—that the measures which had been urged were evidently intended to serve the proprietary interest with great prejudice to that of the people; that I was much obliged to him (the Governor) for his professions of regard to me, and that he might rely on everything in my power to make his administration as easy to him as possible, hoping at the same time that he had not brought with him the same unfortunate instructions his predecessor had been hampered with. On this he did not then explain himself. But when he afterwards came to do business with the Assembly, they appeared again; the disputes were renewed; and I was as active as ever in the opposition, being the penman, first, of the request to have a communication of the instructions and, then, of the remarks upon them, which may be found in the votes of the time and in the historical review I afterwards published. But between us personally no enmity arose; we were often together; he was a man of letters, had seen much of the world, and was very entertaining and pleasing in conversation. He gave me the first information that my old friend Jas. Ralph was still alive, that he was esteemed one of the best political writers in England, had been employed in the dispute between Prince Frederick and the King, and had obtained a pension of three hundred [£] a year; that his reputation was indeed small as a poet, Pope having damned his poetry in the *Dunciad*, but his prose was thought as good as any man's.

The Assembly finally, finding the Proprietaries obstinately persisted in manacling their deputies with instructions inconsistent not only with the privileges of the people but with the service of the Crown, resolved to petition the King against them, and appointed me their agent to go over to England to present and support the petition.[56] The House had sent up a bill to the Governor granting a sum of £60,000 for the King's use (£10,000 of which was subjected to the orders of the then General, Lord Loudon), which the Governor absolutely refused to pass in compliance with his instructions. I had agreed with Captain Morris, of the packet at New York, for my passage, and my stores were put on board, when Lord Loudon arrived at Philadelphia, expressly, as he told me, to endeavor an accommodation between the Governor and Assembly, that His Majesty's service might not be obstructed by their dissensions. Accordingly, he desired the Governor and myself to meet him, that he might hear what was to be said on both sides. We met and discussed the business. In behalf of the Assembly I urged all the arguments that may be found in the public papers of that time, which were of my writing and are printed with the minutes of the Assembly; and the Governor pleaded his instructions, the bond he had given to observe them, and his ruin if he disobeyed, yet seemed not unwilling to hazard himself if Lord Loudon would advise it. This His Lordship did not choose to do, though I once thought I had nearly prevailed with him to do it; but finally he rather chose to urge the compliance of the Assembly; and he entreated me to use my endeavors with them for that purpose, declaring he could spare none of the King's troops for the defense of our frontiers, and that if we did not continue to provide for that defense ourselves, they must remain exposed to the enemy. I acquainted the House with what had passed; and presenting them with a set of resolutions I had drawn up declaring our rights and that we did not relinquish our claim to those rights but only suspended the exercise of them on this occasion through *force,* against which we protested, they at length agreed to drop that bill and frame another conformable to the proprietary instructions. This of course the Governor passed, and I was then at liberty to proceed on my voyage. But in the meantime the packet had sailed with my sea stores, which was some loss to me, and my only recompense was His Lordship's thanks for my service, all the credit of obtaining the accommodation falling to his share.

He set out for New York before me; and as the time for dispatching the packet boats was in his disposition and there were two then remaining there, one of which he said was to sail very soon, I requested to know the precise time that I might not miss her by any delay of mine. His answer was, "I have given out that she is to sail on Saturday next, but I may let you know, *entre nous,* that if you are there by Monday morning you will be in time, but do not delay longer." By some accidental hindrance at a ferry, it was Monday noon before I arrived, and I was much afraid she might have sailed as the wind was fair, but I was soon made easy by the information that she was still in the harbor and would not move till the next day.

One would imagine that I was now on the very point of departing for Europe. I thought so; but I was not then so well acquainted with His Lordship's character, of which *indecision* was one of the strongest features. I shall give some instances. It was about the beginning of April that I came to New York, and I think it was near the end of June before we sailed. There were then two of the packet boats which had been long in port but were detained for the General's letters, which were always to be ready tomorrow. Another packet arrived, and she too was detained, and before we sailed a fourth was expected. Ours was the first to be dispatched, as having been there longest. Passengers were engaged in all, and some extremely impatient to be gone, and the merchants uneasy about their letters, and the orders they had given for insurance (it being wartime), and for fall goods. But their anxiety availed nothing; His Lordship's letters were not ready. And yet whoever waited on him found him always at his desk, pen in hand, and concluded he must needs write abundantly. Going myself one morning to pay my respects, I found in his anti-chamber one Innis, a messenger of Philadelphia, who had come from thence express with a packet from Governor Denny for the General. He delivered to me some letters from my friends there, which occasioned my inquiring when he was to return and where he lodged, that I might send some letters by him. He told me he was ordered to call tomorrow at nine for the General's answer to the Governor and should set off immediately. I put my letters into his hands the same day. A fortnight after I met him again in the same place.

"So you are soon returned, Innis!"

"Returned! No, I am not gone yet."

"How so?"

"I have called here by order every morning these two weeks past for His Lordship's letter, and it is not yet ready."

"Is it possible, when he is so great a writer, for I see him constantly at his scritoire."

"Yes," says Innis, "but he is like St. George on the signs, *always on horseback, and never rides on.*"

This observation of the messenger was, it seems, well founded; for when in England, I understood that Mr. Pit gave it as one reason for removing this General and sending Amherst and Wolf, that "the ministers never heard from him, and could not know what he was doing."

This daily expectation of sailing, and all the three packets going down to Sandy Hook to join the fleet there, the passengers thought it best to be on board, lest by a sudden order the ships should sail and they be left behind. There, if I remember right, we were about six weeks, consuming our sea stores and obliged to procure more. At length the fleet sailed, the General and all his army on board, bound to Louisburg with intent to besiege and take that fortress; all the packet boats in company, ordered to attend the General's ship, ready to receive his dispatches when they should be ready. We were out five days before we got a letter with leave to part, and then our ship quitted the fleet and steered for England. The other two packets he still detained, carried them with him to Halifax, where he stayed some time to exercise the men in sham attacks upon sham forts, then altered his mind as to besieging Louisburg and returned to New York with all his troops, together with the two packets above mentioned and all their passengers. During his absence the French and savages had taken Fort George on the frontier of that province, and the savages had massacred many of the garrison after capitulation. I saw afterwards in London Capt. Bonnell, who commanded one of those packets. He told me that when he had been detained a month, he acquainted His Lordship that his ship was grown foul to a degree that must necessarily hinder her fast sailing—a point of consequence for a packet boat—and requested an allowance of time to heave her down and clean her bottom. He was asked how long time that would require. He answered three days. The General replied, "If you can do it in one day, I give leave; otherwise not, for you must certainly sail the day after tomorrow." So he never obtained leave, though detained afterwards from day to day during full three months. I saw also in London one of Bonnell's passengers who was so enraged against His Lordship for deceiving and detaining him so long at New York and then carrying him to Halifax and back again, that he swore he would sue him for damages. Whether he did or not, I never heard; but as he represented the injury to his affairs, it was very considerable. On the whole I then wondered much how such a man came to be entrusted with so important a business as the conduct of a great army; but having since seen more of the great world, and the means of obtaining and motives for giving places, my wonder is diminished. General Shirley, on whom the command of the army devolved upon the death of Braddock, would in my opinion, if continued in place, have made a much better campaign than that of Loudon in 1757, which was frivolous, expensive, and disgraceful to our nation beyond conception. For though Shirley was not a bred soldier, he was sensible and sagacious in himself, and attentive to good advice from others, capable of forming judicious plans, and quick and active in carrying them into execution. Loudon, instead of defending the Colonies with his great army, left them totally exposed while he paraded it idly at Halifax, by which means Fort George was lost; besides, he deranged all our mercantile operations and distressed our trade by a long embargo on the exportation of provisions, on pretense of keeping supplies from being obtained by the enemy, but in reality for beating down their price in favor of the contractors, in whose profits, it was said—perhaps from suspicion only—he had a share. And when at length the embargo was taken off, by neglecting to send notice of it to Charlestown, the Carolina fleet was detained near three months longer, whereby their bottoms were so much damaged by the worm that a great part of them foundered in the passage home. Shirley was, I believe, sincerely glad of being relieved from so burdensome a charge as the conduct of an army must be to a man unacquainted with military business. I was at the entertainment given by the City of New York to Lord Loudon on his taking upon him the command. Shirley, though thereby superseded, was present also. There was a great company of officers, citizens, and strangers, and some chairs having been borrowed in the neighborhood, there was one among them very low which fell to the lot of Mr. Shirley. Perceiving it as I sat by him, I said, "They have given you, sir, too low a seat." "No matter," says he, "Mr. Franklin, I find *a low seat the easiest!*"

While I was, as aforementioned, detained at New York, I received all the accounts of the provisions, etc., that I had furnished to Braddock, some of which accounts could not sooner be obtained from the different persons I had employed to assist in the business. I presented them to Lord Loudon, desiring to be paid the balance. He caused them to be regularly examined by the proper officer, who, after comparing every article with its voucher, certified them to be right and the balance due, for which His

Lordship promised to give me an order on the paymaster. This, however, was put off from time to time, and though I called often for it by appointment, I did not get it. At length, just before my departure, he told me he had on better consideration concluded not to mix his accounts with those of his predecessors. "And you," says he, "when in England, have only to exhibit your accounts at the Treasury, and you will be paid immediately." I mentioned, but without effect, the great and unexpected expense I had been put to by being detained so long at New York, as a reason for my desiring to be presently paid; and on my observing that it was not right I should be put to any further trouble or delay in obtaining the money I had advanced, as I charged no commissions for my service, "O, sir," says he, "you must not think of persuading us that you are no gainer. We understand better those affairs and know that everyone concerned in supplying the army finds means in the doing it to fill his own pockets." I assured him that was not my case and that I had not pocketed a farthing. But he appeared clearly not to believe me, and indeed I have since learned that immense fortunes are often made in such employments. As to my balance, I am not paid it to this day, of which more hereafter.

Our captain of the packet had boasted much before we sailed of the swiftness of his ship. Unfortunately, when we came to sea, she proved the dullest of ninety-six sail, to his no small mortification. After many conjectures respecting the cause, when we were near another ship almost as dull as ours (which, however, gained upon us), the captain ordered all hands to come aft and stand as near the ensign staff as possible. We were, passengers included, about forty persons. While we stood there, the ship mended her pace and soon left her neighbor far behind, which proved clearly what our captain suspected, that she was loaded too much by the head. The casks of water, it seems, had been all placed forward. These he therefore ordered to be removed farther aft, on which the ship recovered her character and proved the best sailer in the fleet. The captain said she had once gone at the rate of thirteen knots, which is accounted thirteen miles per hour. We had on board as a passenger Captain Kennedy of

the Royal Navy, who contended that it was impossible, that no
ship ever sailed so fast, and that there must have been some
error in the division of the log line or some mistake in heaving
the log. A wager ensued between the two captains, to be decided
when there should be sufficient wind. Kennedy thereupon examined rigorously the log line, and being satisfied with that, he determined to throw the log himself. Accordingly, some days after
when the wind blew very fair and fresh and the captain of the
packet (*Lutwidge*) said he believed she then went at the rate of
thirteen knots, Kennedy made the experiment and owned his
wager lost. The above fact I give for the sake of the following
observation. It has been remarked as an imperfection in the art
of shipbuilding that it can never be known till she is tried whether
a new ship will or will not be a good sailer, for that the model
of a good sailing ship has been exactly followed in a new one,
which has proved, on the contrary, remarkably dull.[57] I apprehend this may be partly occasioned by the different opinions of
seamen respecting the modes of lading, rigging, and sailing of a
ship. Each has his system. And the same vessel laden by the
judgment and orders of one captain shall sail better or worse than
when by the orders of another. Besides, it scarce ever happens
that a ship is formed, fitted for the sea, and sailed by the same
person. One man builds the hull, another rigs her, a third lades
and sails her. No one of these has the advantage of knowing all
the ideas and experience of the others, and therefore cannot draw
just conclusions from a combination of the whole. Even in the
simple operation of sailing when at sea, I have often observed
different judgments in the officers who commanded the successive
watches, the wind being the same. One would have the sails
trimmed sharper or flatter than another, so that they seemed to
have no certain rule to govern by. Yet I think a set of experiments might be instituted: first, to determine the most proper
form of the hull for swift sailing; next, the best dimensions and
properest place for the masts; then, the form and quantity of
sails, and their position as the winds may be; and lastly, the
dispositon of the lading. This is the age of experiments, and such
a set accurately made and combined would be of great use. I am

therefore persuaded that ere long some ingenious philosopher will undertake it—to whom I wish success.

We were several times chased in our passage, but out-sailed everything and in thirty days had soundings. We had a good observation, and the captain judged himself so near our port (Falmouth) that if we made a good run in the night, we might be off the mouth of the harbor in the morning, and by running in the night might escape the notice of the enemy's privateers, who often cruised near the entrance of the Channel. Accordingly, all the sail was set that we could possibly make, and the wind being very fresh and fair, we went right before it and made great way. The captain, after his observation, shaped his course—as he thought—so as to pass wide of the Scilly Isles; but it seems there is sometimes a strong indraught setting up St. George's Channel which deceives seamen and caused the loss of Sir Cloudsley Shovel's squadron. This indraught was probably the cause of what happened to us. We had a watchman placed in the bow to whom they often called, "Look well out before, there"; and he as often answered, "Aye, aye!" but perhaps had his eyes shut and was half asleep at the time, they sometimes answering, as is said, mechanically. For he did not see a light just before us which had been hid by the studding sails from the man at helm and from the rest of the watch, but by an accidental yaw of the ship was discovered and occasioned a great alarm—we being very near it, the light appearing to me as big as a cart wheel. It was midnight, and our captain fast asleep. But Capt. Kennedy jumping upon deck and seeing the danger ordered the ship to wear round, all sails standing—an operation dangerous to the masts, but it carried us clear, and we escaped shipwreck, for we were running right upon the rocks on which the lighthouse was erected. This deliverance impressed me strongly with the utility of light-houses and made me resolve to encourage the building more of them in America, if I should live to return there.

In the morning it was found by the soundings, etc., that we were near our port, but a thick fog hid the land from our sight. About nine o'clock the fog began to rise and seemed to be lifted up from the water like the curtain at a playhouse, discovering underneath the town of Falmouth, the vessels in its harbor, and the fields that surrounded it. A most pleasing spectacle to those who had been so long without any other prospects than the uniform view of a vacant ocean! And it gave us the more pleasure, as we were now freed from the anxieties which the state of war occasioned.

I set out immediately with my son [a] for London, and we only stopped a little by the way to view Stonehenge on Salisbury Plain, and Lord Pembroke's house and gardens, with his very curious antiquities, at Wilton.

We arrived in London the 27th of July, 1757.[b] As soon as I was settled in a lodging Mr. Charles had provided for me, I went to visit Dr. Fothergill, to whom I was strongly recommended and whose counsel respecting my proceedings I was advised to obtain. He was against an immediate complaint to government and thought the proprietaries should first be personally applied to, who might possibly be induced by the interposition and persuasion of some private friends to accommodate matters amicably. I then waited on my old friend and correspondent, Mr. Peter Collinson, who told me that John Hanbury, the great Virginia merchant, had requested to be informed when I should arrive that he might carry me to Lord Granville's, who was then President of the Council, and wished to see me as soon as possible. I agreed to go with him the next morning. Accordingly, Mr. Hanbury called for me and took me in his carriage to that nobleman's, who received me with great civility; and after some questions respecting the present state of affairs in America, and discourse thereupon, he said to me, "You Americans have wrong ideas of the nature of your constitution; you contend that the King's instructions to his governors are not laws and think yourselves at liberty to regard or disregard them at your own discretion. But those instructions are not like the pocket instructions given to a minister going abroad for regulating his conduct in some trifling point of ceremony. They are first drawn up by judges learned in the laws;

---

[a] [William Franklin.]
[b] [Here ends the third part of the *Autobiography*. The following is the fourth part, written shortly before Franklin's death.]

they are then considered, debated, and perhaps amended in Council, after which they are signed by the King. They are then, so far as relates to you, the *law of the land;* for *the King is the Legislator of the Colonies.*" I told His Lordship this was new doctrine to me. I had always understood from our charters that our laws were to be made by our Assemblies, to be presented, indeed, to the King for his royal assent, but that being once given the King could not repeal or alter them. And as the Assemblies could not make permanent laws without his assent, so neither could he make a law for them without theirs. He assured me I was totally mistaken. I did not think so, however. And His Lordship's conversation having a little alarmed me as to what might be the sentiments of the court concerning us, I wrote it down as soon as I returned to my lodgings. I recollected that about twenty years before a clause in a bill brought into parliament by the ministry had proposed to make the King's instructions laws in the Colonies; but the clause was thrown out by the Commons, for which we adored them as our friends and friends of liberty, till by their conduct toward us in 1765, it seemed that they had refused that point of sovereignty to the King only that they might reserve it for themselves.

After some days, Dr. Fothergill having spoken to the proprietaries, they agreed to a meeting with me at Mr. T. Penn's house in Spring Garden. The conversation at first consisted of mutual declarations of disposition to reasonable accommodation, but I suppose each party had its own ideas of what should be meant by "reasonable." We then went into consideration of our several points of complaint which I enumerated. The proprietaries justified their conduct as well as they could, and I the Assembly's. We now appeared very wide, and so far from each other in our opinions as to discourage all hope of agreement. However, it was concluded that I should give them the heads of our complaints in writing, and they promised then to consider them. I did so soon after; but they put the paper into the hands of their solicitor, Ferdinando John Paris, who managed for them all their law business in their great suit with the neighboring proprietary of Maryland, Lord Baltimore, which had subsisted seventy years, and wrote for them all their papers and messages in their dispute with the Assembly. He was a proud, angry man; and as I had occasionally in the answers of the Assembly treated his papers with some severity, they being really weak in point of argument, and haughty in expression, he had conceived a mortal enmity to me, which discovering itself whenever we met, I declined the proprietary's proposal that he and I should discuss the heads of complaint between our two selves and refused treating with any one but them. They then by his advice put the paper into the hands of the Attorney and Solicitor General for their opinion and counsel upon it, where it lay unanswered a year wanting eight days, during which time I made frequent demands of an answer from the proprietaries but without obtaining any other than that they had not yet received the opinion of the Attorney and Solicitor General. What it was when they did receive it, I never learned, for they did not communicate it to me, but sent a long message to the Assembly drawn and signed by Paris reciting my paper, complaining of its want of formality as a rudeness on my part, and giving a flimsy justification of their conduct, adding that they should be willing to accommodate matters if the Assembly would send over "some person of candor" to treat with them for that purpose, intimating thereby that I was not such.

The want of formality or rudeness was probably my not having addressed the paper to them with their assumed titles of true and absolute proprietaries of the Province of Pennsylvania, which I omitted as not thinking it necessary in a paper, the intention of which was only to reduce to a certainty by writing what in conversation I had delivered *viva voce*. But during this delay, the Assembly having prevailed with Governor Denny to pass an act taxing the proprietary estate in common with the estates of the people, which was the grand point in dispute, they omitted answering the message.

When this act, however, came over, the proprietaries counseled by Paris determined to oppose its receiving the royal assent. Accordingly, they petitioned the King in Council, and a hearing was appointed, in which two lawyers were employed by them against the act and two by me in support of it. They alleged that the act was intended to load the proprietary estate in order to spare those of the people, and that if it were suffered to continue in force and the proprietaries, who were in odium with the people, left to their mercy in proportioning the taxes, they would inevitably be ruined. We replied that the act had no such intention and would have no such effect, that the assessors were honest and discreet men, under an oath to assess fairly and equitably, and that any advantage each of them might expect in lessening his own tax by augmenting that of the proprietaries was too trifling to induce them to perjure themselves. This is the purport of what I remember as urged by both sides, except that we insisted strongly on the mischievous consequences that must attend a repeal; for that the money (£100,000) being printed and given to the King's use, expended in his service, and now spread among the people, the repeal would strike it dead in their hands, to the ruin of many and the total discouragement of future grants; and the selfishness of the proprietors in soliciting such a general catastrophe, merely from a groundless fear of their estate being taxed too highly, was insisted on in the strongest terms. On this Lord Mansfield, one of the Council, rose, and beckoning to me, took me into the clerks' chamber, while the lawyers were pleading, and asked me if I was really of opinion that no injury would be done the proprietary estate in the execution of the act. I said, "Certainly." "Then," says he, "you can have little objection to enter into an engagement to assure that point." I answered, "None at all." He then called in Paris, and after some discourse His Lordship's proposition was accepted on both sides; a paper to the purpose was drawn up by the clerk of the Council, which I signed with Mr. Charles, who was also an agent of the province for their ordinary affairs, when Lord Mansfield returned to the council chamber, where finally the law was allowed to pass. Some changes were, however, recommended, and we also engaged they should be made by a subsequent law; but the Assembly did not think them necessary. For one year's tax having been levied by the act before the order of Council arrived, they appointed a committee to examine the proceedings of the assessors, and on this committee they put several particular friends of the proprietaries. After a full inquiry they unanimously signed a report that they found the tax had been assessed with perfect equity. The Assembly looked on my entering into the first part of the engagement as an essential service to the province, since it secured the credit of the paper money then spread over all the country; and they gave me their thanks in form when I returned. But the proprietaries were enraged at Governor Denny for having passed the act and turned him out, with threats of suing him for breach of instructions which he had given bond to observe. He, however, having done it at the instance of the General and for His Majesty's service, and having some powerful interest at court, despised the threats, and they were never put in execution.

# HUMANITARIAN ESSAYS
# AND OTHER WRITINGS

# OBSERVATIONS ON WAR AND PRIVATEERING *

By the original law of nations, war and extirpation were the punishment of injury. Humanizing by degrees, it admitted slavery instead of death; a further step was the exchange of prisoners instead of slavery; another, to respect more the property of private persons under conquest and be content with acquired dominion. Why should not this law of nations go on improving? Ages have intervened between its several steps; but as knowledge of late increases rapidly, why should not those steps be quickened? Why should it not be agreed to, as the future law of nations, that in any war hereafter the following description of men should be undisturbed, have the protection of both sides, and be permitted to follow their employments in security? viz.

1. Cultivators of the earth, because they labor for the subsistence of mankind.

2. Fishermen, for the same reason.

3. Merchants and traders in unarmed ships, who accommodate different nations by communicating and exchanging the necessaries and conveniences of life.

4. Artists and mechanics, inhabiting and working in open towns.

It is hardly necessary to add that the hospitals of enemies should be unmolested—they ought to be assisted. It is for the interest of humanity in general that the occasions of war, and the inducements to it, should be diminished. If rapine be abolished, one of the encouragements to war is taken away; and peace therefore more likely to continue and be lasting.

---

* [First published in *American Museum,* Vol. VII, p. 101. The second section (p. 172), On Privateering, is taken from a letter of March 14, 1785, to Benjamin Vaughan. The letter concerned the criminal laws and privateering; for the section on the criminal laws see p. 175.]

The practice of robbing merchants on the high seas—a remnant of the ancient piracy—though it may be accidentally beneficial to particular persons, is far from being profitable to all engaged in it or to the nation that authorizes it. In the beginning of a war some rich ships are surprised and taken. This encourages the first adventurers to fit out more armed vessels, and many others to do the same. But the enemy, at the same time become more careful, arm their merchant ships better and render them not so easy to be taken; they go also more under the protection of convoys. Thus, while the privateers to take them are multiplied, the vessels subject to be taken and the chances of profit are diminished; so that many cruises are made wherein the expenses overgo the gains and, as is the case in other lotteries, though particulars have got prizes, the mass of adventurers are losers, the whole expense of fitting out all the privateers during a war being much greater than the whole amount of goods taken.

Then there is the national loss of all the labor of so many men during the time they have been employed in robbing, who besides spend what they get in riot, drunkenness, and debauchery, lose their habits of industry, are rarely fit for any sober business after a peace, and serve only to increase the number of highwaymen and housebreakers. Even the undertakers, who have been fortunate, are by sudden wealth led into expensive living, the habit of which continues when the means of supporting it cease, and finally ruins them; a just punishment for their having wantonly and unfeelingly ruined many honest, innocent traders and their families, whose substance was employed in serving the common interest of mankind.

Justice is as strictly due between neighbor nations as between neighbor citizens. A highwayman is as much a robber when he plunders in a gang as when single; and a nation that makes an unjust war is only a great gang. After employing your people in robbing the Dutch, strange is it that, being put out of that employ by peace, they still continue robbing, and rob one another? *Piraterie,* as the French call it, or privateering, is the universal bent of the English nation, at home and abroad, wherever settled.

No less than seven hundred privateers were, it is said, commissioned in the last war! These were fitted out by merchants to prey upon other merchants who had never done them any injury. Is there probably any one of those privateering merchants of London who were so ready to rob the merchants of Amsterdam that would not as readily plunder another London merchant of the next street, if he could do it with the same impunity? The avidity, the *alieni appetens,* is the same; it is the fear alone of the gallows that makes the difference. How then can a nation which, among the honestest of its people, has so many thieves by inclination, and whose government encouraged and commissioned no less than seven hundred gangs of robbers, how can such a nation have the face to condemn the crime in individuals and hang up twenty of them in a morning? It naturally puts one in mind of a Newgate [58] anecdote. One of the prisoners complained that in the night somebody had taken his buckles out of his shoes. "What the devil!" says another, "have we then *thieves* amongst us? It must not be suffered. Let us search out the rogue and pump him to death."

There is, however, one late instance of an English merchant who will not profit by such ill-gotten gain. He was, it seems, part owner of a ship which the other owners thought fit to employ as a letter of marque and which took a number of French prizes. The booty being shared, he has now an agent here inquiring, by an advertisement in the *Gazette,* for those who suffered the loss, in order to make them, as far as in him lies, restitution. This conscientious man is a Quaker. The Scotch Presbyterians were formerly as tender, for there is still extant an ordinance of the town council of Edinburgh, made soon after the Reformation, "forbidding the purchase of prize goods, under pain of losing the freedom of the burgh for ever, with other punishment at the will of the magistrate; the practice of making prizes being contrary to good conscience and the rule of treating Christian brethren as we would wish to be treated; and such goods *are not to be sold by any godly men within this burgh."* The race of these godly men in Scotland is probably extinct, or their principles abandoned, since, as far as that nation had a hand in promoting the war against the Colonies, prizes and confiscations are believed to have been a considerable motive.

It has been for some time a generally received opinion that a military man is not to inquire whether a war be just or unjust; he is to execute his orders. All princes who are disposed to become tyrants must probably approve of this opinion, and be willing to establish it; but is it not a dangerous one? Since, on that principle, if the tyrant commands his army to attack and destroy, not only an unoffending neighbor nation, but even his own subjects, the army is bound to obey. A Negro slave, in our colonies, being commanded by his master to rob or murder a neighbor, or do any other immoral act, may refuse, and the magistrate will protect him in his refusal. The slavery then of a soldier is worse than that of a Negro! A conscientious officer, if not restrained by the apprehension of its being imputed to another cause, may indeed resign rather than be employed in an unjust war; but the private men are slaves for life, and they are perhaps incapable of judging for themselves. We can only lament their fate, and still more that of a sailor, who is often dragged by force from his honest occupation and compelled to imbrue his hands in, perhaps, innocent blood. But methinks it well behooves merchants (men more enlightened by their education, and perfectly free from any such force or obligation) to consider well of the justice of a war before they voluntarily engage a gang of ruffians to attack their fellow merchants of a neighboring nation, to plunder them of property, and perhaps ruin them and their families if they yield it; or to wound, maim, or murder them if they endeavor to defend it. Yet these things are done by Christian merchants, whether a war be just or unjust; and it can hardly be just on both sides. They are done by English and American merchants, who, nevertheless, complain of private theft, and hang by dozens the thieves they have taught by their own example.

It is high time, for the sake of humanity, that a stop were put to this enormity. The United States of America, though better situated than any European nation to make profit by privateering (most of the trade of Europe with the West Indies passing before their doors) are, as far as in them lies, endeavoring to abolish the practice by offering, in all their treaties with other powers, an article engaging solemnly that, in case of future war, no privateer shall be commissioned on either side, and that unarmed merchant ships, on both sides, shall pursue their voyages un-molested. This will be a happy improvement of the law of na-tions. The humane and the just cannot but wish general success to the proposition.

## ON THE CRIMINAL LAWS *

If we really believe, as we profess to believe, that the law of Moses was the law of God, the dictate of divine wisdom, infinitely superior to human, on what principles do we ordain death as the punishment of an offense which, according to that law, was only to be punished by a restitution of fourfold? To put a man to death for an offense which does not deserve death, is it not mur-der? And, as the French writer says, *Doit on punir un délit contre la societé par un crime contre la nature?* [59]

Superfluous property is the creature of society. Simple and mild laws were sufficient to guard the property that was merely necessary. The savage's bow, his hatchet, and his coat of skins were sufficiently secured, without law, by the fear of personal resentment and retaliation. When, by virtue of the first laws, part of the society accumulated wealth and grew more powerful, they enacted others more severe and would protect their property at the expense of humanity. This was abusing their power, and commencing a tyranny. If a savage, before he entered society, had been told, "Your neighbor, by this means, may become owner of a hundred deer; but if your brother or your son or yourself, having no deer of your own and being hungry, should kill one, an infamous death must be the consequence," he would probably

---

* [Extract from a letter to Benjamin Vaughan, March 14, 1785. For the second part of the letter, "On Privateering," see p. 172.]

have preferred his liberty, and his common right of killing any deer, to all the advantages of society that might be proposed to him.

That it is better a hundred guilty persons should escape than that one innocent person should suffer, is a maxim that has been long and generally approved; never, that I know of, controverted. Even the sanguinary author of the *Thoughts* [60] agrees to it, adding well, "that the very thought of *injured* innocence, and much more that of *suffering* innocence, must awaken all our tenderest and most compassionate feelings, and at the same time raise our highest indignation against the instruments of it." "But," he adds, "there is no danger of *either,* from a strict adherence to the laws."—Really! Is it then impossible to make an unjust law? And if the law itself be unjust, may it not be the very "instrument" which ought "to raise the author's, and everybody's highest indignation"? I see, in the last newspapers from London, that a woman is capitally convicted at the Old Bailey [61] for privately stealing out of a shop some gauze, value fourteen shillings and threepence; is there any proportion between the injury done by a theft, value fourteen shillings and threepence, and the punishment of a human creature by death on a gibbet? Might not that woman by her labor have made the reparation ordained by God in paying fourfold? Is not all punishment inflicted beyond the merit of the offense so much punishment of innocence? In this light, how vast is the annual quantity of not only *injured* but *suffering* innocence in almost all the civilized states of Europe!

But it seems to have been thought that this kind of innocence may be punished by way of *preventing* crimes. I have read, indeed, of a cruel Turk in Barbary, who, whenever he bought a new Christian slave, ordered him immediately to be hung up by the legs, and to receive a hundred blows of a cudgel on the soles of his feet, that the severe sense of the punishment, and fear of incurring it thereafter, might prevent the faults that should merit it. Our author himself would hardly approve entirely of this Turk's conduct in the government of slaves; and yet he appears to recommend something like it for the government of English subjects, when he applauds the reply of Judge Burnet to the convict horse-stealer, who, being asked what he had to say why judgment of death should not pass against him and answering that it was hard to hang a man for *only* stealing a horse, was told by the judge, "Man, thou art not to be hanged *only* for stealing a horse, but that horses may not be stolen." The man's answer, if candidly examined, will, I imagine, appear reasonable, as being founded on the eternal principle of justice and equity, that punishments should be proportioned to offenses; and the judge's reply brutal and unreasonable, though the writer "wishes all judges to carry it with them whenever they go to the circuit, and to bear it in their minds, as containing a wise reason for all the penal statutes which they are called upon to put into execution. It at once illustrates," says he, "the true grounds and reasons of all capital punishments whatsoever, namely, that every man's property, as well as his life, may be held sacred and inviolate." Is there then no difference in value between property and life? If I think it right that the crime of murder should be punished with death, not only as an equal punishment of the crime, but to prevent other murders, does it follow that I must approve of inflicting the same punishment for a little invasion on my property by theft? If I am not myself so barbarous, so bloody-minded, and revengeful as to kill a fellow creature for stealing from me fourteen shillings and threepence, how can I approve of a law that does it? Montesquieu, who was himself a judge, endeavors to impress other maxims. He must have known what humane judges feel on such occasions, and what the effects of those feelings; and so far from thinking that severe and excessive punishments pre vent crimes, he asserts, as quoted by our French writer, that

> L'atrocité des loix en empêche l'exécution.
> L'orsque la peine est sans mésure, on est souvent obligé de lui préférer l'impunité.
> La cause de tous les relâchemens vient de l'impunité des crimes, et non de la modération des peines."

It is said by those who know Europe generally that there are more thefts committed and punished annually in England than in all the other nations put together. If this be so, there must be a cause or causes for such depravity in our common people. May not one be the deficiency of justice and morality in our national government, manifested in our oppressive conduct to subjects, and unjust wars on our neighbors? View the long-persisted-in unjust, monopolizing treatment of Ireland, at length acknowledged! View the plundering government exercised by our merchants in the Indies; the confiscating war made upon the American colonies; and, to say nothing of those upon France and Spain, view the late war upon Holland, which was seen by impartial Europe in no other light than that of a war of rapine and pillage; the hopes of an immense and easy prey being its only apparent, and probably its true and real motive and encouragement.

## A PARABLE AGAINST PERSECUTION [a]

1. And it came to pass after these things that Abraham sat in the door of his tent, about the going of the sun.

2. And behold a man bent with age, coming from the way of the wilderness leaning on a staff.

3. And Abraham arose and met him and said unto him, "Turn in, I pray thee, and wash thy feet and tarry all night; and thou shalt rise early in the morning and go thy way."

---

[a] [Published as a communication from Franklin in Lord Kames: *Sketches in the History of Man*, Vol. II, pp. 472-473, with the following comment by Lord Kames: "The following Parable against Persecution was communicated to me by Dr. Franklin of Philadelphia, a man who makes a great figure in the learned world: and who would make a greater figure for benevolence and candor, were virtue as much regarded in this declining age as knowledge. . . . Were it really a chapter of Genesis one is apt to think that persecution could never have shown a bare face among Jews or Christians. But alas! that is a vain thought."]

4. And the man said, "Nay; for I will abide under this tree."

5. But Abraham pressed him greatly; so he turned and they went into the tent; and Abraham baked unleavened bread, and they did eat.

6. And when Abraham saw that the man blessed not God, he said unto him, "Wherefore dost thou not worship the most high God, creator of heaven and earth?"

7. And the man answered and said, "I do not worship thy God, neither do I call upon his name, for I have made to myself a god, which abideth always in my house and provideth me with all things."

8. And Abraham's zeal was kindled against the man, and he arose and fell upon him, and drove him forth with blows into the wilderness.

9. And God called unto Abraham, saying, "Abraham, where is the stranger?"

10. And Abraham answered and said, "Lord, he would not worship thee, neither would he call upon thy name; therefore have I driven him out from before my face into the wilderness."

11. And God said, "Have I borne with him these hundred and ninety and eight years, and nourished him and clothed him, notwithstanding his rebellion against me, and couldst not thou, who art thyself a sinner, bear with him one night?"

12. And Abraham said, "Let not the anger of my Lord wax hot against his servant; lo, I have sinned; forgive me, I pray thee."

13. And Abraham arose and went forth into the wilderness and diligently sought for the man and found him, and returned with him to the tent; and when he had entreated him kindly, he sent him away on the morrow with gifts.

14. And God spake again unto Abraham saying, "For this thy sin shall thy seed be afflicted four hundred years in a strange land.

15. "But for thy repentance will I deliver them, and they shall come forth with power and with gladness of heart and with much substance."

## A LETTER ON RELIGIOUS TOLERATION [a]

I understand from the public papers that in the debates on the bill for relieving the dissenters in the point of subscription to the church articles, sundry reflections were thrown out against the people, importing that they themselves are of a persecuting intolerant spirit, for that when they had the superiority, they persecuted the church, and still persecute it in America, where they compel its members to pay taxes for maintaining the presbyterian or independent worship, and at the same time refuse them a toleration in the full exercise of their religion, by the administrations of a bishop.

If we look back into history for the character of the present sects in Christianity, we shall find few that have not, in their turns, been persecutors and complainers of persecution. The primitive Christians thought persecution extremely wrong in the pagans, but practiced it on one another. The first Protestants of the Church of England blamed persecution in the Romish Church, but practiced it against the Puritans; these found it wrong in the bishops, but fell into the same practice both here and in New England.—To account for this we should remember that the doctrine of *toleration* was not then known, or had not prevailed in the world. Persecution was therefore not so much the fault of the sect as of the times. It was not in those days deemed wrong *in itself*. The general opinion was only that those *who are in error* ought not to persecute *the truth,* but the *possessors of truth* were in the right to persecute *error* in order to destroy it. Thus every sect, believing itself possessed of *all truth* and that every tenet differing from theirs was *error,* conceived that when the power was in their hands, persecution was a duty required of them by that God whom they supposed to be offended with heresy.—By degrees, more moderate *and more modest* sentiments have taken place in the Christian world; and among Protestants particularly, all disclaim persecution, none vindicate it, and few practice it.—

---

[a] [First published in a newspaper in England, June 3, 1772, and then anonymously as an appendix to the pamphlet: *Two Letters to the Prelates.*]

We should then cease to reproach each other with what was done by our ancestors, but judge of the present character of sects or churches by their *present conduct* only.

Now to determine on the justice of this charge against the present dissenters, particularly those in America, let us consider the following facts. They went from England to establish a new country for themselves, *at their own expense,* where they might enjoy the free exercise of religion in their own way. When they had purchased the territory of the natives, they granted the lands out in townships, requiring for it neither purchase-money nor quit-rent, but this condition only to be complied with, that the freeholders should support a gospel minister (meaning probably one of the then governing sects) and a free school, within the township. Thus, what is commonly called Presbyterianism became the *established religion* of that country. All went on well this way, while the same religious opinions were general, the support of minister and school being raised by a proportionate tax on the lands. But, in process of time, some becoming Quakers, some Baptists, and, of late years, some returning to the Church of England (through the laudable endeavors and a *proper application* of their funds by the society for propagating the gospel), objections were made to the payment of a tax appropriated to the support of a church they disapproved and had forsaken. The civil magistrates, however, continued for a time to collect and apply the tax according to the original laws, which remained in force; and they did it the more freely, as thinking it just and equitable that the holders of lands should pay what was contracted to be paid when they were granted, as the only consideration for the grant, and what had been considered by all subsequent purchasers as a perpetual incumbrance on the estate, bought therefore at a proportionately cheaper rate; a payment which, it was thought, no honest man ought to avoid under pretext of his having changed his religious persuasion; and this, I suppose, is one of the best grounds of demanding tithes of dissenters now in England. But the practice being clamored against by the Episcopalians as persecution, the legislature of the province of Massachusetts Bay, nearly thirty years since, passed an act for their

relief, requiring, indeed, the tax to be paid as usual, but directing that several sums, levied from members of the Church of
England should be paid over to the minister of that church with
whom such members usually attended divine worship; which minister had power given him to receive, and, on occasion, *to recover
the same by law.*

It seems that legislature considered that the end of the tax was
to secure and improve the morals of the people, and promote their
happiness, by supporting among them the public worship of God
and the preaching of the gospel; that where particular people
fancied a particular mode, that mode might probably, therefore,
be of most use to those people, and that if the good was done,
it was not so material in what mode or by whom it was done.
The consideration that their brethren, the dissenters in England,
were still compelled to pay tithes to the clergy of the church, had
not weight enough with the legislature to prevent this moderate
act, which still continues in full force; and I hope no uncharitable
conduct of the church toward the dissenters will ever provoke
them to repeal it.

With regard to *a bishop,* I know not upon what ground the
dissenters, either here or in America, are charged with refusing
the benefit of such an officer to the church in that country. *Here*
they seem to have naturally no concern in the affair. *There* they
have no power to prevent it, if government should think fit to
send one. They would probably *dislike,* indeed, to see an order
of men established among them from whose persecutions their
fathers fled into that wilderness, and whose future domination
they might possibly fear, *not knowing that their natures are
changed.*—But the non-appointment of bishops for America seems
to arise from another quarter. The same wisdom of government,
probably, that prevents the sitting of convocations, and forbids,
by *noli prosequi's,* the persecution of dissenters for non-subscrip-
tion, avoids establishing bishops where the minds of people are
not yet prepared to receive them cordially, lest the public peace
should be endangered.

And now let us see how this *persecution-account* stands between
the parties.

In New England, where the legislative bodies are almost to a man dissenters from the Church of England:

1. There is no test to prevent churchmen holding offices.

2. The sons of churchmen have the full benefit of the universities.

3. The taxes for support of public worship, when paid by churchmen, are given to the Episcopal minister.

In Old England:

1. Dissenters are excluded from all offices of profit and honor.

2. The benefits of education in the universities are appropriated to the sons of churchmen.

3. The clergy of the dissenters receive none of the tithes paid by their people, who must be at the additional charge of maintaining their own separate worship.—

But it is said that the dissenters of America *oppose* the introduction of a bishop.

In fact, it is not alone the dissenters there that give the opposition (if *not encouraging* must be termed *opposing*) but the laity in general dislike the project, and some even of the clergy. The inhabitants of Virginia are almost all Episcopalians; the church is fully established there, and the council and general assembly are, perhaps to a man, its members, yet, when lately, at a meeting of the clergy, a resolution was taken to apply for a bishop, against which several however protested, the assembly of the province, at the next meeting, expressed their disapprobation of the thing in the strongest manner, by unanimously ordering the thanks of the house to the protesters; for many of the American laity of the church think it some advantage—whether their own young men come to England for ordination and improve themselves at the same time by conversation with the learned here, or the congregations are supplied by Englishmen, who have had the benefit of education in English universities, and are ordained before they came abroad. They do not, therefore, see the necessity of a bishop merely for ordination; and confirmation is among them deemed a ceremony of no very great importance, since few seek it in England, where bishops are in plenty.—These sentiments prevail with many churchmen there, not to promote a design which they think must sooner or later saddle them with great expenses to support it.—As to the dissenters, their minds might probably be more conciliated to the measure if the bishops here should, in their wisdom and goodness, think fit to set their sacred character in a more friendly light, by dropping their opposition to the dissenters' application for relief in subscription, and declaring their willingness that dissenters should be capable of offices, enjoy the benefit of education in the universities, and the privilege of appropriating their tithes to the support of their own clergy. In all these points of toleration they appear far behind the present dissenters of New England, and it may seem to some a step below the dignity of bishops to follow the example of such inferiors. I do not, however, despair of their doing it some time or other, since nothing of the kind is too hard for *true Christian humility*.

## ON THE SLAVE TRADE *

Reading in the newspapers the speech of Mr. Jackson in Congress against meddling with the affair of slavery, or attempting to mend the condition of slaves, it put me in mind of a similar speech, made about one hundred years since, by Sidi Mehemet Ibrahim, a member of the divan of Algiers, which may be seen in Martin's account of his consulship, 1687. It was against granting the petition of the sect called Erika, or purists, who prayed for the abolition of piracy and slavery, as being unjust.—Mr. Jackson does not quote it; perhaps he has not seen it. If therefore, some of its reasonings are to be found in his eloquent speech, it may only show that men's interests operate, and are operated

---

* [This excellent parody on a speech by Mr. Jackson was first published in *American Museum,* Vol. IX, p. 336.]

on, with surprising similarity in all countries and climates, whenever they are under similar circumstances. The African speech, as translated, is as follows:

"Alla Bismillah, etc., God is great, and Mahomet is his prophet.

"Have these Erika considered the consequences of granting their petition? If we cease our cruises against the Christians, how shall we be furnished with the commodities their countries produce, and which are so necessary for us? If we forbear to make slaves of their people, who, in this hot climate, are to cultivate our lands? Who are to perform the common labors of our city and of our families? Must we not then be our own slaves? And is there not more compassion and more favor due to us Mussulmen than to those Christian dogs?—We have now above fifty thousand in and near Algiers. This number, if not kept up by fresh supplies, will soon diminish and be gradually annihilated. If, then, we cease taking and plundering the infidel ships and making slaves of the seamen and passengers, our lands will become of no value for want of cultivation; the rents of houses in the city will sink one-half; and the revenues of government arising from the share of prizes must be totally destroyed.—And for what? To gratify the whim of a whimsical sect, who would have us not only forbear making more slaves, but even manumit those we have. But who is to indemnify their masters for the loss? Will the state do it? Is our treasury sufficient? Will the Erika do it? Can they do it? Or would they, to do what they think justice to the slaves, do a greater injustice to the owners? And if we set our slaves free, what is to be done with them? Few of them will return to their native countries; they know too well the greater hardships they must there be subject to. They will not embrace our holy religion; they will not adopt our manners; our people will not pollute themselves by intermarrying with them. Must we maintain them as beggars in our streets, or suffer our properties to be the prey of their pillage? For men accustomed to slavery will not work for a livelihood when not compelled.—And what is there so pitiable in their present condition? Were they not slaves in their own countries? Are not Spain, Portugal, France, and the Italian states governed by despots, who hold all their subjects in slavery, without exception? Even England treats her sailors as slaves, for they are, whenever the government pleases, seized and confined in ships of war, condemned not only to work, but to fight for small wages or a mere subsistence, not better than our slaves are allowed by us. Is their condition then made worse by their falling into our hands? No; they have only exchanged one slavery for another, and I may say better; for here they are brought into a land where the sun of Islamism gives forth its light and shines in full splendor, and they have an opportunity of making themselves acquainted with the true doctrine, and thereby saving their immortal souls. Those who remain at home have not that happiness. Sending the slaves home, then, would be sending them out of light into darkness.

"I repeat the question, what is to be done with them? I have heard it suggested that they may be planted in the wilderness, where there is plenty of land for them to subsist on, and where they may flourish as a free state.—But they are, I doubt, too little disposed to labor without compulsion, as well as too ignorant to establish good government; and the wild Arabs would soon molest and destroy or again enslave them. While serving us, we take care to provide them with everything; and they are treated with humanity. The laborers in their own countries are, as I am informed, worse fed, lodged, and clothed. The condition of most of them is therefore already mended, and requires no further improvement. Here their lives are in safety. They are not liable to be impressed for soldiers, and forced to cut one another's Christian throats, as in the wars of their own countries. If some of the religious-mad bigots, who now tease us with their silly petitions, have, in a fit of blind zeal, freed their slaves, it was not generosity, it was not humanity that moved them to the action; it was from the conscious burden of a load of sins, and hope, from the supposed merits of so good a work, to be excused from damnation.— How grossly are they mistaken in imagining slavery to be disavowed by the Alcoran! Are not the two precepts, to quote no more, 'Masters, treat your slaves with kindness—Slaves, serve your masters with cheerfulness and fidelity,' clear proofs to the contrary? Nor can the plundering of infidels be in that sacred book forbidden; since it is well known from it that God has given the world, and all that it contains, to his faithful Mussulmen, who are to enjoy it, of right, as fast as they can conquer it. Let us then hear no more of this detestable proposition, the manumission of Christian slaves, the adoption of which would, by depreciating our lands and houses, and thereby depriving so many good citizens of their properties, create universal discontent, and provoke insurrections, to the endangering of government and producing general confusion. I have, therefore, no doubt that this wise council will prefer the comfort and happiness of a whole nation of true believers to the whim of a few Erika, and dismiss the petition."

The result was, as Martin tells us, that the divan came to this resolution: "That the doctrine that the plundering and enslaving the Christians is unjust is at best problematical; but that it is the interest of this state to continue the practice is clear; therefore, let the petition be rejected." And it was rejected accordingly.

And since like motives are apt to produce, in the minds of men, like opinions and resolutions, may we not venture to predict from this account that the petitions to the Parliament of England for abolishing the slave trade, to say nothing of other legislatures, and the debates upon them, will have a similar conclusion.

# ON THE FREEDOM OF THE PRESS *

## ACCOUNT OF THE HIGHEST COURT OF THE JUDICATURE IN PENNSYLVANIA, VIZ., THE COURT OF THE PRESS

*Power of this Court*

It may receive and promulgate accusations of all kinds, against all persons and characters among the citizens of the state, and

---

* [First published in *American Museum*, Vol. VI, p. 295.]

even against all inferior courts; and may judge, sentence, and condemn to infamy, not only private individuals, but public bodies, etc., with or without inquiry or hearing, at the court's discretion.

### Whose Favor, or for Whose Emolument this Court is Established

In favor of about one citizen in five hundred, who, by education, or practice in scribbling, has acquired a tolerable style as to grammar and construction, so as to bear printing; or who is possessed of a press and a few types. This five-hundredth part of the citizens have the privilege of accusing and abusing the other four hundred and ninety-nine parts, at their pleasure; or they may hire out their pens and press to others for that purpose.

### Practice of this Court

It is not governed by any of the rules of the common courts of law. The accused is allowed no grand jury to judge of the truth of the accusation before it is publicly made; nor is the name of the accuser made known to him; nor has he an opportunity of confronting the witnesses against him, for they are kept in the dark, as in the Spanish court of inquisition. Nor is there any petty jury of his peers sworn to try the truth of the charges. The proceedings are also sometimes so rapid that an honest good citizen may find himself suddenly and unexpectedly accused, and in the same morning judged and condemned and sentence pronounced against him that he is a rogue and a villain. Yet if an officer of this court receives the slightest check for misconduct in this his office, he claims immediately the rights of a free citizen by the Constitution and demands to know his accuser, to confront the witnesses, and to have a fair trial by a jury of his peers.

### Foundation of Its Authority

It is said to be founded on an article in the state constitution which establishes the liberty of the press—a liberty which every Pennsylvanian would fight and die for, though few of us, I believe, have distinct ideas of its nature and extent. It seems, indeed, somewhat like the liberty of the press that felons have, by the common law of England, before conviction; that is, to be either pressed to death or hanged. If, by the liberty of the press were understood merely the liberty of discussing the propriety of public measures and political opinions, let us have as much of it as you please; but if it means the liberty of affronting, calumniating, and defaming one another, I, for my part, own myself willing to part with my share of it, whenever our legislators shall please so to alter the law; and shall cheerfully consent to exchange my liberty of abusing others for the privilege of not being abused myself.

## By Whom this Court is Commissioned or Constituted

It is not by any commission from the supreme executive council, who might previously judge of the abilities, integrity, knowledge, etc., of the persons to be appointed to this great trust of deciding upon the characters and good fame of the citizens; for this court is above that council and may accuse, judge, and condemn it at pleasure. Nor is it hereditary, as is the court of dernier resort in the peerage of England. But any man who can procure pen, ink, and paper, with a press, a few types, and a huge pair of blacking balls, may commissionate himself, and his court is immediately established in the plenary possession and exercise of its rights. For if you make the least complaint of the judge's conduct, he daubs his blacking balls in your face whenever he meets you; and, besides tearing your private character to splinters, marks you out for the odium of the public as an enemy to the liberty of the press.

## Of the Natural Support of this Court

Its support is founded in the depravity of such minds as have not been mended by religion, nor improved by good education.

> There is a lust in man no charm can tame,
> Of loudly publishing his neighbour's shame.

Hence,

> On eagles' wings, immortal scandals fly,
> While virtuous actions are but born and die.
> —Dryden.

Whoever feels pain in hearing a good character of his neighbor will feel a pleasure in the reverse. And of those who, despairing to rise to distinction by their virtues, are happy if others can be depressed to a level with themselves, there are a number sufficient in every great town to maintain one of these courts by their subscription. A shrewd observer once said that in walking the streets of a slippery morning, one might see where the good-natured people lived, by the ashes thrown on the ice before the doors; probably he would have formed a different conjecture of the temper of those whom he might find engaged in such subscriptions.

## Of the Checks Proper to be Established against the Abuses of Power in those Courts

Hitherto there are none. But since so much has been written and published on the federal Constitution; and the necessity of checks, in all other parts of good government, has been so clearly and learnedly explained, I find myself so far enlightened as to suspect some check may be proper in this part also; but I have been at a loss to imagine any that may not be construed an infringement of the sacred liberty of the press. At length, however, I think I have found one that, instead of diminishing general liberty, shall augment it; which is by restoring to the people a species of liberty of which they have been deprived by our laws; I mean the liberty of the cudgel! In the rude state of society, prior to the existence of laws, if one man gave another ill language, the affronted person might return it by a box on the ear; and if repeated, by a good drubbing, and this without offending against any law; but now the right of making such returns is denied, and they are punished as breaches of the peace, while the right of abusing seems to remain in full force, the laws made against it being rendered ineffectual by the liberty of the press.

My proposal then is to leave the liberty of the press untouched, to be exercised in its full extent, force, and vigor, but to permit the liberty of the cudgel to go with it, *pari passu*. Thus, my fellow citizens, if an impudent writer attacks your reputation— dearer perhaps to you than your life—and puts his name to the charge, you may go to him as openly and break his head. If he conceals himself behind the printer, and you can nevertheless discover who he is, you may, in like manner, waylay him in the night, attack him behind, and give him a good drubbing. If your adversary hires better writers than himself to abuse you more effectually, you may hire brawny porters, stronger than yourself, to assist you in giving him a more effectual drubbing. Thus far goes my project as to *private* resentment and retribution. But if the public should ever happen to be affronted, as it ought to be, with the conduct of such writers, I would not advise proceeding immediately to these extremities, but that we should in moderation content ourselves with tarring and feathering and tossing them in a blanket.

If, however, it should be thought that this proposal of mine may disturb the public peace, I would then humbly recommend to our legislators to take up the consideration of both liberties, that of the press and that of the cudgel, and by an explicit law mark their extent and limits; and at the same time that they secure the person of a citizen from assaults, they would likewise provide for the security of his reputation.

## NEW MODE OF LENDING MONEY *

I send you herewith a bill for ten louis d'ors. I do not pretend to give such a sum. I only *lend* it to you. When you shall return to your country, you cannot fail getting into some business that will in time enable you to pay all your debts. In that case, when you meet with another honest man in similar distress, you must *pay me* by lending this sum to him, enjoining him to *discharge the debt* by a like operation, when he shall be able and shall meet with such another opportunity. I hope it may thus go through many hands before it meet with a *knave* to stop its progress. This

---

* [A letter written April 22, 1784, and published in the *Gentleman's Magazine*, September, 1797.]

is a trick of mine for doing a good deal with a little money. I am not rich enough to afford *much* in good works, and so am obliged to be cunning and make the most of a *little*.

## ON BRINGING THE CONVENIENCES OF LIFE TO NEW ZEALAND [a]

Britain is said to have produced originally nothing but *sloes*. What vast advantages have been communicated to her by the fruits, seeds, roots, herbage, animals, and arts of other countries! We are by their means become a wealthy and mighty nation, abounding in all good things. Does not some *duty* hence arise from us toward other countries still remaining in our former state?

Britain is now the first maritime power in the world. Her ships are innumerable, capable by their form, size, and strength of sailing all seas. Our seamen are equally bold, skillful, and hardy; dexterous in exploring the remotest regions, and ready to engage in voyages to unknown countries, though attended with the greatest dangers. The inhabitants of those countries, our *fellow men*, have canoes only; not knowing iron, they cannot build ships; they have little astronomy, and no knowledge of the compass to guide them; they cannot therefore come to us, or obtain any of our advantages. From these circumstances, does not some duty seem to arise from us to them? Does not Providence by these distinguishing favors seem to call on us to do something ourselves for the common interest of humanity?

Those who think it their duty to ask bread and other blessings daily from heaven, would they not think it equally a duty to communicate of those blessings when they have received them and show their gratitude to their great Benefactor by the only means in their power, promoting the happiness of his other children?

---

[a] [Written August 29, 1771, and privately printed. The scheme was a joint plan by Franklin and his friend Dalrymple. Only the part written by Franklin is here reprinted.]

Ceres is said to have made a journey through many countries to teach the use of corn and the art of raising it. For this single benefit the grateful nations deified her. How much more may Englishmen deserve such honor by communicating the knowledge and use not of corn only, but of all the other enjoyments earth can produce and which they are now in possession of. *Communiter bona profundere, Deum est.*

Many voyages have been undertaken with views of profit or of plunder or to gratify resentment; to procure some advantage to ourselves, or do some mischief to others; but a voyage is now proposed to visit a distant people on the other side of the globe, not to cheat them, not to rob them, not to seize their lands or enslave their persons, but merely to do them good and make them, as far as in our power lies, to live as comfortably as ourselves.

It seems a laudable wish that all the nations of the earth were connected by a knowledge of each other and a mutual exchange of benefits, but a commercial nation particularly should wish for a general civilization of mankind, since trade is always carried on to much greater extent with people who have the arts and conveniences of life than it can be with naked savages. We may therefore hope in this undertaking to be of some service to our country, as well as to those poor people who, however distant from us, are in truth related to us, and whose interests do, in some degree, concern every one who can say, *Homo sum,* etc.

## INFORMATION TO THOSE WHO WOULD REMOVE TO AMERICA [a]

Many persons in Europe having directly or by letters expressed to the writer of this, who well is acquainted with North America, their desire of transporting and establishing themselves in that country, but who appear to him to have formed, through igno-

---

[a] [Published as a pamphlet in 1784.]

rance, mistaken ideas, and expectations of what is to be obtained there, he thinks it may be useful and prevent inconvenient, expensive, and fruitless voyages of improper persons, if he gives some clearer and truer notions of that part of the world than appear to have hitherto prevailed.

He finds it is imagined by numbers that the inhabitants of North America are rich, capable of rewarding, and disposed to reward all sorts of ingenuity; that they are at the same time ignorant of all the sciences, and, consequently, that strangers possessing talents in the belles lettres, fine arts, etc., must be highly esteemed, and so well paid as to become easily rich themselves; that there is also an abundance of profitable offices to be disposed of, which the natives are not qualified to fill; and that, having few persons of family among them, strangers of birth must be greatly respected, and of course easily obtain the best of those offices, which will make all their fortunes; that the governments too, to encourage emigrations from Europe, not only pay the expense of personal transportation, but give lands gratis to strangers, with Negroes to work for them, utensils of husbandry, and stocks of cattle. These are all wild imaginations; and those who go to America with expectations founded upon them will surely find themselves disappointed.

The truth is that though there are in that country few people so miserable as the poor of Europe, there are also very few that in Europe would be called rich; it is rather a general happy mediocrity that prevails. There are few great proprietors of the soil, and few tenants; most people cultivate their own lands, or follow some handicraft or merchandise; very few rich enough to live idly upon their rents or incomes, or to pay the high prices given in Europe for painting, statues, architecture, and the other works of art that are more curious than useful. Hence the natural geniuses that have arisen in America with such talents have uniformly quit that country for Europe, where they can be more suitably rewarded. It is true that letters and mathematical knowledge are in esteem there, but they are at the same time more common than is apprehended; there being already existing nine colleges or universities, viz. four in New England, and one in each of the provinces of New York, New Jersey, Pennsylvania, Maryland, and Virginia, all furnished with learned professors; besides a number of smaller academies; these educate many of their youth in the languages and those sciences that qualify men for the professions of divinity, law, or physic. Strangers indeed are by no means excluded from exercising those professions, and the quick increase of inhabitants gives them a chance of employ, which they have in common with the natives. Of civil offices or employments there are few, no superfluous ones as in Europe; and it is a rule established in some of the states that no office should be so profitable as to make it desirable. The thirty-sixth article of the constitution of Pennsylvania runs expressly in these words: "As every freeman, to preserve his independence (if he has not a sufficient estate) ought to have some profession, calling, trade, or farm, whereby he may honestly subsist, there can be no necessity for, nor use in, establishing offices of profit; the usual effects of which are dependence and servility, unbecoming free-men, in the possessors and expectants; faction, contention, corruption, and disorder among the people. Wherefore, whenever an office, through increase of fees or otherwise, becomes so profitable as to occasion many to apply for it, the profits ought to be lessened by the legislature."

These ideas prevailing more or less in all the United States, it cannot be worth any man's while, who has a means of living at home, to expatriate himself, in hopes of obtaining a profitable civil office in America; and as to military offices, they are at an end with the war, the armies being disbanded. Much less is it advisable for a person to go thither who has no other quality to recommend him but his birth. In Europe it has indeed its value; but it is a commodity that cannot be carried to a worse market than to that of America, where people do not inquire concerning a stranger, "What is he?" but "What can he do?" If he has any useful art, he is welcome; and if he exercises it and behaves well, he will be respected by all that know him; but a mere man of quality, who on that account wants to live upon the public by some office or salary, will be despised and disregarded. The husbandman is in honor there, and even the mechanic, because their employments are useful. The people have a saying that God Almighty is himself a mechanic, the greatest in the universe; and he is respected and admired more for the variety, ingenuity, and utility of his handiworks than for the antiquity of his family. They are pleased with the observation of a Negro, and frequently mention it, that "Boccarora (meaning the white man) make de black man workee, make de horse workee, make de ox workee, make ebery ting workee; only de hog. He de hog, no workee; he eat, he drink, he walk about, he go to sleep when he please, he libb like a gentleman." According to these opinions of the Americans, one of them would think himself more obliged to a genealogist who could prove for him that his ancestors and relations for ten generations had been ploughmen, smiths, carpenters, turners, weavers, tanners, or even shoemakers, and consequently that they were useful members of society; than if he could only prove that they were gentlemen, doing nothing of value, but living idly on the labor of others, mere *fruges consumere nati,* and otherwise *good for nothing,* till by their death their estates, like the carcass of the Negro's gentleman hog, "come to be *cut up.*"

With regard to encouragements for strangers from government, they are really only what are derived from good laws and liberty. Strangers are welcome, because there is room enough for them all, and therefore the old inhabitants are not jealous of them; the laws protect them sufficiently, so that they have no need of the patronage of great men; and everyone will enjoy securely the profits of his industry. But if he does not bring a fortune with him, he must work and be industrious to live. One or two years' residence gives him all the rights of a citizen; but the government does not at present, whatever it may have done in former times, hire people to become settlers, by paying their passages, giving land, Negroes, utensils, stock, or any other kind of emolument whatever. In short, America is the land of labor, and by no means what the English call "Lubberland," and the French "Pays de Cocagne," where the streets are said to be paved with half-peck loaves, the houses tiled with pancakes, and where fowls fly about ready-roasted, crying "Come eat me!"

Who then are the kind of persons to whom an emigration to

America may be advantageous? And what are the advantages they may reasonably expect?

Land being cheap in that country, from the vast forests still void of inhabitants and not likely to be occupied in an age to come, insomuch that the propriety of a hundred acres of fertile soil full of wood may be obtained near the frontiers, in many places, for eight or ten guineas, hearty young laboring men, who understand the husbandry of corn and cattle, which is nearly the same in that country as in Europe, may easily establish themselves there. A little money saved of the good wages they receive there, while they work for others, enables them to buy the land and begin their plantation, in which they are assisted by the good will of their neighbors, and some credit. Multitudes of poor people from England, Ireland, Scotland, and Germany have by this means in a few years become wealthy farmers, who, in their own countries, where all the lands are fully occupied and the wages of labor low, could never have emerged from the mean condition wherein they were born.

From the salubrity of the air, the healthiness of the climate, the plenty of good provisions, and the encouragement to early marriages, by the certainty of subsistence in cultivating the earth, the increase of inhabitants by natural generation is very rapid in America, and becomes still more so by the accession of strangers; hence there is a continual demand for more artisans of all the necessary and useful kinds, to supply those cultivators of the earth with houses and with furniture and utensils of the grosser sorts, which cannot so well be brought from Europe. Tolerably good workmen in any of those mechanic arts are sure to find employ, and to be well paid for their work, there being no restraints preventing strangers from exercising any art they understand, nor any permission necessary. If they are poor, they begin first as servants or journeymen, and if they are sober, industrious, and frugal, they soon become masters, establish themselves in business, marry, raise families, and become respectable citizens.

Also persons of moderate fortunes and capitals who, having a number of children to provide for, are desirous of bringing them up to industry, and to secure estates for their posterity, have opportunities of doing it in America which Europe does not afford. There they may be taught and practice profitable mechanic arts without incurring disgrace on that account, but on the contrary acquiring respect by such abilities. There small capitals laid out in lands, which daily become more valuable by the increase of people, afford a solid prospect of ample fortunes thereafter for those children. The writer of this has known several instances of large tracts of land bought, on what was then the frontier of Pennsylvania, for ten pounds per hundred acres, which, when the settlements had been extended far beyond them, sold readily, without any improvement made upon them, for three pounds per acre. The acre in America is the same as the English acre, or the acre of Normandy.

Those who desire to understand the state of government in America would do well to read the constitutions of the several states and the Articles of Confederation that bind the whole together for general purposes under the direction of one assembly called the Congress. These constitutions have been printed, by order of Congress, in America; two editions of them have also been printed in London, and a good translation of them into French has lately been published at Paris.

Several of the princes of Europe of late, from an opinion of advantage to arise by producing all commodities and manufactures within their own dominions, so as to diminish or render useless their importations, have endeavored to entice workmen from other countries, by high salaries, privileges, etc. Many persons, pretending to be skilled in various great manufactures, imagining that America must be in want of them and that the Congress would probably be disposed to imitate the princes above mentioned, have proposed to go over, on condition of having their passages paid, lands given, salaries appointed, exclusive privileges for terms of years, etc. Such persons, on reading the Articles of Confederation, will find that the Congress have no power committed to them, or money put into their hands, for such purposes, and that if any such encouragement is given, it must be by the government of some separate state. This, however, has rarely been done in America; and when it has been done, it has rarely succeeded, so as to establish a manufacture which the country was not yet so ripe for as to encourage private persons to set it up; labor being generally too dear there, and hands difficult to be kept together, everyone desiring to be a master, and the cheapness of land inclining many to leave trades for agriculture. Some indeed have met with success, and are carried on to advantage; but they are generally such as require only a few hands, or wherein great part of the work is performed by machines. Goods that are bulky and of so small value as not well to bear the expense of freight may often be made cheaper in the country than they can be imported; and the manufacture of such goods will be profitable wherever there is a sufficient demand. The farmers in America produce indeed a good deal of wool and flax; and none is exported, it is all worked up; but it is in the way of domestic manufacture, for the use of the family. The buying up quantities of wool and flax, with the design to employ spinners, weavers, etc., and form great establishments, producing quantities of linen and woolen goods for sale, has been several times attempted in different provinces; but those projects have generally failed, goods of equal value being imported cheaper. And when the governments have been solicited to support such schemes by encouragements, in money, or by imposing duties on importation of such goods, it has been generally refused on this principle: that if the country is ripe for the manufacture, it may be carried on by private persons to advantage; and if not, it is a folly to think of forcing nature. Great establishments of manufacture require great numbers of poor to do the work for small wages; those poor are to be found in Europe, but will not be found in America till the lands are all taken up and cultivated and the excess of people who cannot get land want employment. The manufacture of silk, they say, is natural in France, as that of cloth in England, because each country produces in plenty the first material; but if England will have a manufacture of silk as well as that of cloth, and France of cloth as well as that of silk, these unnatural operations must be supported by mutual prohibitions or high duties on the importation of each other's goods; by which means the workmen are enabled to tax the home consumer by greater prices, while the higher wages they receive make them neither happier nor richer, since they only drink more and work less. Therefore the governments in America do nothing to encourage such projects. The people, by this means, are not imposed on either by the merchant or mechanic; if the merchant demands too much profit on imported shoes, they buy of the shoemaker; and if he asks too high a price, they take them of the merchant: thus the two professions are checks on each other. The shoemaker, however, has, on the whole, a considerable profit upon his labor in America, beyond what he had in Europe, as he can add to his price a sum nearly equal to all the expenses of freight and commission, risk or insurance, etc., necessarily charged by the merchant. And the case is the same with the workmen in every other mechanic art. Hence it is that artisans generally live better and more easily in America than in Europe; and such as are good economists make a comfortable provision for age and for their children. Such may, therefore, remove with advantage to America.

In the old long-settled countries of Europe, all arts, trades, professions, farms, etc., are so full that it is difficult for a poor man who has children to place them where they may gain, or learn to gain, a decent livelihood. The artisans, who fear creating future rivals in business, refuse to take apprentices, but upon conditions of money, maintenance, or the like, which the parents are unable to comply with. Hence the youth are dragged up in ignorance of every gainful art, and obliged to become soldiers, or servants, or thieves, for a subsistence. In America, the rapid increase of inhabitants takes away that fear of rivalship, and artisans willingly receive apprentices from the hope of profit by their labor during the remainder of the time stipulated after they shall be instructed. Hence it is easy for poor families to get their children instructed; for the artisans are so desirous of apprentices that many of them will even give money to the parents to have boys from ten to fifteen years of age bound apprentices to them till the age of twenty-one; and many poor parents have, by that means, on their arrival in the country, raised money enough to buy land sufficient to establish themselves, and to subsist the rest of their family by agriculture. These contracts for apprentices are made before a magistrate, who regulates the agreement according to reason and justice, and, having in view the formation of a future useful citizen, obliges the master to engage by a written indenture not only that during the time of service stipulated the apprentice shall be duly provided with meat, drink, apparel, washing, and lodging, and at its expiration with a complete new suit of clothes, but also that he shall be taught to read, write, and cast accounts; and that he shall be well instructed in the art or profession of his master, or some other, by which he may afterward gain a livelihood, and be able in his turn to raise a family. A copy of this indenture is given to the apprentice or his friends, and the magistrate keeps a record of it, to which recourse may be had in case of failure by the master in any point of performance. This desire among the masters to have more hands employed in working for them induces them to pay the passages of young persons of both sexes who, on their arrival, agree to serve them one, two, three, or four years; those who have already learned a trade agreeing for a shorter term, in proportion to their skill, and the consequent immediate value of their service; and those who have none agreeing for a longer term, in consideration of being taught an art their poverty would not permit them to acquire in their own country.

The almost general mediocrity of fortune that prevails in America obliging its people to follow some business for subsistence, those vices that arise usually from idleness are in great measure prevented. Industry and constant employment are great preservatives of the morals and virtue of a nation. Hence bad examples to youth are more rare in America, which must be a comfortable consideration to parents. To this may be truly added that serious religion, under its various denominations, is not only tolerated, but respected and practiced. Atheism is unknown there; infidelity rare and secret; so that persons may live to a great age in that country without having their piety shocked by meeting with either an atheist or an infidel. And the Divine Being seems to have manifested his approbation of the mutual forbearance and kindness with which the different sects treat each other, by the remarkable prosperity with which he has been pleased to favor the whole country.


# THE WAY TO WEALTH *

COURTEOUS READER:

I have heard that nothing gives an author so great pleasure as to find his works respectfully quoted by other learned authors. This pleasure I have seldom enjoyed, for though I have been, if I may say it without vanity, an eminent author of *Almanacks* annually now a full quarter of a century, my brother authors in the same way, for what reason I know not, have ever been very sparing in their applauses, and no other author has taken the least notice of me, so that, did not my writings produce me some solid *pudding,* the great deficiency of *praise* would have quite discouraged me.

I concluded at length that the people were the best judges of my merit, for they buy my works; and, besides, in my rambles where I am not personally known, I have frequently heard one or other of my adages repeated, with, "as *Poor Richard* says," at the end of it; this gave me some satisfaction, as it showed not only that my instructions were regarded, but discovered likewise some respect for my authority; and I own that to encourage the practice of remembering and repeating those wise sentences I have sometimes *quoted myself* with great gravity.

Judge, then, how much I must have been gratified by an incident I am going to relate to you. I stopped my horse lately where a great number of people were collected at a vendue of merchant goods. The hour of sale not being come, they were conversing on the badness of the times and one of the company called to a plain clean old man with white locks, "Pray, father Abraham, what think you of the times? Won't these heavy taxes quite ruin the country? How shall we be ever able to pay them? What

---

ª [Published as a Preface to *Poor Richard's Almanack,* 1758, and known also as: "Poor Richard Improved."]

would you advise us to?" Father Abraham stood up and replied,
"If you'd have my advice, I'll give it you in short, for 'A word
to the wise is enough,' and 'Many words won't fill a bushel,' as
*Poor Richard* says." They joined in desiring him to speak his
mind, and gathering round him, he proceeded as follows:

"Friends," says he, "and neighbors, the taxes are indeed very
heavy, and if those laid on by the government were the only ones
we had to pay, we might more easily discharge them; but we
have many others, and much more grievous to some of us. We are
taxed twice as much by our *idleness,* three times as much by our
*pride,* and four times as much by our *folly;* and from these taxes
the commissioners cannot ease or deliver us by allowing an abatement. However let us hearken to good advice, and something
may be done for us; 'God helps them that help themselves,' as
*Poor Richard* says, in his *Almanack* of 1733.

"It would be thought a hard government that should tax its
people one-tenth part of their *time,* to be employed in its service.
But *idleness* taxes many of us much more, if we reckon all that
is spent in absolute *sloth,* or doing of nothing, with that which
is spent in idle employments or amusements that amount to
nothing. Sloth, by bringing on diseases, absolutely shortens life.
'Sloth, like rust, consumes faster than labor wears; while the used
key is always bright,' as *Poor Richard* says. 'But dost thou love
life, then do not squander time, for that's the stuff life is made
of,' as *Poor Richard* says. How much more than is necessary do
we spend in sleep, forgetting that 'The sleeping fox catches no
poultry,' and that 'There will be sleeping enough in the grave,'
as *Poor Richard* says.

" 'If time be of all things the most precious, wasting time
must be,' as *Poor Richard* says, 'the greatest prodigality'; since,
as he elsewhere tells us, 'Lost time is never found again; and what
we call time enough, always proves little enough.' Let us then up
and be doing, and doing to the purpose; so by diligence shall we
do more with less perplexity. 'Sloth makes all things difficult, but
industry all easy,' as *Poor Richard* says; and 'He that riseth late
must trot all day, and shall scarce overtake his business at night';
while 'Laziness travels so slowly that poverty soon overtakes him,'

as we read in *Poor Richard,* who adds, 'Drive thy business, let not that drive thee'; and 'Early to bed and early to rise makes a man healthy, wealthy, and wise.'

"So what signifies *wishing* and *hoping* for better times. We may make these times better if we bestir ourselves. 'Industry need not wish,' as *Poor Richard* says, 'and he that lives upon hope will die fasting. There are no gains without pains; then help hands, for I have no lands,' or if I have, they are smartly taxed. And, as *Poor Richard* likewise observes, 'He that hath a trade hath an estate; and he that hath a calling hath an office of profit and honor'; but then the *trade* must be worked at, and the *calling* well followed, or neither the *estate* nor the *office* will enable us to pay our taxes. If we are industrious, we shall never starve; for, as *Poor Richard* says, 'At the workingman's house hunger looks in, but dares not enter.' Nor will the bailiff or the constable enter, for 'Industry pays debts, while despair increaseth them,' says *Poor Richard.* What though you have found no treasure, nor has any rich relation left you a legacy, 'Diligence is the mother of good-luck,' as *Poor Richard* says, 'and God gives all things to industry. Then plough deep, while sluggards sleep, and you shall have corn to sell and to keep,' says *Poor Dick.* Work while it is called today, for you know not how much you may be hindered tomorrow, which makes *Poor Richard* say, 'One today is worth two tomorrows,' and further, 'Have you somewhat to do tomorrow, do it today.' If you were a servant, would you not be ashamed that a good master should catch you idle? Are you then your own master, 'be ashamed to catch yourself idle,' as *Poor Dick* says. When there is so much to be done for yourself, your family, your country, and your gracious king, be up by peep of day; 'Let not the sun look down and say, inglorious here he lies.' Handle your tools without mittens; remember that 'The cat in gloves catches no mice,' as *Poor Richard* says. 'Tis true there is much to be done, and perhaps you are weakhanded, but stick to it steadily; and you will see great effects, for 'Constant dropping wears away stones,' and by 'diligence and patience the mouse ate in two the cable'; and 'Little strokes fell great oaks,' as *Poor Richard* says in his *Almanack,* the year I cannot just now remember.

"Methinks I hear some of you say, 'Must a man afford himself no leisure?' I will tell thee, my friend, what *Poor Richard* says: 'Employ thy time well, if thou meanest to gain leisure; and, since thou art not sure of a minute, throw not away an hour.' Leisure is time for doing something useful; this leisure the diligent man will obtain, but the lazy man never; so that, as *Poor Richard* says, 'A life of leisure and a life of laziness are two things.' Do you imagine that sloth will afford you more comfort than labor? No, for as *Poor Richard* says, 'Trouble springs from idleness, and grievous toil from needless ease. Many without labor would live by their wits only, but they break for want of stock.' Whereas industry gives comfort and plenty and respect: 'Fly pleasures, and they'll follow you. The diligent spinner has a large shift; and now I have a sheep and a cow, everybody bids me good morrow'; all which is well said by *Poor Richard.*

"But with our industry, we must likewise be *steady, settled, and careful,* and oversee our own affairs 'with our own eyes,' and not trust too much to others; for, as *Poor Richard* says,

> I never saw an oft-removed tree,
> Nor yet an oft-removed family,
> That throve so well as those that settled be.

And again, 'Three removes is as bad as a fire'; and again, 'Keep thy shop, and thy shop will keep thee'; and again, 'If you would have your business done, go; if not, send.' And again,

> He that by the plough would thrive,
> Himself must either hold or drive.

And again, 'The eye of a master will do more work than both his hands'; and again, 'Want of care does us more damage than want of knowledge'; and again, 'Not to oversee workmen, is to leave them your purse open.' Trusting too much to others' care is the ruin of many; for, as the *Almanack* says, 'In the affairs of this world, men are saved, not by faith, but by the want of it'; but a man's own care is profitable; for, says *Poor Dick,* 'Learning is to the studious,' and 'riches to the careful,' as well as 'power to the bold,' and 'Heaven to the virtuous.' And further,

'If you would have a faithful servant and one that you like, serve yourself.' And again, he advises to circumspection and care, even in the smallest matters, because sometimes 'A little neglect may breed great mischief'; adding, 'for want of a nail the shoe was lost; for want of a shoe the horse was lost; and for want of a horse the rider was lost, being overtaken and slain by the enemy; all for want of care about a horseshoe nail.'

"So much for industry, my friends, and attention to one's own business; but to these we must add *frugality,* if we would make our *industry* more certainly successful. A man may, if he knows not how to save as he gets, 'keep his nose all his life to the grindstone,' and die not worth a 'groat' at last. 'A fat kitchen makes a lean will,' as *Poor Richard* says; and

> Many estates are spent in the getting,
> Since women for tea forsook spinning and knitting,
> And men for punch forsook hewing and splitting.

'If you would be wealthy,' says he in another *Almanack,* 'think of saving as well as of getting: The Indies have not made Spain rich, because her outgoes are greater than her incomes.'

"Away then with your expensive follies, and you will not then have so much cause to complain of hard times, heavy taxes, and chargeable families; for, as *Poor Dick* says,

> Women and wine, game and deceit,
> Make the wealth small and the wants great.

And further, 'What maintains one vice would bring up two children.' You may think, perhaps, that a *little* tea or a *little* punch now and then, diet a *little* more costly, clothes a *little* finer, and a *little* entertainment now and then, can be no *great* matter; but remember what *Poor Richard* says, 'Many a little makes a mickle'; and further, 'Beware of little expenses; a small leak will sink a great ship'; and again, 'Who dainties love shall beggars prove'; and moreover, 'Fools make feasts, and wise men eat them.'

"Here you are all got together at this vendue of *fineries* and *knickknacks.* You call them *goods;* but if you do not take care, they will prove *evils* to some of you. You expect they will be sold *cheap,* and perhaps they may for less than they cost; but if you have no occasion for them, they must be *dear* to you. Remember what *Poor Richard* says; 'Buy what thou hast no need of, and ere long thou shalt sell thy necessaries.' And again, 'At a great pennyworth pause a while'; he means that perhaps the cheapness is *apparent* only, and not *real;* or the bargain, by straitening thee in thy business, may do thee more harm than good. For in another place he says, 'Many have been ruined by buying good penny-worths.' Again, *Poor Richard* says, 'tis 'foolish to lay out money in a purchase of repentance'; and yet this folly is practiced every day at vendues, for want of minding the *Almanack.* 'Wise men,' as *Poor Dick* says, 'learn by others' harms, fools scarcely by their own; but *felix quem faciunt aliena pericula cautum.*' Many a one, for the sake of finery on the back, have gone with a hungry belly, and half-starved their families. 'Silks and satins, scarlet and velvets,' as *Poor Richard* says, 'put out the kitchen fire.'

"These are not the *necessaries* of life; they can scarcely be called the *conveniences;* and yet only because they look pretty, how many *want* to *have* them! The *artificial* wants of mankind thus become more numerous than the *natural;* and, as *Poor Dick* says, 'for one poor person, there are a hundred indigent.' By these and other extravagances the genteel are reduced to poverty, and forced to borrow of those whom they formerly despised, but who through industry and frugality have maintained their standing; in which case it appears plainly that 'A ploughman on his legs is higher than a gentleman on his knees,' as *Poor Richard* says. Perhaps they have had a small estate left them, which they knew not the getting of; they think, ' 'Tis day, and will never be night'; that a little to be spent out of *so much* is not worth minding; 'A child and a fool,' as *Poor Richard* says, 'imagine twenty shillings and twenty years can never be spent' but, 'Always taking out of the meal-tub, and never putting in, soon comes to the bottom'; as *Poor Dick* says, 'When the well's dry, they know the worth of water.' But this they might have known before if they had taken his advice: 'If you would know the value of money, go and try to borrow some; for he that goes aborrowing goes asorrowing'; and indeed so does he that lends to such people, when he goes *to get it in again*. *Poor Dick* further advises, and says,

> Fond pride of dress is sure a very curse;
> E'er fancy you consult, consult your purse.

And again, 'Pride is as loud a beggar as want, and a great deal more saucy.' When you have bought one fine thing, you must buy ten more, that your appearance may be all of a piece; but *Poor Dick* says, ' 'Tis easier to suppress the first desire than to satisfy all that follow it.' And 'tis as truly folly for the poor to ape the rich, as for the frog to swell in order to equal the ox.

> Great estates may venture more,
> But little boats should keep near shore.

'Tis, however, a folly soon punished; for 'Pride that dines on vanity, sups on contempt,' as *Poor Richard* says. And in another place, 'Pride breakfasted with plenty, dined with poverty, and supped with infamy.' And after all, of what use is this 'pride of appearance,' for which so much is risked, so much is suffered? It cannot promote health or ease pain; it makes no increase of merit in the person; it creates envy; it hastens misfortune.

> What is a butterfly? At best
> He's but a caterpillar dressed
> The gaudy fop's his picture just,

as *Poor Richard* says.

"But what madness must it be to *run in debt* for these super-fluities! We are offered, by the terms of this vendue, *six months' credit;* and that perhaps has induced some of us to attend it, because we cannot spare the ready money and hope now to be fine without it. But, ah, think what you do when you run in debt; *you give to another power over your liberty.* If you cannot pay at the time, you will be ashamed to see your creditor; you will be in fear when you speak to him; you will make poor pitiful sneaking excuses, and by degrees come to lose your veracity and sink into base downright lying; for, as *Poor Richard* says, 'The second vice is lying, the first is running in debt.' And again, to the same purpose, 'Lying rides upon debt's back.' Whereas a free-born Englishman ought not to be ashamed or afraid to see or speak to any man living. But poverty often deprives a man of all spirit and virtue: ' 'Tis hard for an empty bag to stand upright,' as *Poor Richard* truly says.

"What would you think of that prince, or that government, who should issue an edict forbidding you to dress like a gentleman or a gentlewoman, on pain of imprisonment or servitude? Would you not say that you were free, have a right to dress as you please, and that such an edict would be a breach of your privileges, and such a government tyrannical? And yet you are about to put yourself under that tyranny, when you run in debt for such dress! Your creditor has authority at his pleasure to deprive you of your liberty, by confining you in jail for life, or to sell you for a servant, if you should not be able to pay him! When you have got your bargain, you may, perhaps, think little of payment; but 'Creditors,' *Poor Richard* tells us, 'have better memories than debtors'; and in another place says, 'Creditors are a superstitious sect, great observers of set days and times.' The day comes round before you are aware, and the demand is made before you are prepared to satisfy it, or if you bear your debt in mind, the term which at first seemed so long, will, as it lessens, appear extremely short. *Time* will seem to have added wings to his heels as well as shoulders. 'Those have a short lent,' says *Poor Richard*, 'who owe money to be paid at Easter.' Then since, as he says, 'The borrower is a slave to the lender, and the debtor to the creditor,' disdain the chain, preserve your freedom, and maintain your independence. Be *industrious* and *free;* be *frugal* and *free*. At present, perhaps, you may think yourself in thriving circumstances, and that you can bear a little extravagance without injury; but,

> For age and want, save while you may;
> No morning sun lasts a whole day,

as *Poor Richard* says. Gain may be temporary and uncertain, but ever while you live expense is constant and certain; and ' 'Tis easier to build two chimneys than to keep one in fuel,' as *Poor Richard* says. So, 'Rather go to bed supperless than rise in debt.'

Get what you can, and what you get hold;
'Tis the stone that will turn all your lead into gold,

as *Poor Richard* says. And when you have got the philosopher's stone, sure you will no longer complain of bad times, or the difficulty of paying taxes.

"This doctrine, my friends, is *reason* and *wisdom;* but after all, do not depend too much upon your own *industry,* and *frugality,* and *prudence,* though excellent things, for they may all be blasted without the blessing of heaven; and, therefore, ask that blessing humbly, and be not uncharitable to those that at present seem to want it, but comfort and help them. Remember, Job suffered, and was afterwards prosperous.

"And now to conclude, 'Experience keeps a dear school, but fools will learn in no other, and scarce in that'; for it is true, 'we may give advice, but we cannot give conduct,' as *Poor Richard* says; however, remember this, 'They that won't be counseled, can't be helped,' as *Poor Richard* says; and further that, 'If you will not hear reason, she'll surely rap your knuckles.' "

Thus the old gentleman ended his harangue. The people heard it and approved the doctrine, and immediately practiced the contrary, just as if it had been a common sermon; for the vendue opened, and they began to buy extravagantly, notwithstanding his cautions and their own fear of taxes. I found the good man had thoroughly studied my *Almanacks,* and digested all I had dropped on these topics during the course of twenty-five years. The frequent mention he made of me must have tired anyone else, but my vanity was wonderfully delighted with it, though I was conscious that not a tenth part of the wisdom was my own, which he ascribed to me, but rather the *gleanings* I had made of the sense of all ages and nations. However, I resolved to be the better for the echo of it; and though I had at first determined to buy stuff for a new coat, I went away resolved to wear my old one a little longer. Reader, if thou wilt do the same, thy profit will be as great as mine. I am, as ever, thine to serve thee,

*July 7, 1757*                                     RICHARD SAUNDERS

# NOTES

## INTRODUCTION

1. The colonies originally fell into two categories: Charter colonies (Connecticut, Massachusetts, and Rhode Island), which were governed, without any direct interference from the Crown, by charters granted to commercial trading companies; and Proprietary colonies, which were founded as royal land grants to individuals or groups of individuals. Under the latter system the Proprietor owned and politically controlled the colony, although the political power was generally delegated to colonial representatives. Pennsylvania, Maryland, and Delaware remained Proprietary colonies until the Revolution. The others, however, at the time of the Revolution had become royal provinces, each represented by a governor who was appointed by the Crown but dependent for his salary on a legislature chosen by the voters of the province.

2. The Stamp Act was imposed on the colonies by the British Parliament in 1765 as a tax on paper—including newspapers, pamphlets, legal documents, and licenses. The tax was bitterly resented by the people of the colonies, and Franklin acted as their representative in this matter before Parliament in 1766.

3. The first government of Massachusetts was theocratic in character. Inspired by Calvin's and subsequent British Puritan teachings, especially by the ideal of a "holy commonwealth," their experiment was intended to realize Christ's reign on earth. Being a union of civil and church government, it was completely dominated by the church, i.e. the Congregational Church. The magistrates were at first little more than sheriffs doing the bidding of the clergy, who interpreted "the law of God." The exercise of civil rights was dependent on Church membership which could be gained only through a cumbersome test and public confession of sins, so that many citizens would forego their political privileges rather than undergo the humiliating Church test. The period was marked by religious intolerance against dissenters among their own ranks in the Congregation and members of other denominations. Some of the leading theologians of this period were John

Cotton (1584-1652) and the so-called Mather dynasty: Richard (1596-1669), Increase (1639-1723), Cotton (1663-1728), and Samuel (1706-1785). (See also the following note on Cotton Mather.)

## TEXT

1. Cotton Mather (1663-1728) was the son of the Reverend Increase Mather (1639-1723) whose high-handed rule of Harvard University led to a general revolt against theocracy. Cotton Mather inherited some of this popular hatred of the "Mather dynasty," although he was theologically more liberal. Besides his pompous history of New England, *Magnalia Christi Americana*, he wrote a book on natural science and religion (*The Christian Philosopher*, 1721) and the *Essays to Do Good* (1710) which were the immediate object of Benjamin Franklin's first satire. (See preceding note, Intr. 3.)

2. Daniel Defoe (1659-1731) was a British novelist and author of political pamphlets. He is best known for his novel, *Robinson Crusoe* (1719).

3. The original manuscript reads "Grub Street ballad," which is derived from a street in London where poor and wretched writers lived.

4. Addison and Steele's famous London daily (1711-1712) remained a model for Franklin. His little *Dissertation on Liberty and Necessity* was based on one of Addison's pieces.

5. Thomas Tryon's *The Way to Health, Long Life and Happiness, or a Discourse of Temperance* (1691).

6. John Locke (1632-1704). His *Essay on Human Understanding* was then just beginning to circulate in New England, and was suspect in the colleges, though less so than the writings of the radical deists, the Earl of Shaftesbury and Anthony Collins, mentioned in the next paragraph.

7. The so-called *Port Royal Logic*, edited by the Jansenists Anton Arnauld and Pierre Nicole and translated from the French by Thomas Spencer Baynes, was a popular text among Puritans.

8. Alexander Pope (1688-1744): English poet and satirist. Among his most famous works are his *Dunciad* (1728, 1729, 1742), a lampoon on dullness and certain poets, and his *Essay on Man* (1733), a poetic survey of human nature.

9. These lines are an adaptation from *Essay on Translated Verse* by the British poet, Lord Roscommon (1630-1685).

10. John Bunyan (1628-1688): English preacher and writer. He is best known for his *Pilgrim's Progress* (1678). His other works include *The Holy City* (1666) and *The Holy War* (1682).

10a. Samuel Richardson (1689-1761): an English writer, known as the originator of the modern novel. His first novel, *Pamela,* was published in 1740.

11. Charles Cotton (1630-1687): English poet. Franklin is referring here to his travesty on Virgil's *Aeneid.*

12. Piece of Eight: a Spanish dollar containing eight reals, each worth 12½ cents.

13. William Burnet (1688-1729) was appointed governor of New York and New Jersey in 1720 and later changed to the governorship of Massachusetts in 1728.

14. Deborah Read married Franklin on September 1, 1730; died December 19, 1774.

15. James Ralph (1695-1762) was an American writer who accompanied Franklin to London in 1724. He remained there and became a free-lance writer and political propagandist. His major work is *The History of England,* from the Restoration through the reign of William III (2 volumes; 1744, 1746).

16. Little Britain: a street in London.

17. Pistole: a Spanish coin worth about four dollars.

17a. I.e., the court district of London. The name was derived from the society of Knights Templars, whose buildings the barristers later occupied.

18. *The Religion of Nature Delineated* was a very popular and moderate expression of deism written by the Anglican clergyman, William Wollaston (1660-1724).

19. Bernard Mandeville (1670-1733) was a Dutch philosopher and satirist who settled in medical practice in London. His *Fable of the Bees, or Private Vices, Public Benefits* (first published as *The Grumbling Hive* in 1705) became a classic exposition of the defense of "enlightened self-love."

20. Henry Pemberton (1694-1771) was a physician and author associated for some time with Sir Isaac Newton. He wrote *A View of Sir I. Newton's Philosophy* (1728).

21. Sir Hans Sloane (1660-1753) was a British physician and naturalist who succeeded Sir Isaac Newton as president of the Royal Society (1727-1741). In addition to his scientific reputation, he was a distinguished collector. His library and curios were

assembled after his death, opened to public view, and, incidentally, became the nucleus of the British Museum (1759).

22.   Edward Young (1683-1765): English poet and dramatist. The work here referred to is Satire IV of a series of seven satires published between 1725 and 1728 under the title, *Love of Fame, the Universal Passion.*

23.   "The origin of the name (chapel) appears to have been that printing was first carried on in England in an ancient chapel converted into a printing house, and the title has been preserved by tradition. The bien venu among the printers answers to the terms 'entrance' and 'footing' among mechanics; thus a journeyman, on entering a printing house, was accustomed to pay one or more gallons of beer for the good of the chapel; this custom was falling into disuse thirty years ago; it is very properly rejected entirely in the United States."—W. T. Franklin, in his edition of 1818.

24.   I.e., he never needed to ask for Monday off to recover from Sunday's dissipation.

25.   This college was then a home for military officers. James Salter (Don Saltero), whose home was also in Chelsea, and who had a collection of curiosities, had formerly been a servant of Sir Hans Sloane. (Cf. note 21.)

26.   The swim here recorded covered a distance of about three miles. Franklin was an exceptionally strong swimmer, and he thoroughly enjoyed the water. He discussed the art and technique of swimming in letters to Oliver Neave (date unknown) and to Barbeu Dubourg (1773), both of which are printed in Nathan G. Goodman's *The Ingenious Dr. Franklin,* pp. 41-49.

27.   Sir William Wyndham (1687-1740) was a prominent figure in British politics.

28.   During the colonial period there were two kinds of "bought" or bonded servants. The first group included both those who were seeking a better life in the New World and those who wished to escape from trouble in England. A "crimps bill," or affidavit affirming that the indentured servant was sailing of his own free will, was required of all those migrating for that purpose. The bill was the shipmaster's protection against charges that the immigrant had been kidnapped or deceived by false promises of wealth into signing the bill to cover his passage and later found that he was bound into service to pay off his debt. The second group of bonded servants included British criminals who had been given a choice between punishment in England and being sold by the British Crown for service in America. The

American colonists objected strongly to the latter practice, which was justified by the British on the grounds that the criminals might change their natures with a change in climate. In the *Pennsylvania Gazette* of May 9, 1751, Franklin, expressing the colonists' disapproval, sarcastically suggested as a counter-proposal that Americans who objected to the brutal killing of rattlesnakes might send them to England in the hope that the change of climate would render them harmless.

29.  John Dryden (1631-1700): famous English poet and dramatist who became Poet Laureate and Historiographer Royal in 1670. The passage given by Franklin is a misquotation from Dryden's *Oedipus*, Act III, Scene 1. The exact wording is:

> Whatever is, is in its causes just;
> Since all things are by fate. But purblind man
> Sees but a part o' th' chain; the nearest link;
> His eyes not carrying to that equal beam
> That poises all above.

30.  Keimer's weekly newspaper was called *The Universal Instructor in all Arts and Sciences and Pennsylvania Gazette*. Franklin became the owner of the paper on October 2, 1729, and changed the title to *The Pennsylvania Gazette,* a semi-weekly, full of Franklin's wit and wisdom.

30a.  According to Farrand, Franklin, before sailing for France, left a chest full of his papers in the care of his friend, Joseph Galloway. During the Revolution, Joseph Galloway went over to the British side and the chest fell into the hands of Mrs. Galloway, who protected it from confiscation by the enemy. At her death, it is probable that Abel James, a highly respected Philadelphia merchant, acted as executor of Mrs. Galloway's estate and in that way came into possession of the first part of the *Autobiography*. (See Max Farrand, ed., *Benjamin Franklin's Memoirs,* Parallel Text Edition, p. xx.)

30b.  Benjamin Vaughan (1751-1835) was a British diplomat, sympathetic with the causes of the American colonists and a close friend of Franklin. In 1779 he published a collection of Franklin's writings, the only edition of his non-scientific papers to be published during his lifetime. Later, in 1789, Vaughan was the recipient of one of the two "fair copies" which Franklin had made of the first three parts of the *Autobiography*. (See "Note on the Text," p. xix.)

31.  Joseph Addison (1672-1719): English poet, essayist, and statesman. His drama, *Cato,* was published in 1713 and received immediate acclaim. (Cf. note 4.)

32. "Thou, Philosophy, life's guide, that seekest the virtues and drivest out the vices, one day well lived by thy precepts is preferable to an endless life of sinning."

33. James Thomson (1700-1748) was a Scottish poet and dramatist. His allegorical poem, "The Castle of Indolence," is generally considered his masterpiece.

34. *Poor Richard's Almanack* was published by Franklin continuously from 1733 to 1758 and contained, in addition to Franklin's essays, humorous sketches, and proverbs, the usual almanac material—weather forecasts, road conditions, important historical dates, etc. *The Way to Wealth* (p. 202) is the Preface to the edition of 1758 and contains most of Franklin's best sayings over the entire period of publication.

35. This and the discourse appeared on June 23 and July 7, 1730.

36. The Union Fire Company was organized on December 7, 1736. Franklin's interest in this and in fireproof construction is discussed in his letters of June 26, 1770, and February 10, 1771, to Samuel Rhoads. Both letters can be found in A. H. Smyth: *Life and Writings of Benjamin Franklin*, V, pp. 265 and 305.

37. George Whitefield (1714-1770) [Franklin's spelling incorrect]: English evangelist and founder of the Calvinistic Methodists. His arrival in America as an itinerant evangelist, associated in England with the Methodist movement, was the beginning of the "Great Awakening" which stirred all the colonies for more than a decade.

38. Anthony Benezet (1730-1784) was an educator born in France. He became a Quaker in 1727, moved to Philadelphia in 1731, and associated himself with the anti-slavery movement. In 1767 he published *A Caution to Great Britain and Her Colonies, in a Short Representation of the Calamitous State of the Enslaved Negroes of the British Dominion.*

39. The American Philosophical Society rapidly became the chief academy of sciences in the country and is still one of the most important foundations for the promotion of scientific interests. The Society dates its founding back to 1727, when the Junto was organized by Franklin.

40. James Logan (1674-1751): business secretary to the Penn family and a prominent citizen of Philadelphia after he moved there from Ireland in 1699.

41. William Penn (1644-1718): English lawyer and statesman. He was influential in framing the charter of the West Jersey

colony in America in 1677. Later he founded the proprietary colony of Pennsylvania (1681).

42. The Dunkers were a sect of German-American Baptists who came to America in 1719. The church organization was perfected in 1723, and the front section of the mother church, located in Germantown, Philadelphia, was built in 1770.

43. The present University of Pennsylvania traces its origin to the Charity School, founded in 1740, and to its successor, the Academy organized by Franklin in 1749. It became the College of Philadelphia in 1775 and in 1791 changed its name to the University of Pennsylvania.

44. A magic square is one composed of vertical and horizontal rows of numbers arranged in such a way that the sums of the numbers in each of the rows—horizontal, vertical, and diagonal— are equal. Two of Franklin's squares are reproduced in Nathan G. Goodman's *The Ingenious Dr. Franklin*, pp. 106-109.

45. The Pennsylvania Hospital (1751) was the first hospital in the colony and became, under the influence of Dr. Benjamin Rush, a leader in the treatment of mental diseases.

46. Gilbert Tennent (1703-1764) was, with Whitefield (see note 37) and Jonathan Edwards, one of the chief preachers during the "Great Awakening"; and the "log college" which he founded in New Jersey became an important Seminary. The meeting house here alluded to is the Second Presbyterian Church in Philadelphia, founded by Gilbert Tennent in 1743.

47. Copies of Franklin's lamps light the pavement in front of Independence Hall (Philadelphia) today.

48. Doctor John Fothergill (1712-1780): a noted British physician. In 1774 he aided Franklin in drafting a scheme of reconciliation between England and the American colonies.

49. This march of the French troops was in connection with the siege of Yorktown, which fell on October 19, 1781.

50. David Hume (1711-1776): the famous Scottish philosopher and historian.

51. Franklin refers to the town now called "Gnadenhütten." It is described as follows in *Lippincott's Gazetteer of the World* (Philadelphia and London, 1922 ed.), p. 730: "Gnadenhütten ('Tents of grace') was once a village of Christian Indians under Moravian instruction."—M. Farrand.

52. A town about fifty miles north of Philadelphia.

53. Peter Collinson (1094-1768) [Franklin's spelling incorrect]: an English naturalist and antiquarian, and a Fellow of the Royal Society (F.R.S.). He was responsible for introducing

Franklin's scientific experiments to the Royal Society and for publishing his volume: *Experiments and Observations on Electricity, Made at Philadelphia in America, by Benjamin Franklin*, London, 1751. This was translated into French in 1773.

54. This and others of Franklin's original primitive electrical machines can be seen in the Library Company of Philadelphia and in the Benjamin Franklin Memorial and the Franklin Institute, also in Philadelphia.

55. Considerable doubt has been thrown recently on the historicity of the "kite experiment." Just what the experiment was and who actually performed it is not clear. In any case, the first important experiment designed by Franklin to draw electricity from the clouds was performed with a lightning rod in France in 1753.

56. Franklin's first foreign mission (1757) was a success. He brought about the assessment of the surveyed lands of the Proprietaries of Pennsylvania, the Penns.

57. Franklin's knowledge of shipbuilding and maritime matters in general was extensive. He charted the Gulf Stream, experimented on the relationship between the depth of water and the speed of boats, and wrote on various other maritime matters. See especially his letter to David Le Roy, August 1785, in A. H. Smyth: *Life and Writings of Benjamin Franklin*, IX, pp. 372-413.

58. Newgate: a prison in London, established in 1218, reconstructed several times, and finally demolished in 1902.

59. Franklin is here referring to a pamphlet entitled: *Observations concernant l'Exécution de l'Article II de la Déclaration sur le Vol*.

60. The reference here is to a pamphlet: *Thoughts on Executive Justice*.

61. Old Bailey: England's chief criminal court.

# The American Heritage Series